Rick and Morty
Ever After

ONI PRESS

AN ONI PRESS PUBLICATION

[adult swim]

RICK AND MORTY™ CREATED BY **DAN HARMON** AND **JUSTIN ROILAND**

WRITTEN BY 𝕾𝖆𝖒 𝕸𝖆𝖌𝖌𝖘
ILLUSTRATED BY 𝕾𝖆𝖗𝖆𝖍 𝕾𝖙𝖊𝖗𝖓 AND 𝕰𝖒𝖒𝖊𝖙𝖙 𝕳𝖊𝖑𝖊𝖓
COLORED BY 𝕾𝖆𝖗𝖆𝖍 𝕾𝖙𝖊𝖗𝖓
LETTERED BY 𝕮𝖗𝖆𝖓𝖐!

EDITED BY 𝕾𝖆𝖗𝖆𝖍 𝕲𝖆𝖞𝖉𝖔𝖘 AND 𝕽𝖔𝖇𝖊𝖗𝖙 𝕸𝖊𝖞𝖊𝖗𝖘
DESIGNED BY 𝕶𝖆𝖙𝖊 𝖅. 𝕾𝖙𝖔𝖓𝖊

ONI PRESS

[adult swim]

Rick and Morty

Ever After

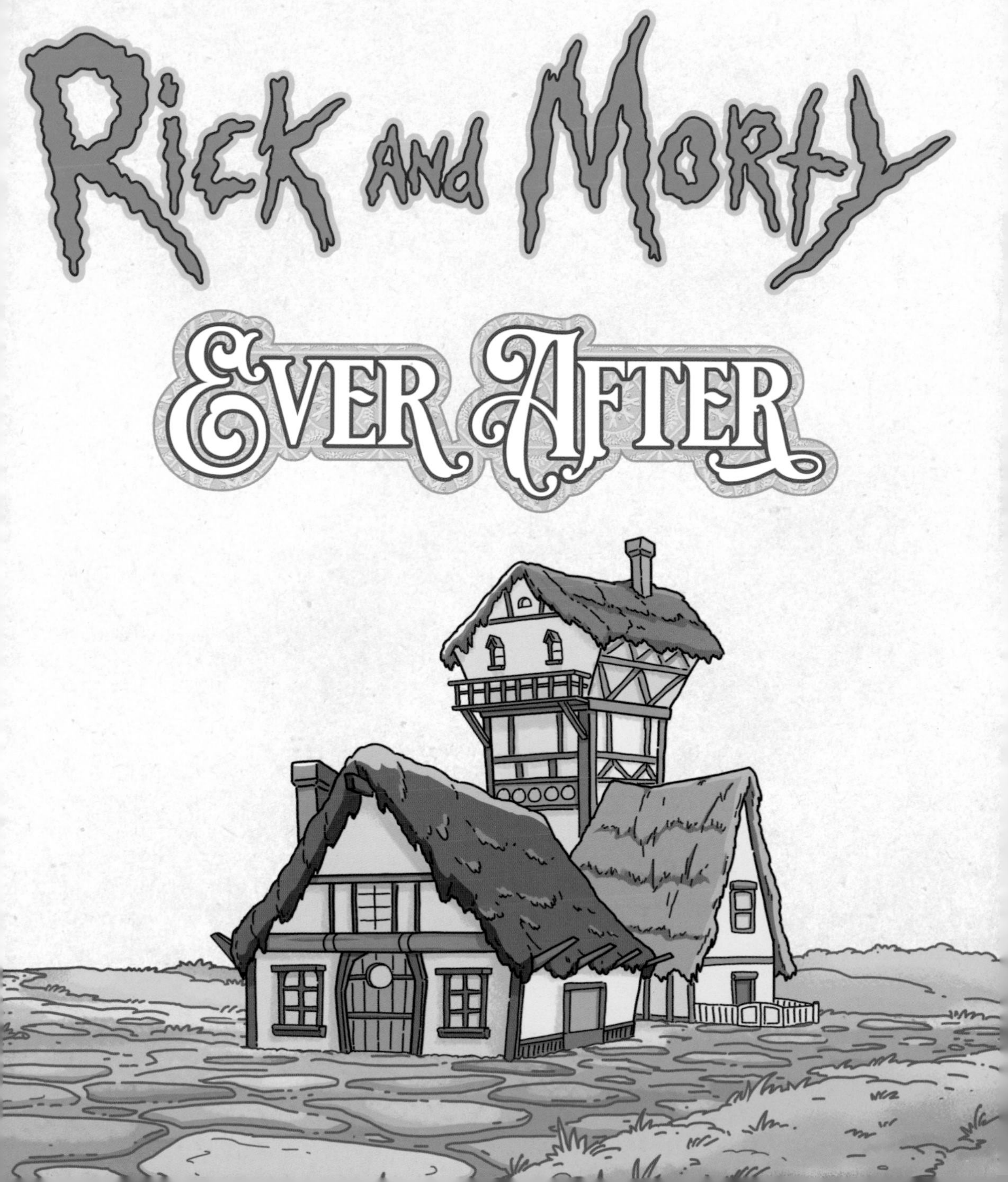

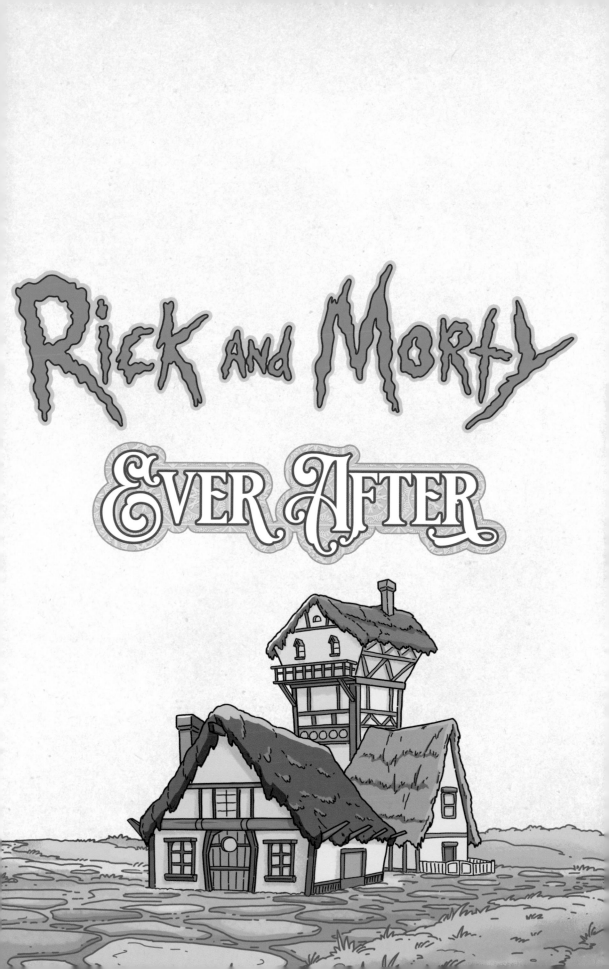

—— Published by Oni-Lion Forge Publishing Group, LLC ——

JAMES LUCAS JONES, PRESIDENT & PUBLISHER

SARAH GAYDOS, EDITOR IN CHIEF

CHARLIE CHU, E.V.P. OF CREATIVE & BUSINESS DEVELOPMENT

BRAD ROOKS, DIRECTOR OF OPERATIONS

AMBER O'NEILL, SPECIAL PROJECTS MANAGER

MARGOT WOOD, DIRECTOR OF MARKETING & SALES

DEVIN FUNCHES, SALES & MARKETING MANAGER

KATIE SAINZ, MARKETING MANAGER

TARA LEHMANN, PUBLICIST

TROY LOOK, DIRECTOR OF DESIGN & PRODUCTION

KATE Z. STONE, SENIOR GRAPHIC DESIGNER

SONJA SYNAK, GRAPHIC DESIGNER

HILARY THOMPSON, GRAPHIC DESIGNER

SARAH ROCKWELL, GRAPHIC DESIGNER

ANGIE KNOWLES, DIGITAL PREPRESS LEAD

VINCENT KUKUA, DIGITAL PREPRESS TECHNICIAN

JASMINE AMIRI, SENIOR EDITOR

SHAWNA GORE, SENIOR EDITOR

AMANDA MEADOWS, SENIOR EDITOR

ROBERT MEYERS, SENIOR EDITOR, LICENSING

DESIREE RODRIGUEZ, EDITOR

GRACE SCHEIPETER, EDITOR

ZACK SOTO, EDITOR

CHRIS CERASI, EDITORIAL COORDINATOR

STEVE ELLIS, VICE PRESIDENT OF GAMES

BEN EISNER, GAME DEVELOPER

MICHELLE NGUYEN, EXECUTIVE ASSISTANT

JUNG LEE, LOGISTICS COORDINATOR

JOE NOZEMACK, PUBLISHER EMERITUS

ONIPRESS.COM   LIONFORGE.COM

@ONIPRESS 🅕 🅧 🅘 🅣 @LIONFORGE

[adult swim]™

ADULTSWIM.COM 🅕 🅧 @RICKANDMORTY

THIS VOLUME COLLECTS ISSUES **#1–4**
OF THE ONI PRESS SERIES *RICK AND MORTY™: EVER AFTER*

FIRST EDITION: MAY 2021

ISBN 978-1-62010-881-9
εISBN 978-1-62010-882-6

PRINTED IN CHINA.

LIBRARY OF CONGRESS CONTROL NUMBER: 2020939587

1 2 3 4 5 6 7 8 9 10

SPECIAL THANKS TO JUSTIN ROILAND, DAN HARMON, JOSH ANDERSON, VICTORIA SELOVER, AND JASON STRUSS.

Chapter One

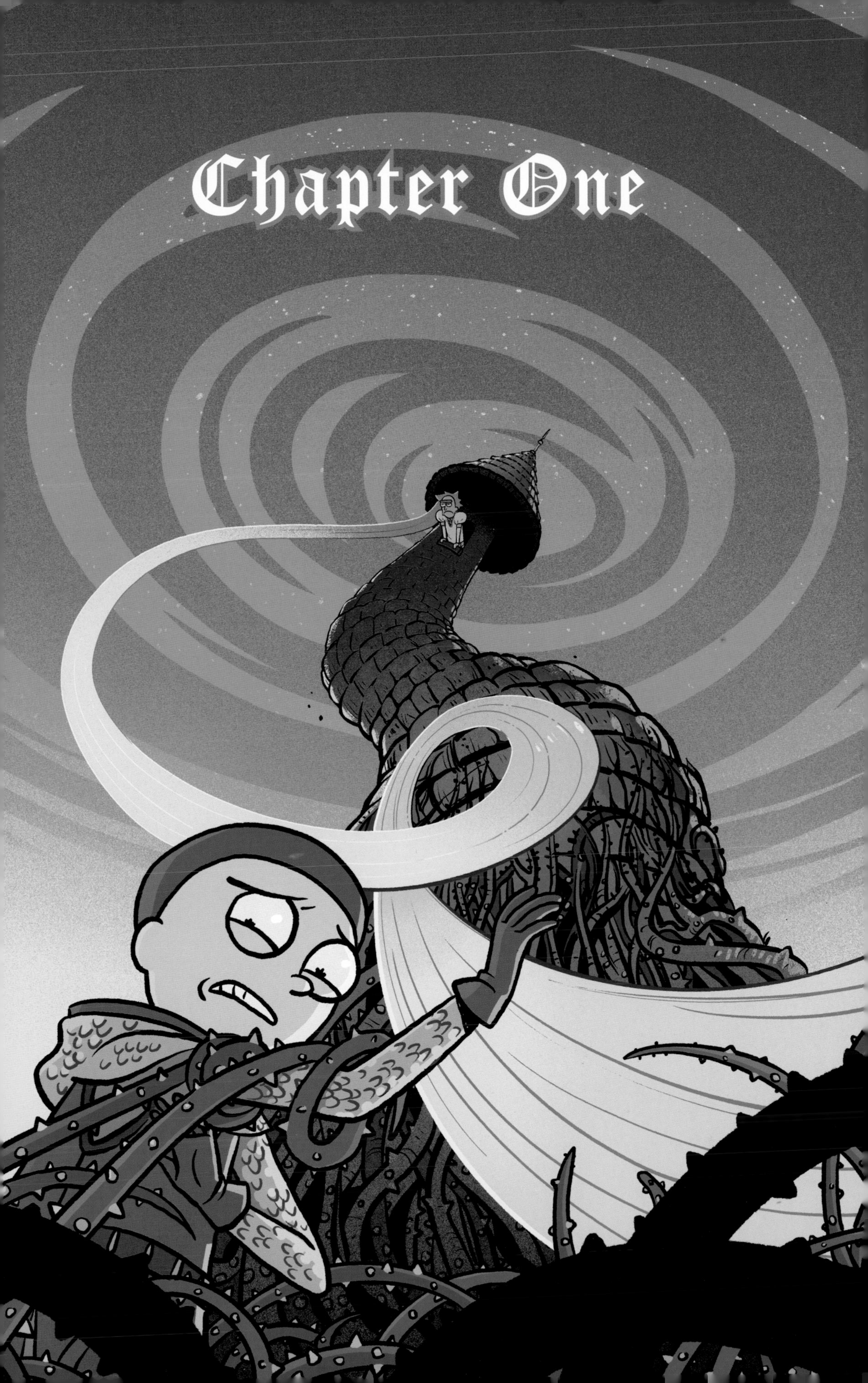

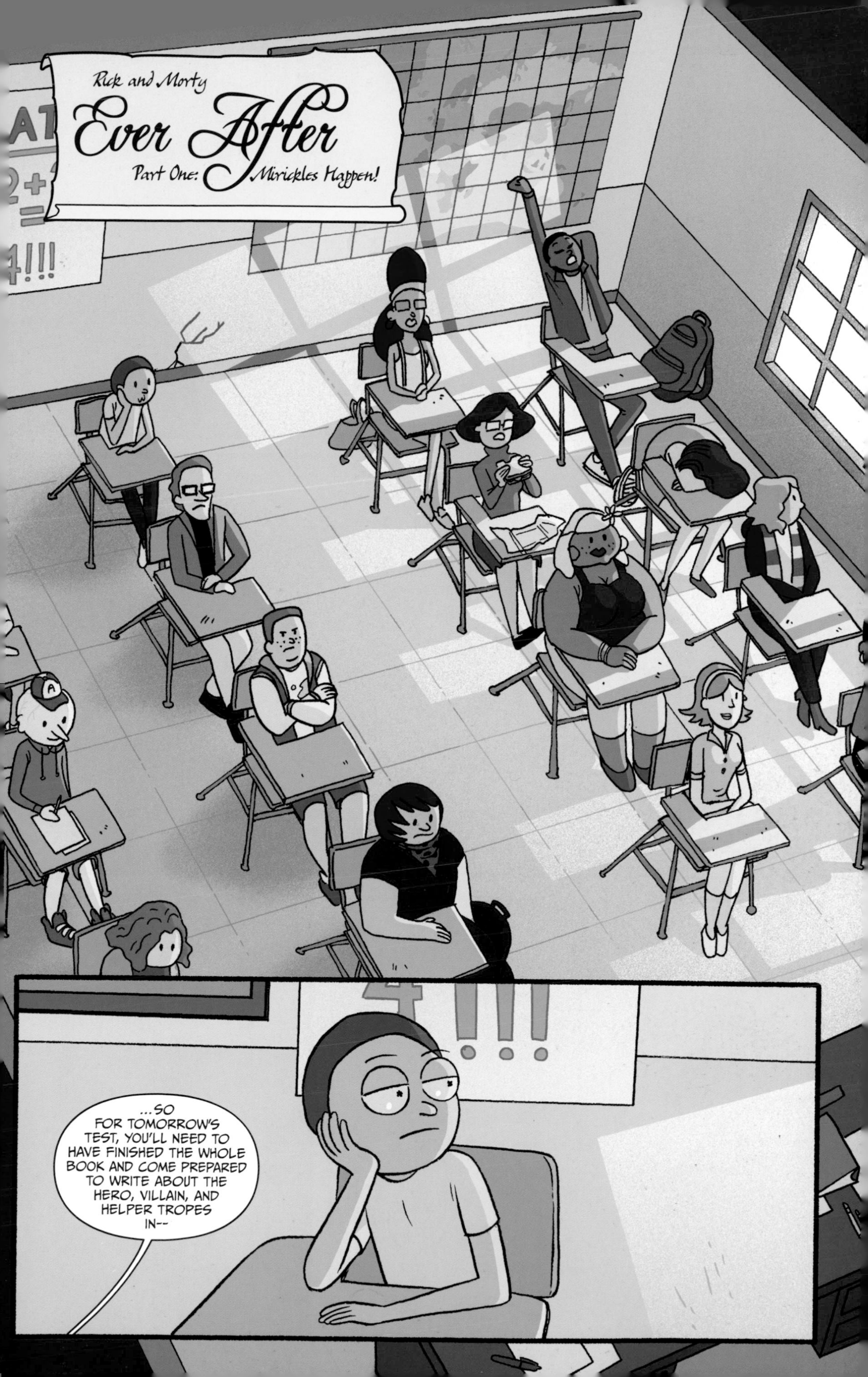
Rick and Morty
Ever After
Part One: Mirickles Happen!
4!!!
...SO FOR TOMORROW'S TEST, YOU'LL NEED TO HAVE FINISHED THE WHOLE BOOK AND COME PREPARED TO WRITE ABOUT THE HERO, VILLAIN, AND HELPER TROPES IN--

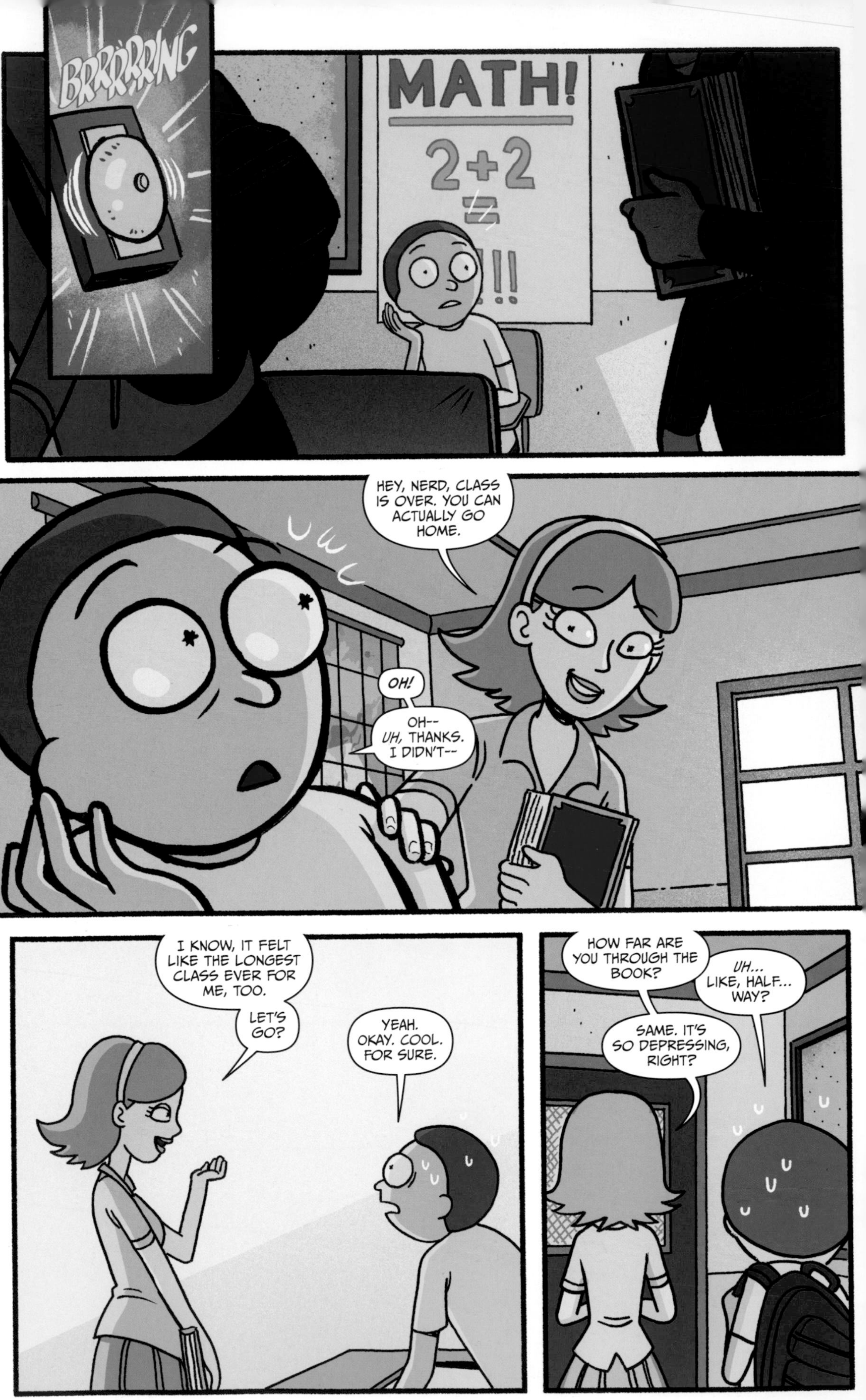
BRRRRRING
MATH!
2+2
=
HEY, NERD, CLASS IS OVER. YOU CAN ACTUALLY GO HOME.
OH!
OH-- UH, THANKS. I DIDN'T--
I KNOW, IT FELT LIKE THE LONGEST CLASS EVER FOR ME, TOO.
LET'S GO?
YEAH. OKAY. COOL. FOR SURE.
HOW FAR ARE YOU THROUGH THE BOOK?
UH... LIKE, HALF... WAY?
SAME. IT'S SO DEPRESSING, RIGHT?

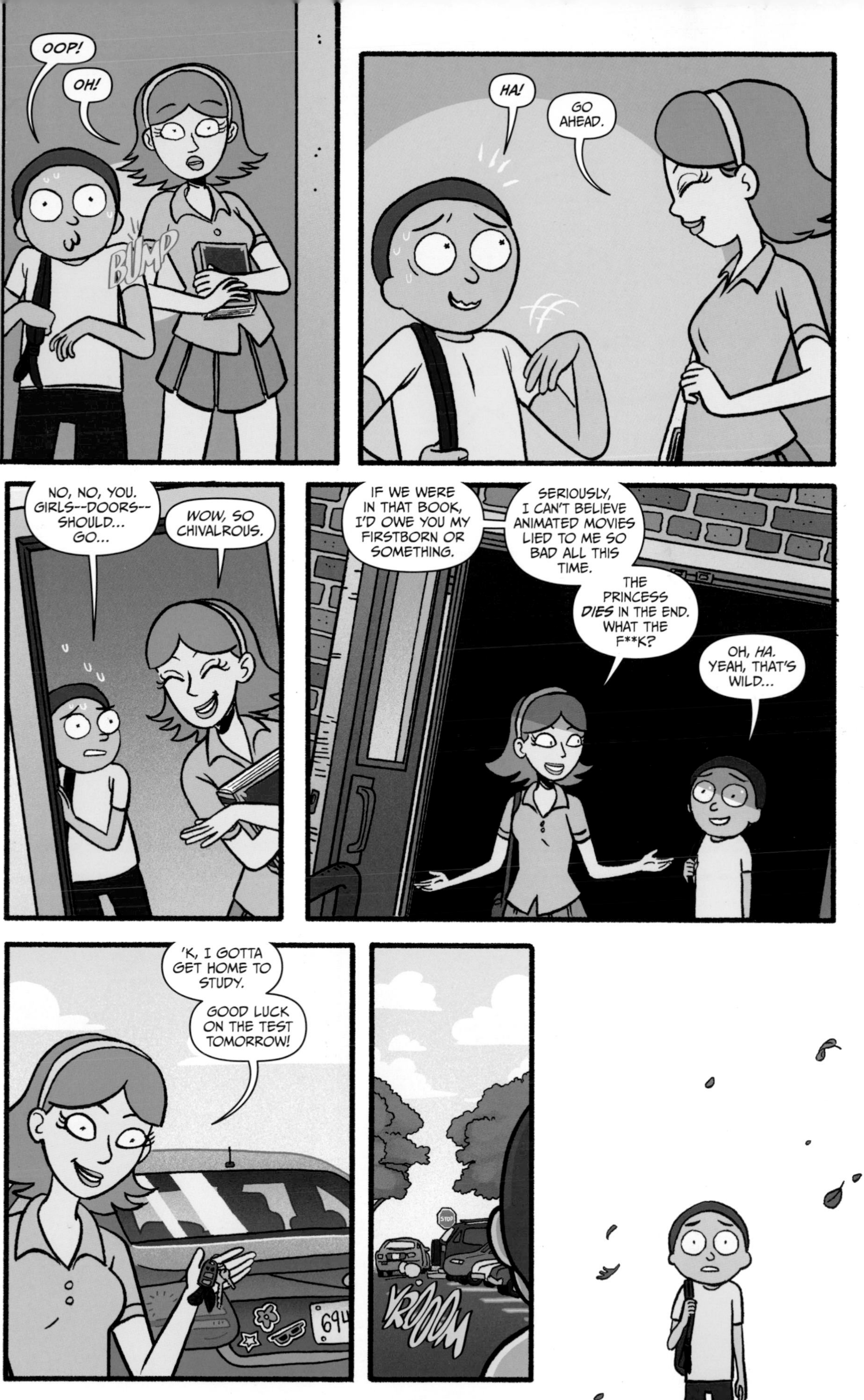
OOP!
OH!
BUMP
HA!
GO AHEAD.
NO, NO, YOU. GIRLS--DOORS--SHOULD... GO...
WOW, SO CHIVALROUS.
IF WE WERE IN THAT BOOK, I'D OWE YOU MY FIRSTBORN OR SOMETHING.
SERIOUSLY, I CAN'T BELIEVE ANIMATED MOVIES LIED TO ME SO BAD ALL THIS TIME.
THE PRINCESS DIES IN THE END. WHAT THE F**K?
OH, HA. YEAH, THAT'S WILD...
'K, I GOTTA GET HOME TO STUDY.
GOOD LUCK ON THE TEST TOMORROW!
STOP
VROOOM

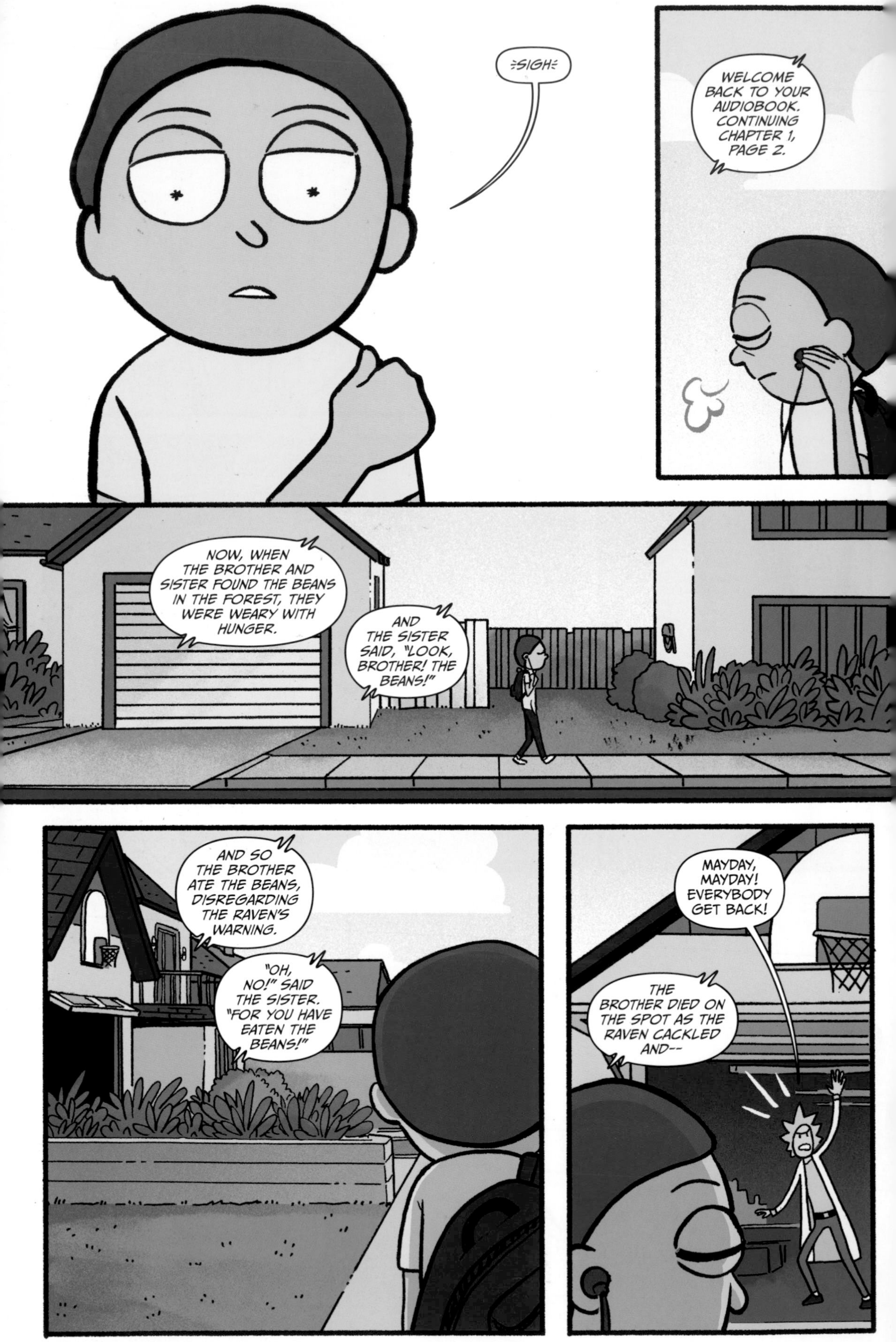
SIGH
WELCOME BACK TO YOUR AUDIOBOOK. CONTINUING CHAPTER 1, PAGE 2.
NOW, WHEN THE BROTHER AND SISTER FOUND THE BEANS IN THE FOREST, THEY WERE WEARY WITH HUNGER.
AND THE SISTER SAID, "LOOK, BROTHER! THE BEANS!"
AND SO THE BROTHER ATE THE BEANS, DISREGARDING THE RAVEN'S WARNING.
"OH, NO!" SAID THE SISTER. "FOR YOU HAVE EATEN THE BEANS!"
MAYDAY, MAYDAY! EVERYBODY GET BACK!
THE BROTHER DIED ON THE SPOT AS THE RAVEN CACKLED AND--

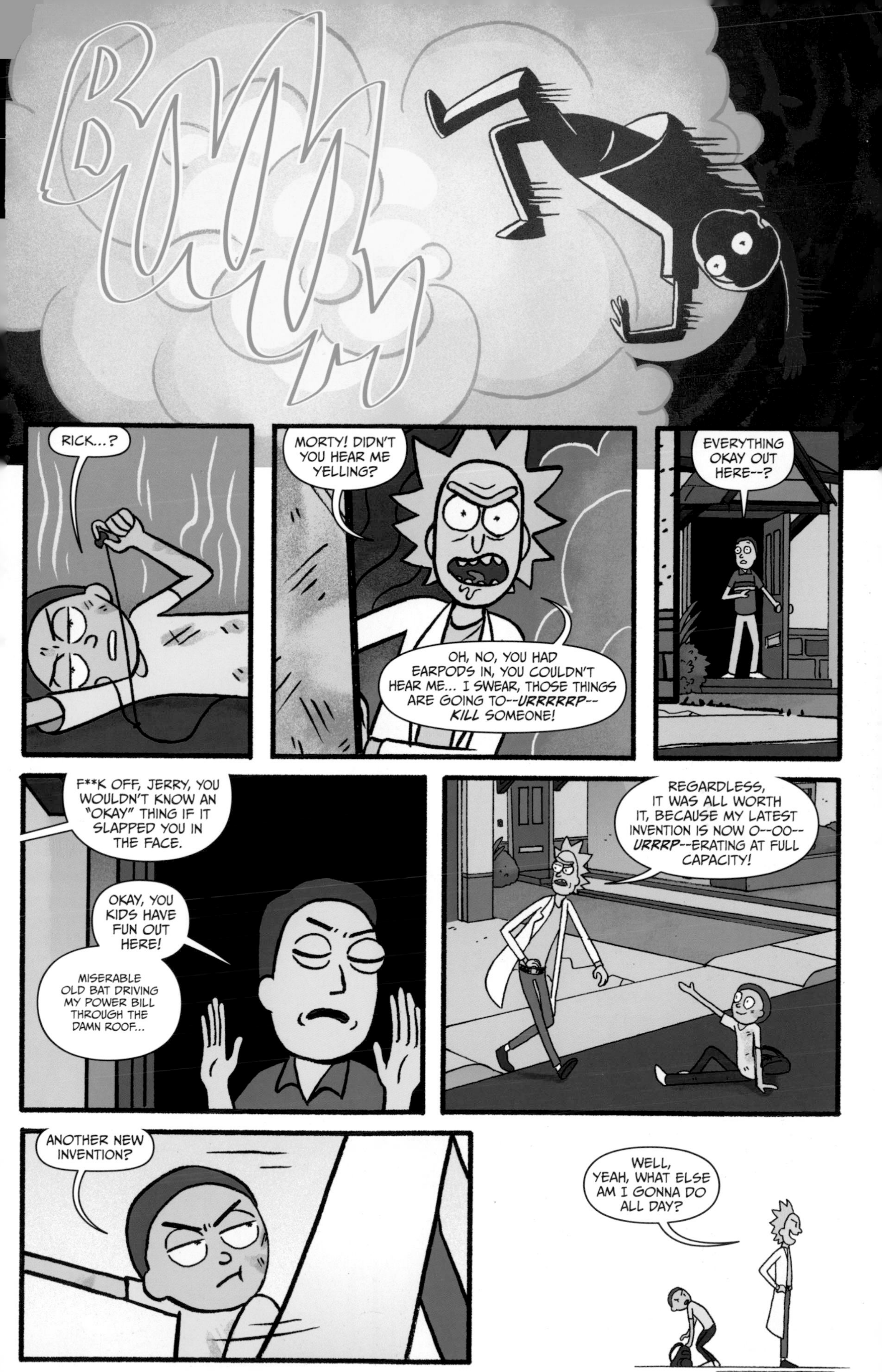
BOOOM
RICK...?
MORTY! DIDN'T YOU HEAR ME YELLING?
OH, NO, YOU HAD EARPODS IN, YOU COULDN'T HEAR ME... I SWEAR, THOSE THINGS ARE GOING TO--URRRRRP--KILL SOMEONE!
EVERYTHING OKAY OUT HERE--?
F**K OFF, JERRY, YOU WOULDN'T KNOW AN "OKAY" THING IF IT SLAPPED YOU IN THE FACE.
OKAY, YOU KIDS HAVE FUN OUT HERE!
MISERABLE OLD BAT DRIVING MY POWER BILL THROUGH THE DAMN ROOF...
REGARDLESS, IT WAS ALL WORTH IT, BECAUSE MY LATEST INVENTION IS NOW O--OO--URRRP--ERATING AT FULL CAPACITY!
ANOTHER NEW INVENTION?
WELL, YEAH, WHAT ELSE AM I GONNA DO ALL DAY?

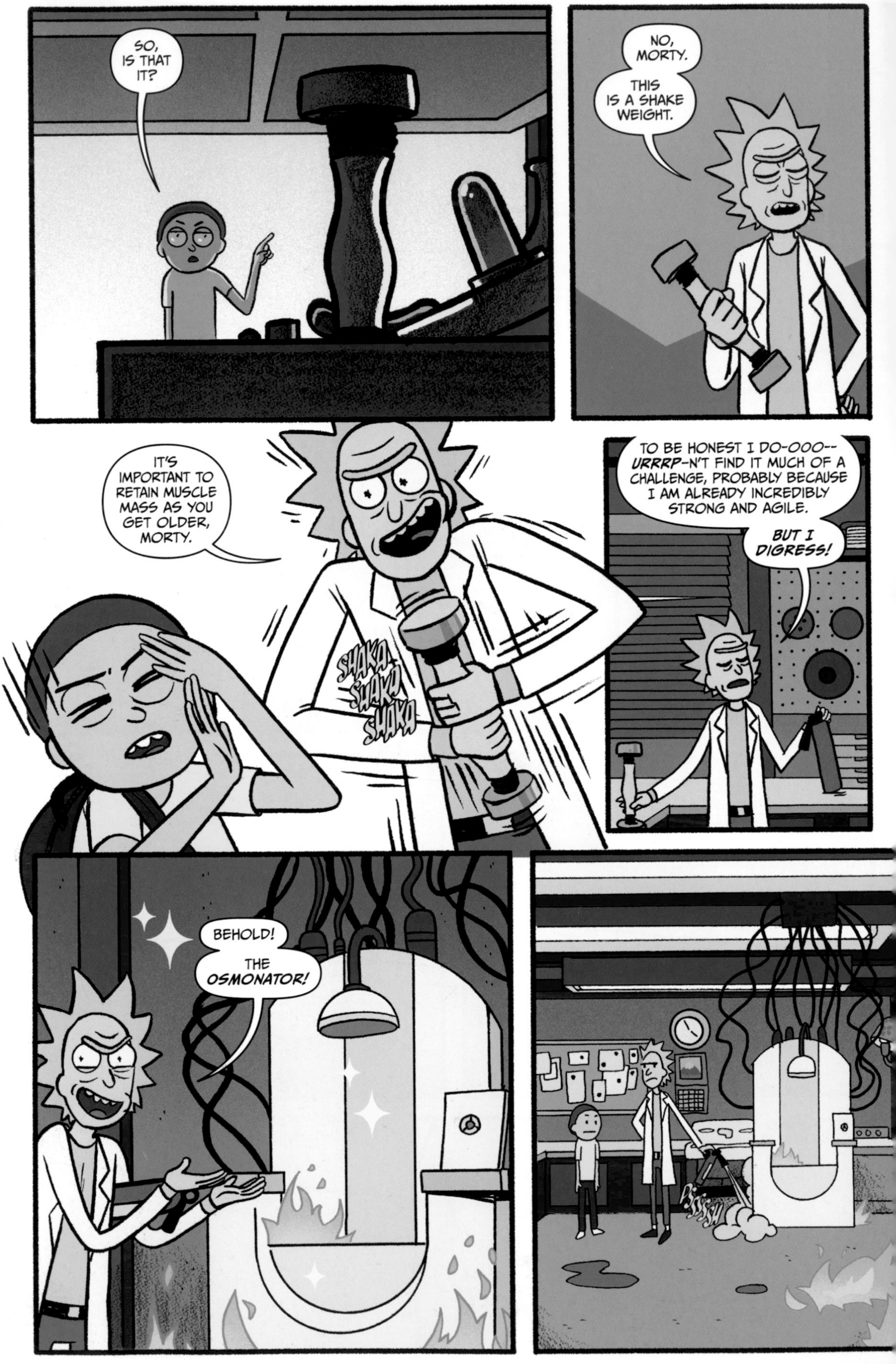
SO, IS THAT IT?
NO, MORTY.
THIS IS A SHAKE WEIGHT.
IT'S IMPORTANT TO RETAIN MUSCLE MASS AS YOU GET OLDER, MORTY.
SHAKA SHAKA SHAKA
TO BE HONEST I DO-OOO-- URRRP-N'T FIND IT MUCH OF A CHALLENGE, PROBABLY BECAUSE I AM ALREADY INCREDIBLY STRONG AND AGILE.
BUT I DIGRESS!
BEHOLD!
THE OSMONATOR!
PSSSSH

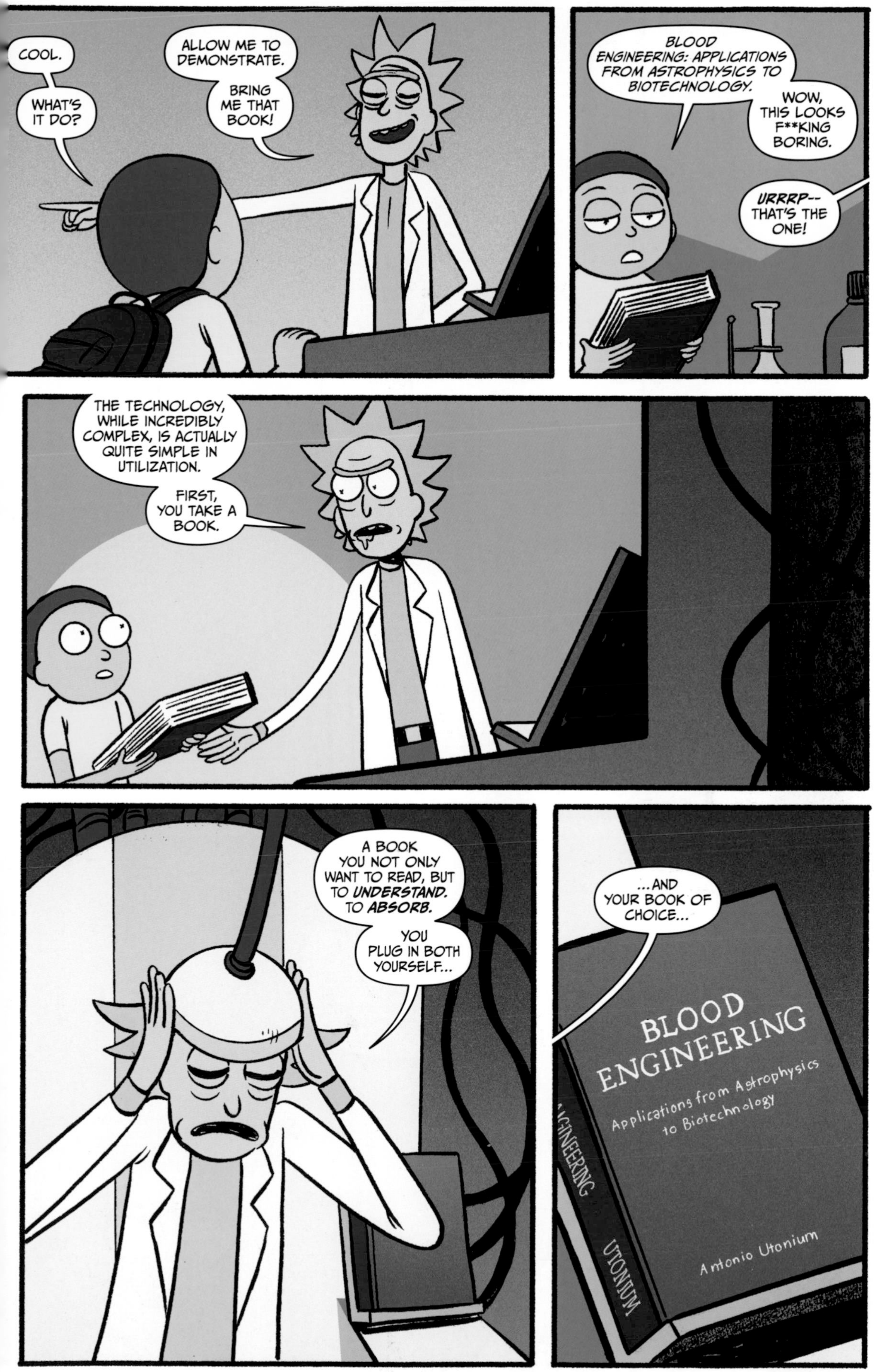
COOL.
WHAT'S IT DO?
ALLOW ME TO DEMONSTRATE.
BRING ME THAT BOOK!
BLOOD ENGINEERING: APPLICATIONS FROM ASTROPHYSICS TO BIOTECHNOLOGY.
WOW, THIS LOOKS F**KING BORING.
URRRP-- THAT'S THE ONE!
THE TECHNOLOGY, WHILE INCREDIBLY COMPLEX, IS ACTUALLY QUITE SIMPLE IN UTILIZATION.
FIRST, YOU TAKE A BOOK.
A BOOK YOU NOT ONLY WANT TO READ, BUT TO *UNDERSTAND.* TO *ABSORB.*
YOU PLUG IN BOTH YOURSELF...
...AND YOUR BOOK OF CHOICE...
BLOOD ENGINEERING
Applications from Astrophysics to Biotechnology
Antonio Utonium
UTONIUM

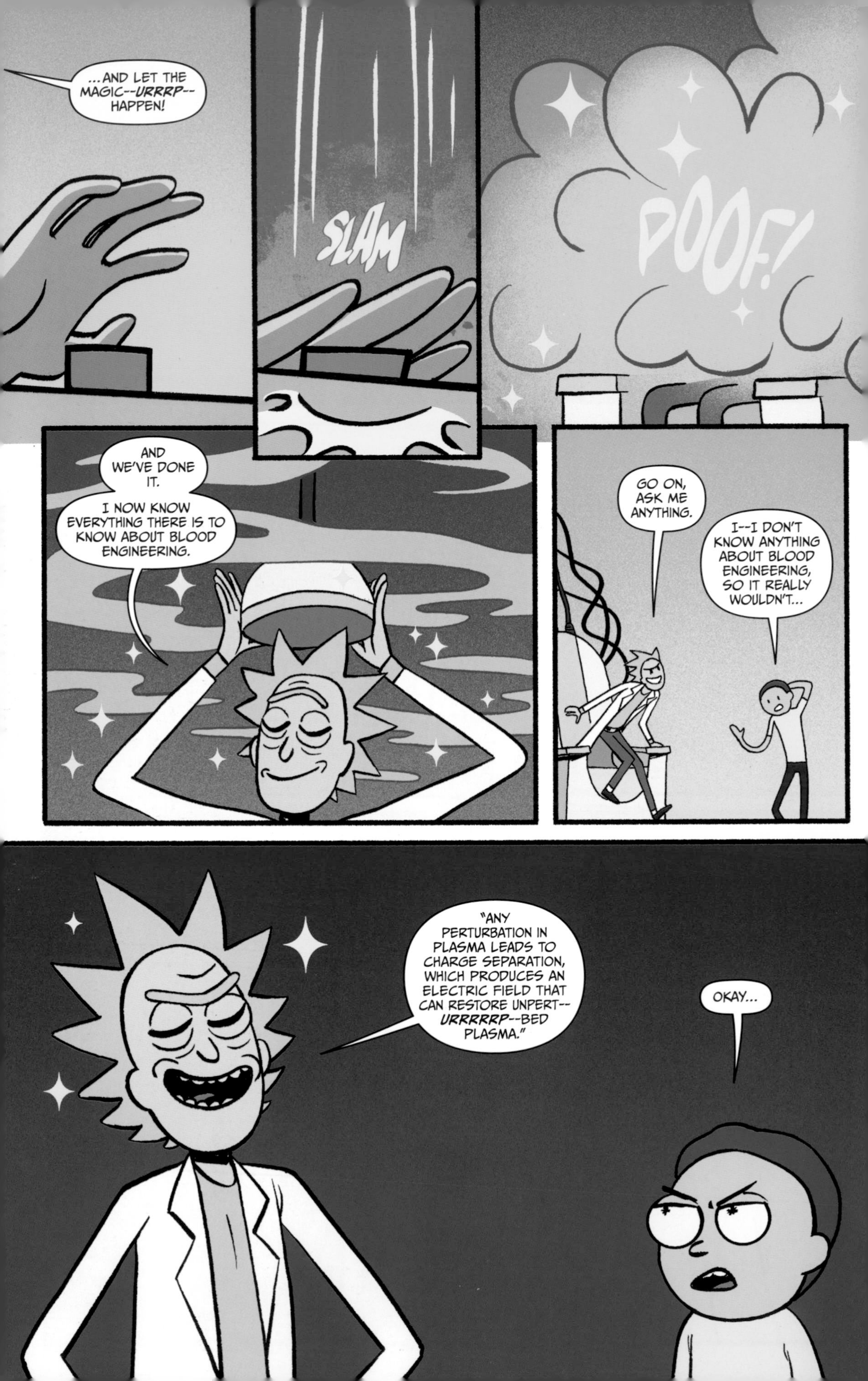
...AND LET THE MAGIC--URRRP--HAPPEN!
SLAM
POOF!
AND WE'VE DONE IT.
I NOW KNOW EVERYTHING THERE IS TO KNOW ABOUT BLOOD ENGINEERING.
GO ON, ASK ME ANYTHING.
I--I DON'T KNOW ANYTHING ABOUT BLOOD ENGINEERING, SO IT REALLY WOULDN'T...
"ANY PERTURBATION IN PLASMA LEADS TO CHARGE SEPARATION, WHICH PRODUCES AN ELECTRIC FIELD THAT CAN RESTORE UNPERT--URRRRRP--BED PLASMA."
OKAY...

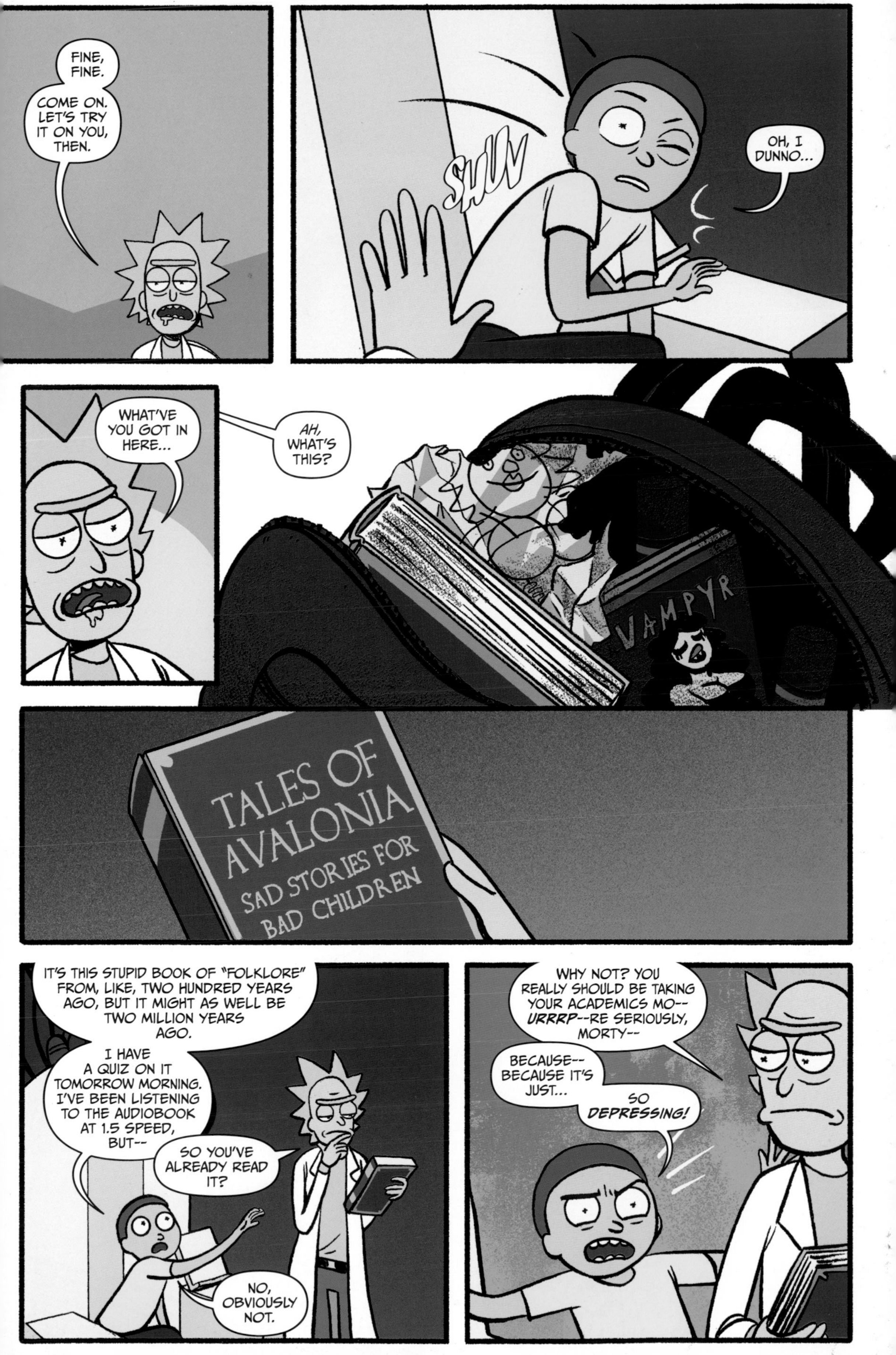
FINE, FINE.
COME ON. LET'S TRY IT ON YOU, THEN.
SHUN
OH, I DUNNO...
WHAT'VE YOU GOT IN HERE...
AH, WHAT'S THIS?
VAMPYR
TALES OF AVALONIA
SAD STORIES FOR BAD CHILDREN
IT'S THIS STUPID BOOK OF "FOLKLORE" FROM, LIKE, TWO HUNDRED YEARS AGO, BUT IT MIGHT AS WELL BE TWO MILLION YEARS AGO.
I HAVE A QUIZ ON IT TOMORROW MORNING. I'VE BEEN LISTENING TO THE AUDIOBOOK AT 1.5 SPEED, BUT--
SO YOU'VE ALREADY READ IT?
NO, OBVIOUSLY NOT.
WHY NOT? YOU REALLY SHOULD BE TAKING YOUR ACADEMICS MO-- URRRP--RE SERIOUSLY, MORTY--
BECAUSE-- BECAUSE IT'S JUST...
SO DEPRESSING!

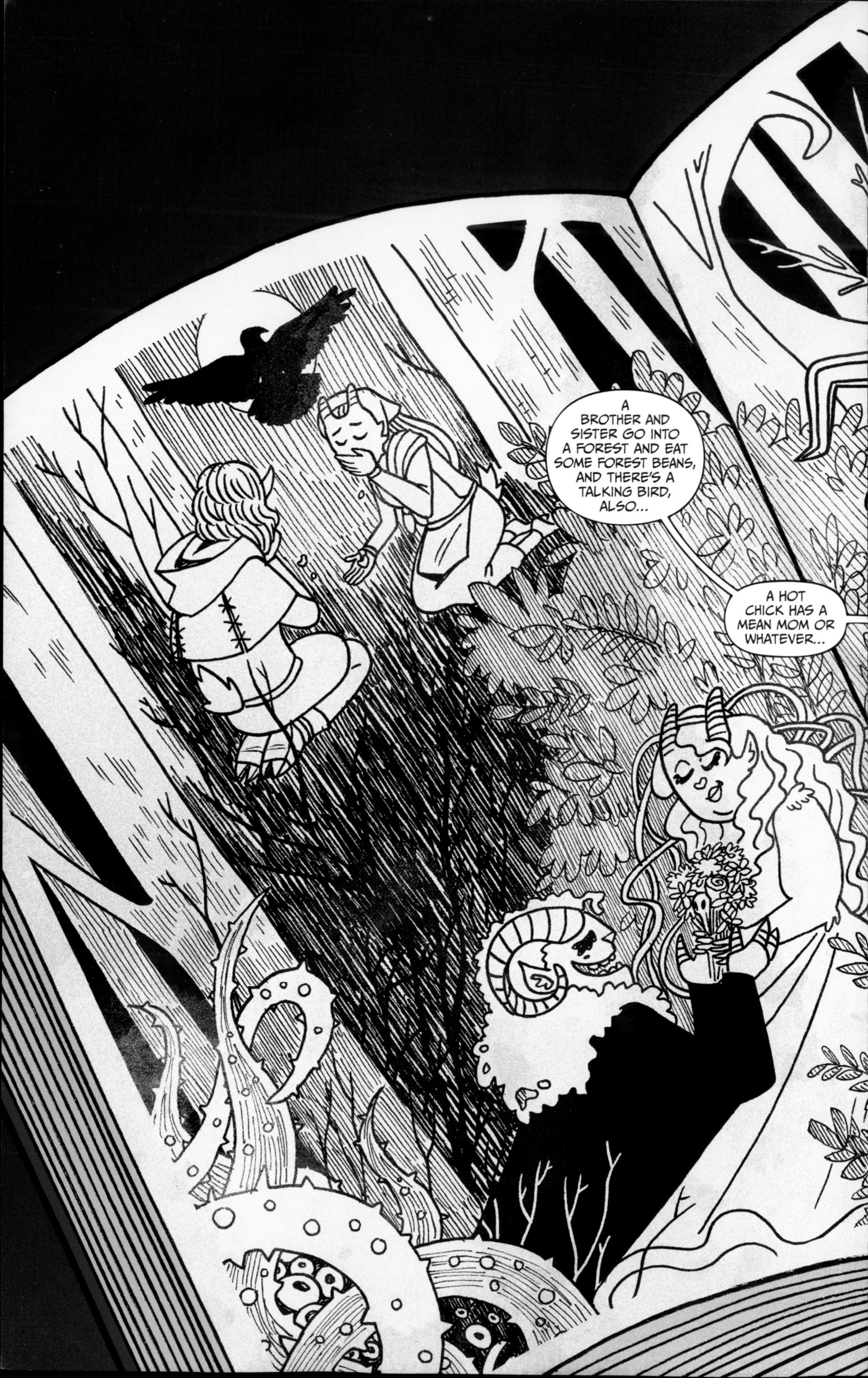
A BROTHER AND SISTER GO INTO A FOREST AND EAT SOME FOREST BEANS, AND THERE'S A TALKING BIRD, ALSO...
A HOT CHICK HAS A MEAN MOM OR WHATEVER...

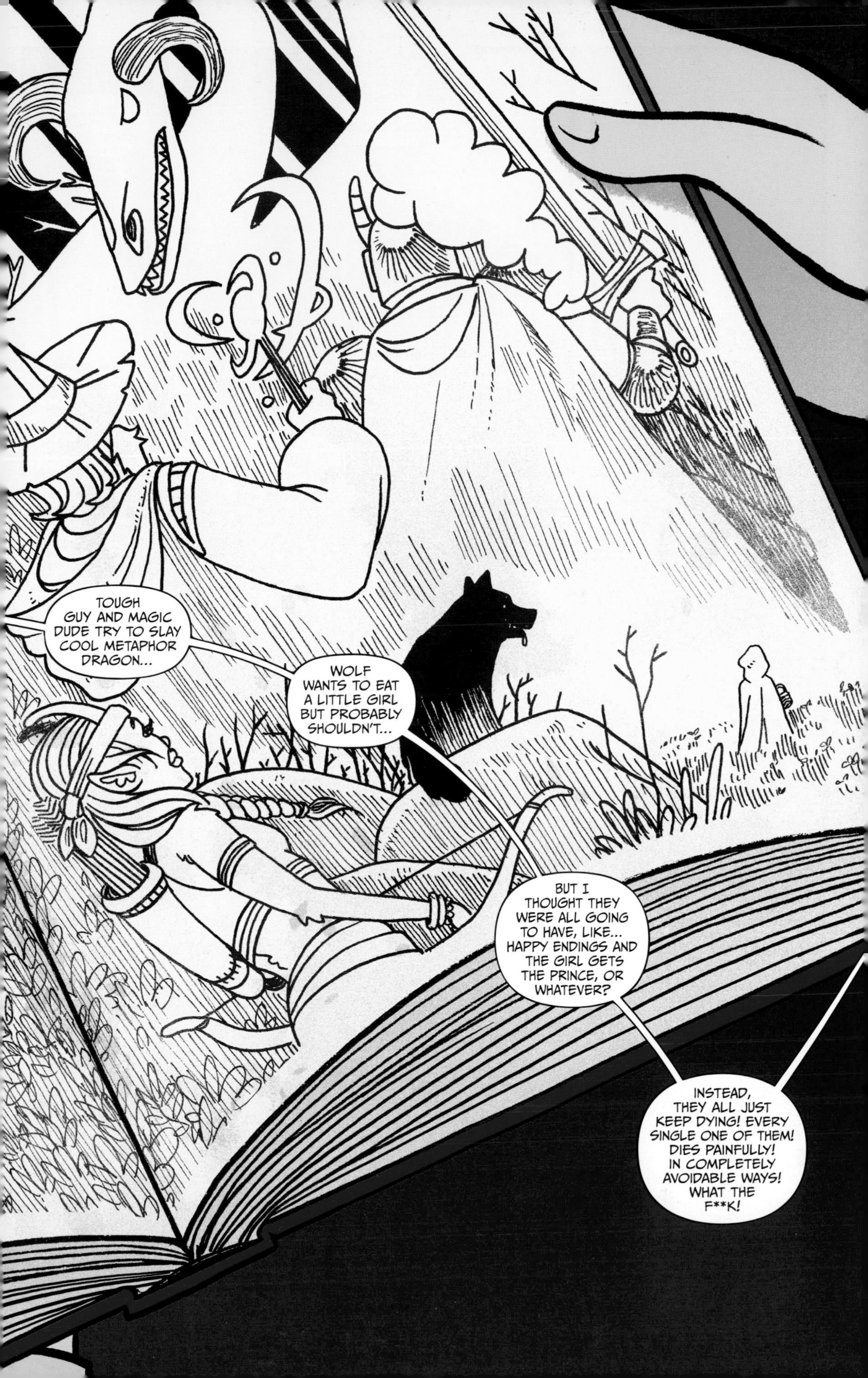

TOUGH GUY AND MAGIC DUDE TRY TO SLAY COOL METAPHOR DRAGON...
WOLF WANTS TO EAT A LITTLE GIRL BUT PROBABLY SHOULDN'T...
BUT I THOUGHT THEY WERE ALL GOING TO HAVE, LIKE... HAPPY ENDINGS AND THE GIRL GETS THE PRINCE, OR WHATEVER?
INSTEAD, THEY ALL JUST KEEP DYING! EVERY SINGLE ONE OF THEM! DIES PAINFULLY! IN COMPLETELY AVOIDABLE WAYS! WHAT THE F**K!

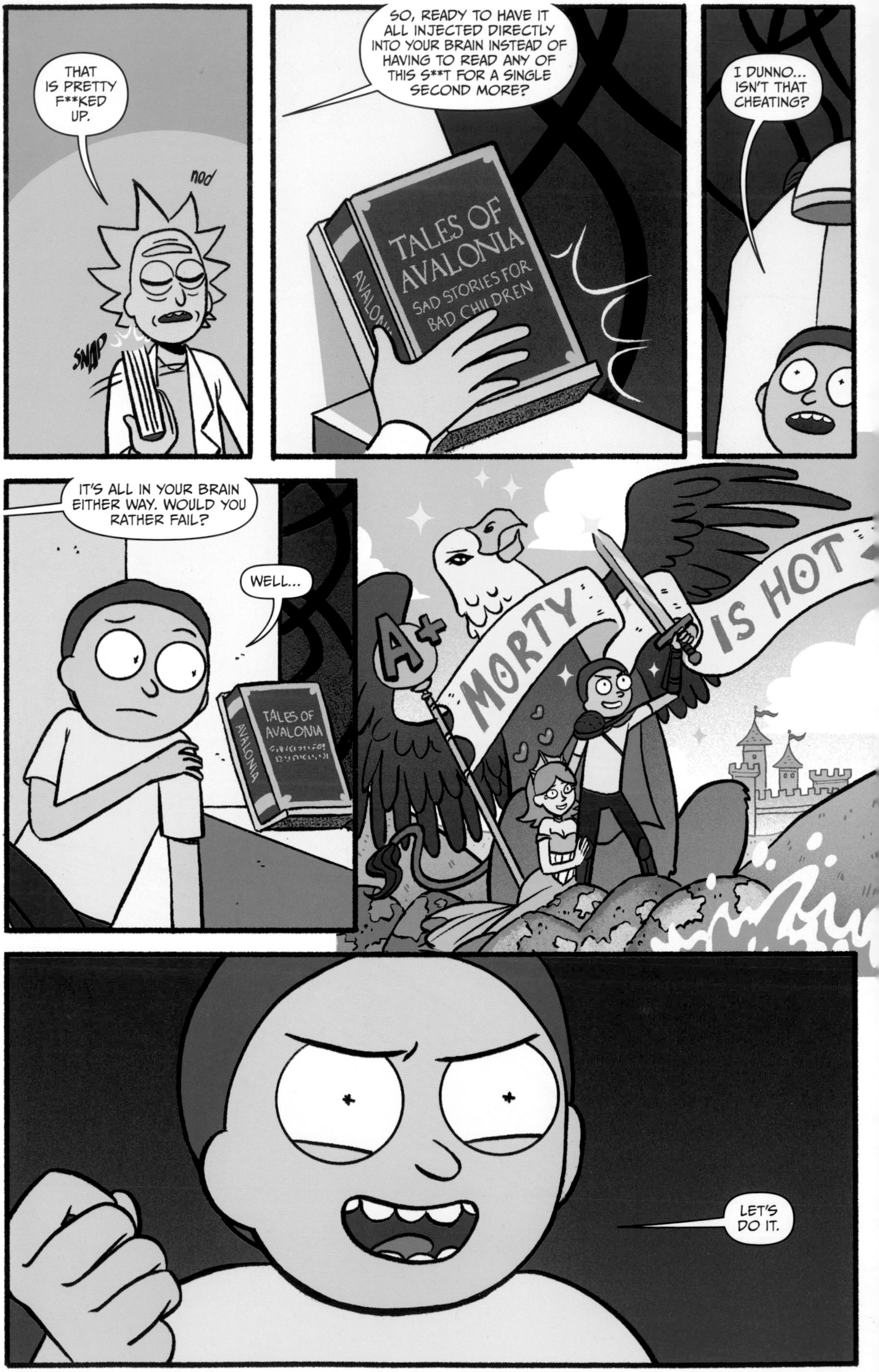
THAT IS PRETTY F**KED UP.
nod
SNAP
SO, READY TO HAVE IT ALL INJECTED DIRECTLY INTO YOUR BRAIN INSTEAD OF HAVING TO READ ANY OF THIS S**T FOR A SINGLE SECOND MORE?
TALES OF AVALONIA
SAD STORIES FOR BAD CHILDREN
I DUNNO... ISN'T THAT CHEATING?
IT'S ALL IN YOUR BRAIN EITHER WAY. WOULD YOU RATHER FAIL?
WELL...
TALES OF AVALONIA
A+
MORTY IS HOT
LET'S DO IT.

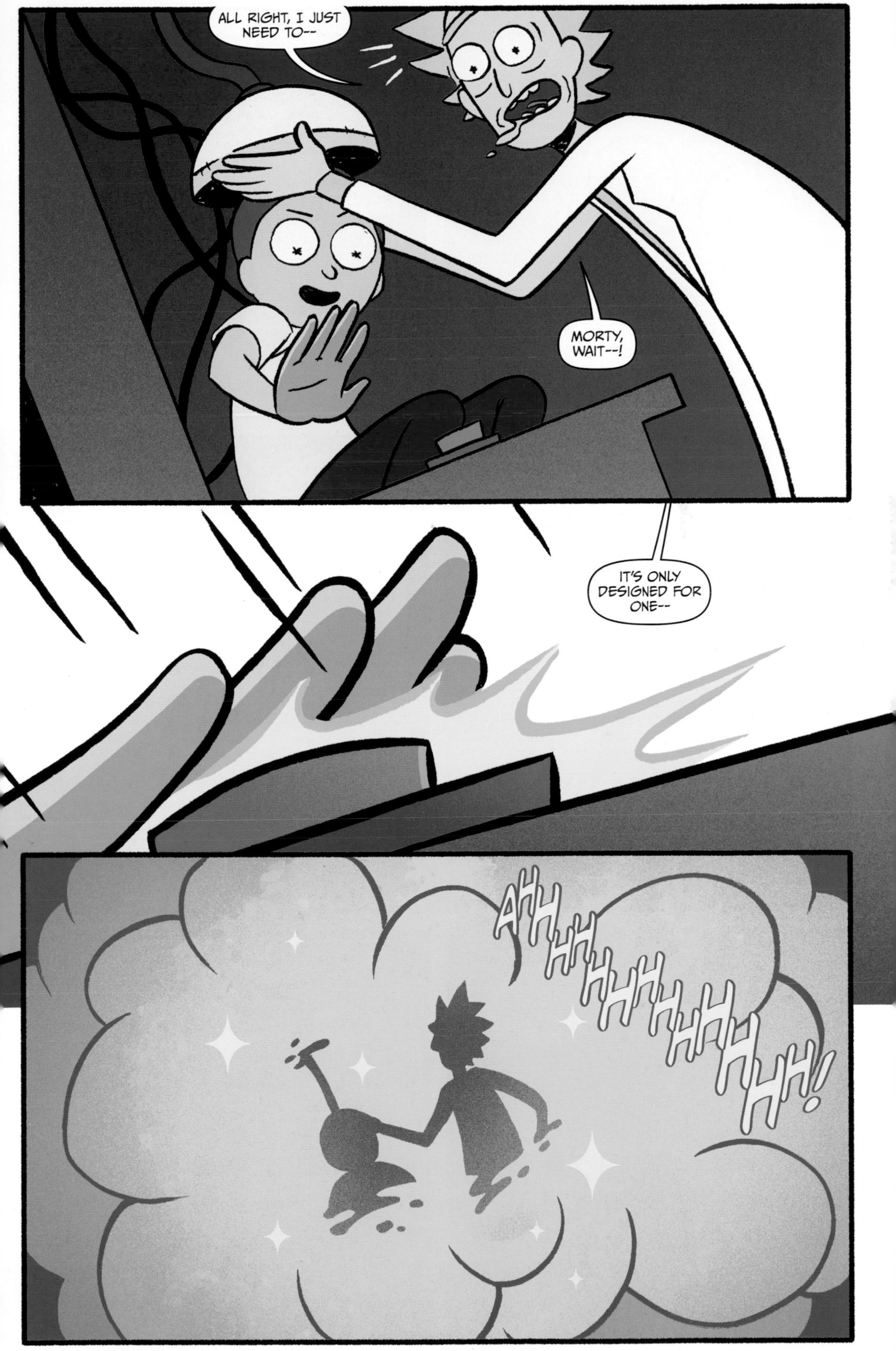
ALL RIGHT, I JUST NEED TO--
MORTY, WAIT--!
IT'S ONLY DESIGNED FOR ONE--
AHHHHHHHHHHHHHHH!

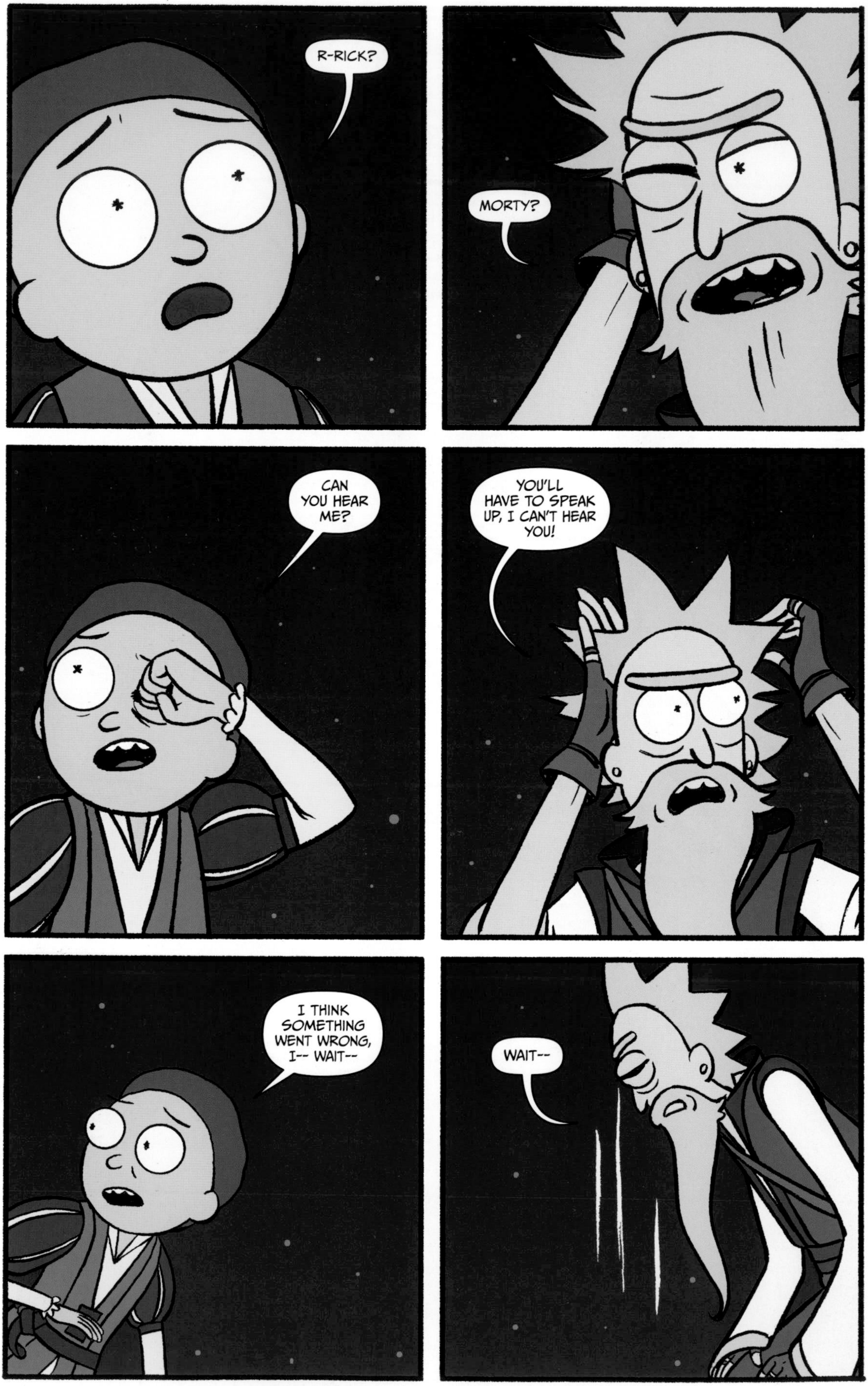
R-RICK?
MORTY?
CAN YOU HEAR ME?
YOU'LL HAVE TO SPEAK UP, I CAN'T HEAR YOU!
I THINK SOMETHING WENT WRONG, I-- WAIT--
WAIT--

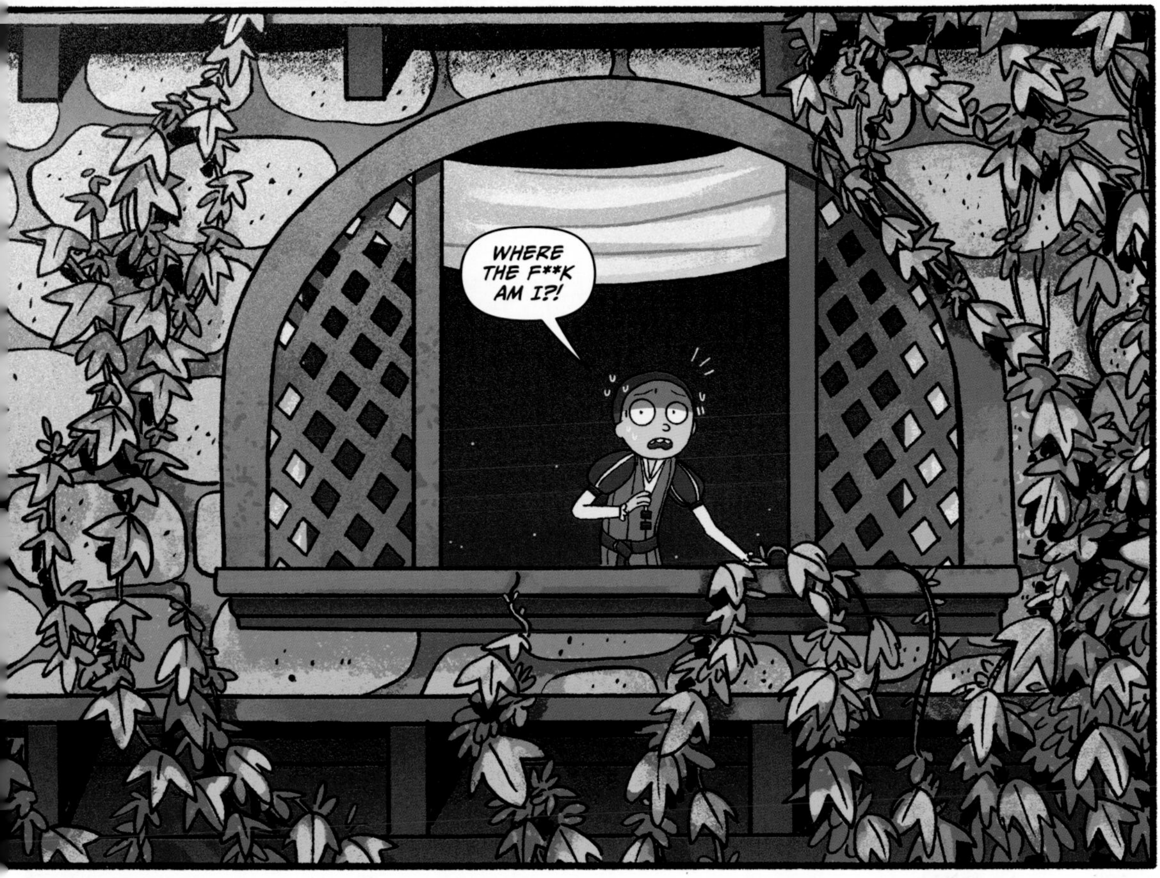
WHERE THE F**K AM I?!

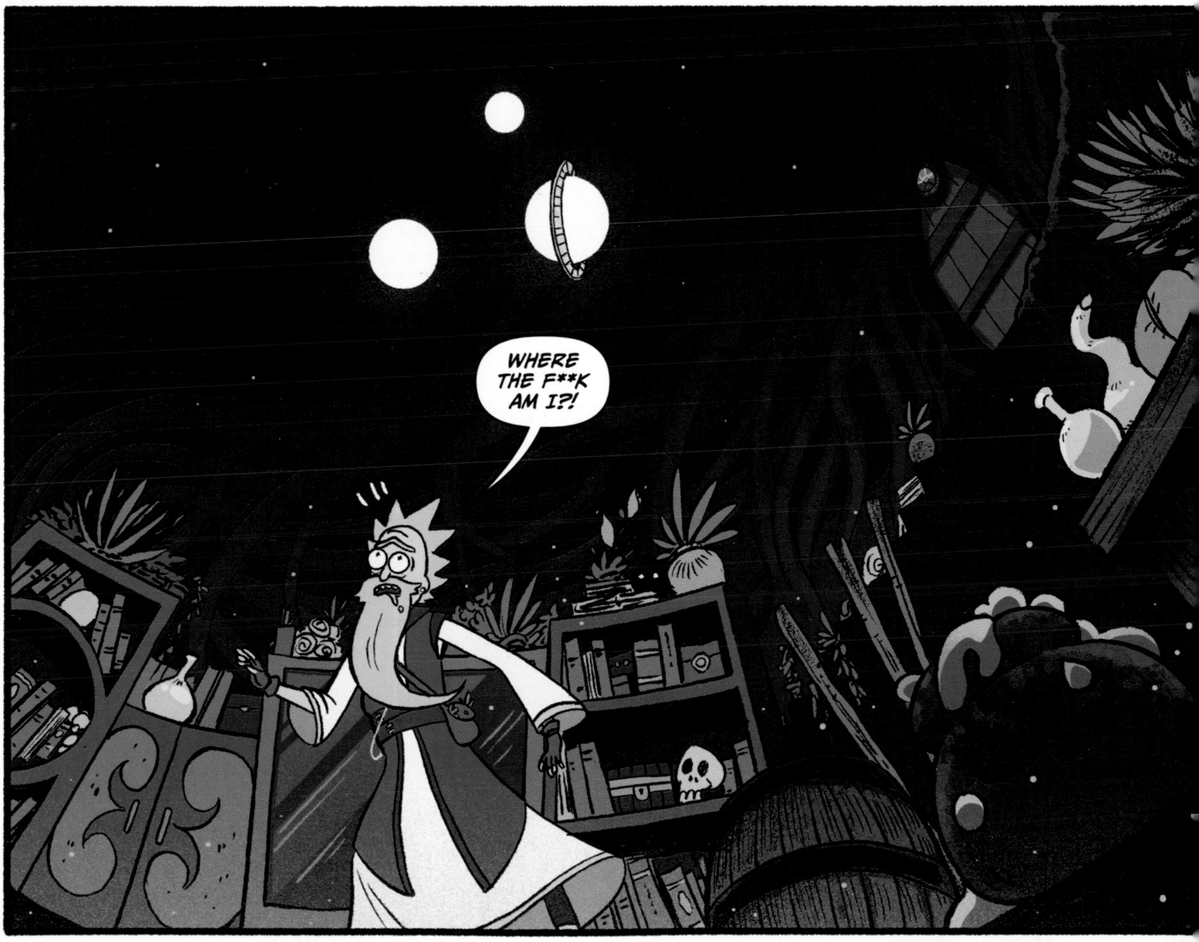
WHERE THE F**K AM I?!

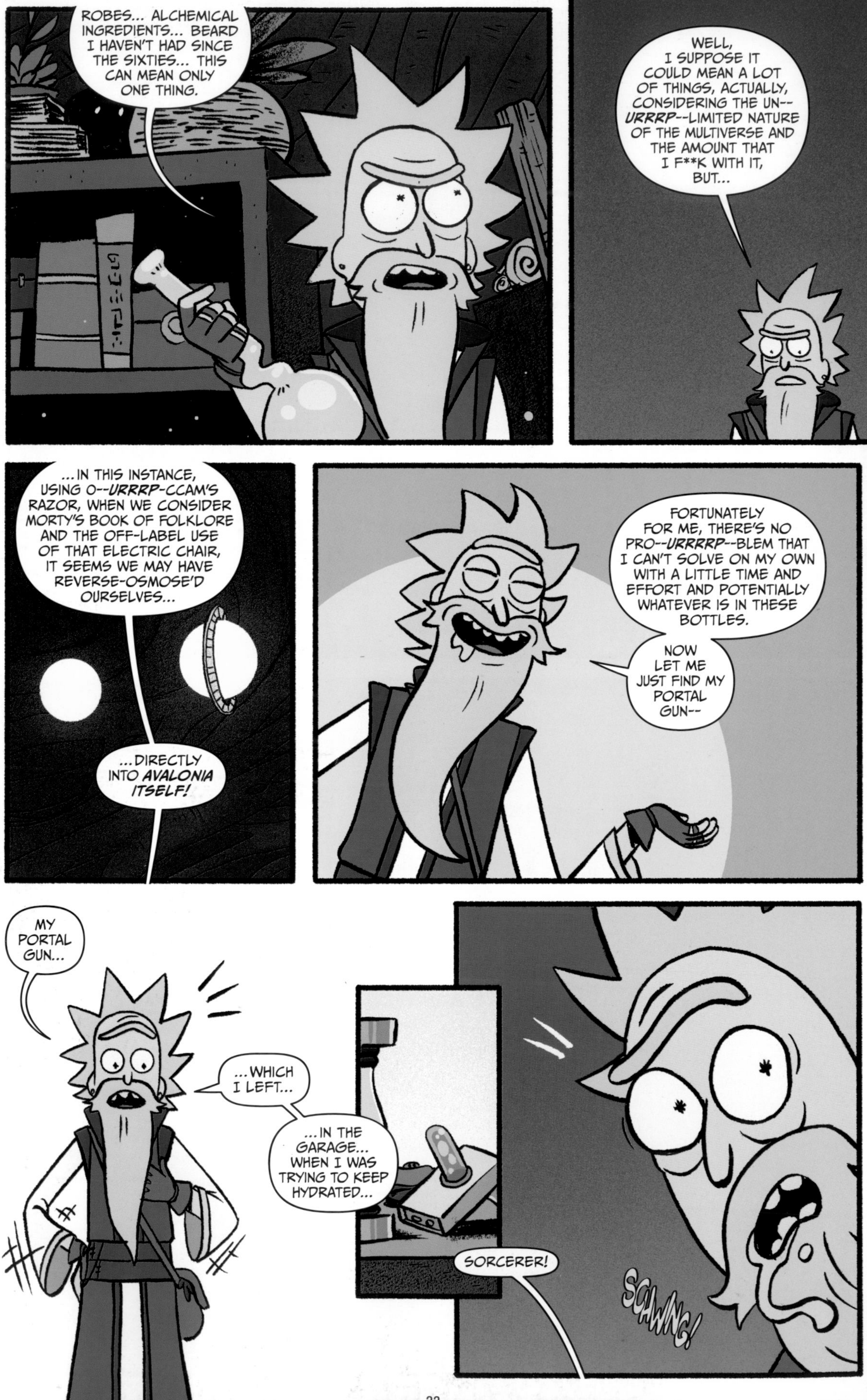
ROBES... ALCHEMICAL INGREDIENTS... BEARD I HAVEN'T HAD SINCE THE SIXTIES... THIS CAN MEAN ONLY ONE THING.
WELL, I SUPPOSE IT COULD MEAN A LOT OF THINGS, ACTUALLY, CONSIDERING THE UN--URRRP--LIMITED NATURE OF THE MULTIVERSE AND THE AMOUNT THAT I F**K WITH IT, BUT...
...IN THIS INSTANCE, USING O--URRRP--CCAM'S RAZOR, WHEN WE CONSIDER MORTY'S BOOK OF FOLKLORE AND THE OFF-LABEL USE OF THAT ELECTRIC CHAIR, IT SEEMS WE MAY HAVE REVERSE-OSMOSE'D OURSELVES...
...DIRECTLY INTO AVALONIA ITSELF!
FORTUNATELY FOR ME, THERE'S NO PRO--URRRRP--BLEM THAT I CAN'T SOLVE ON MY OWN WITH A LITTLE TIME AND EFFORT AND POTENTIALLY WHATEVER IS IN THESE BOTTLES.
NOW LET ME JUST FIND MY PORTAL GUN--
MY PORTAL GUN...
...WHICH I LEFT...
...IN THE GARAGE... WHEN I WAS TRYING TO KEEP HYDRATED...
SORCERER!
SCHWING!

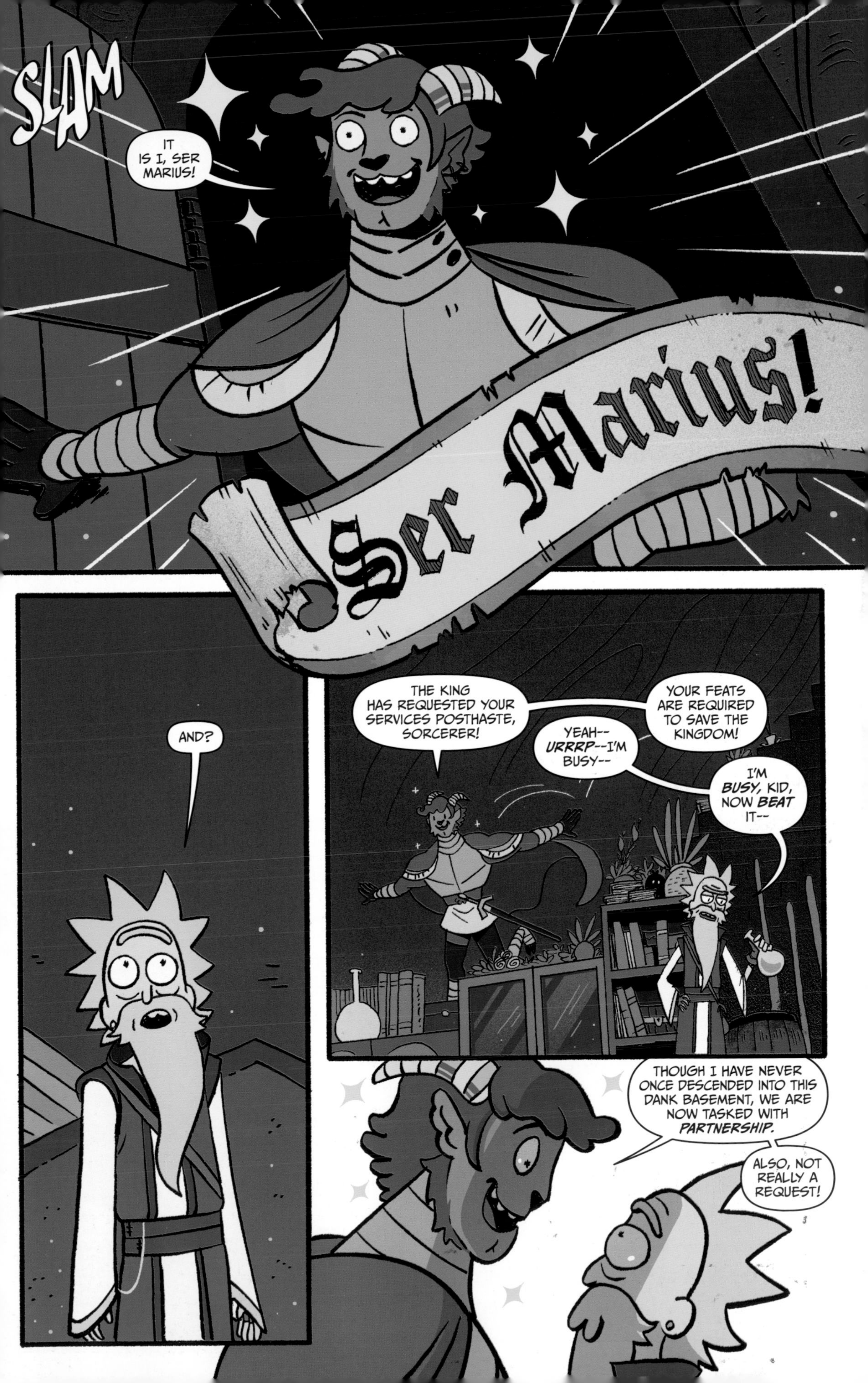
SLAM
IT IS I, SER MARIUS!
Ser Marius!
AND?
THE KING HAS REQUESTED YOUR SERVICES POSTHASTE, SORCERER!
YOUR FEATS ARE REQUIRED TO SAVE THE KINGDOM!
YEAH-- URRRP--I'M BUSY--
I'M BUSY, KID, NOW BEAT IT--
THOUGH I HAVE NEVER ONCE DESCENDED INTO THIS DANK BASEMENT, WE ARE NOW TASKED WITH PARTNERSHIP.
ALSO, NOT REALLY A REQUEST!

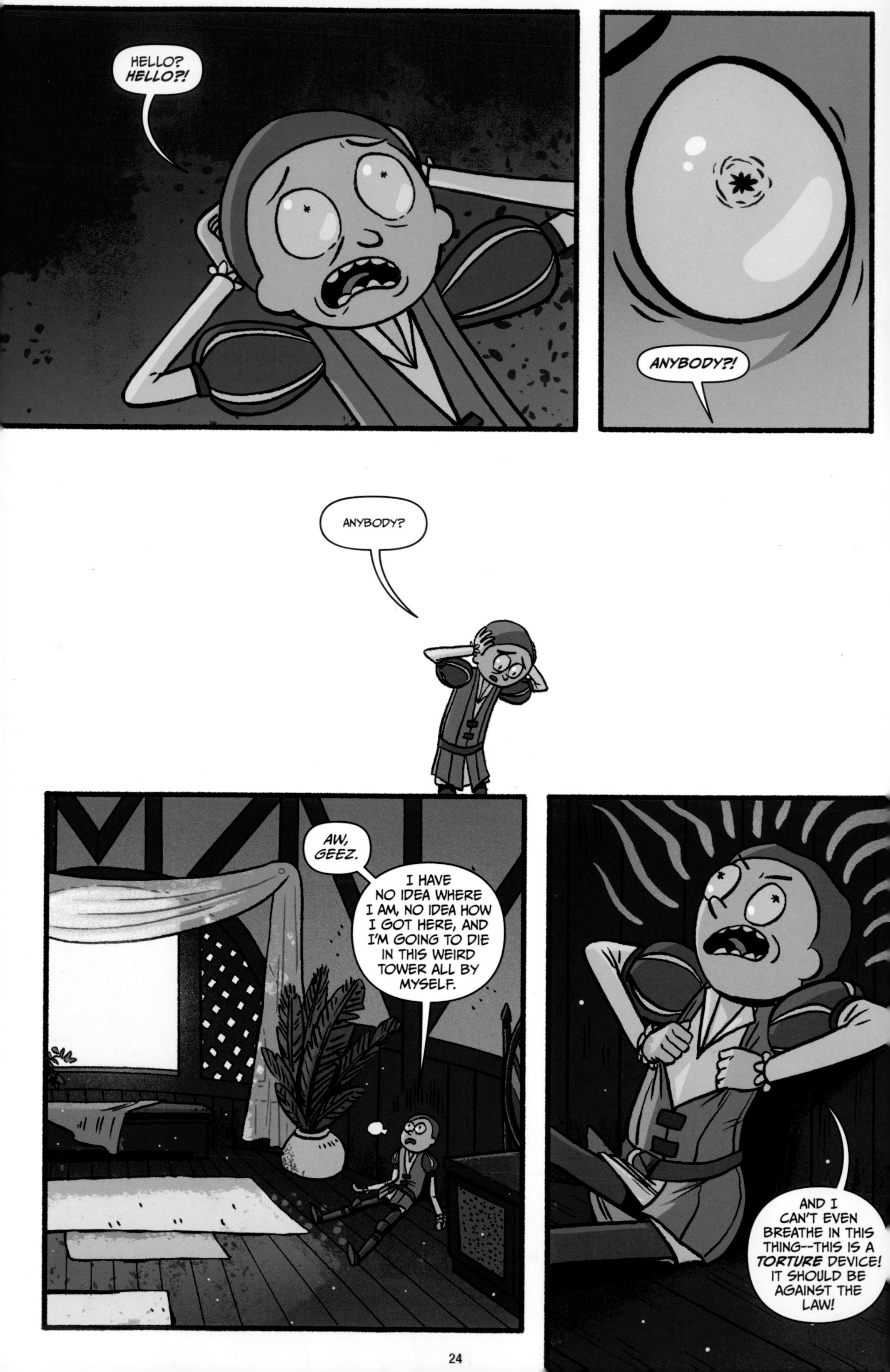
HELLO? HELLO?!
ANYBODY?!
ANYBODY?
AW, GEEZ.
I HAVE NO IDEA WHERE I AM, NO IDEA HOW I GOT HERE, AND I'M GOING TO DIE IN THIS WEIRD TOWER ALL BY MYSELF.
AND I CAN'T EVEN BREATHE IN THIS THING--THIS IS A TORTURE DEVICE! IT SHOULD BE AGAINST THE LAW!

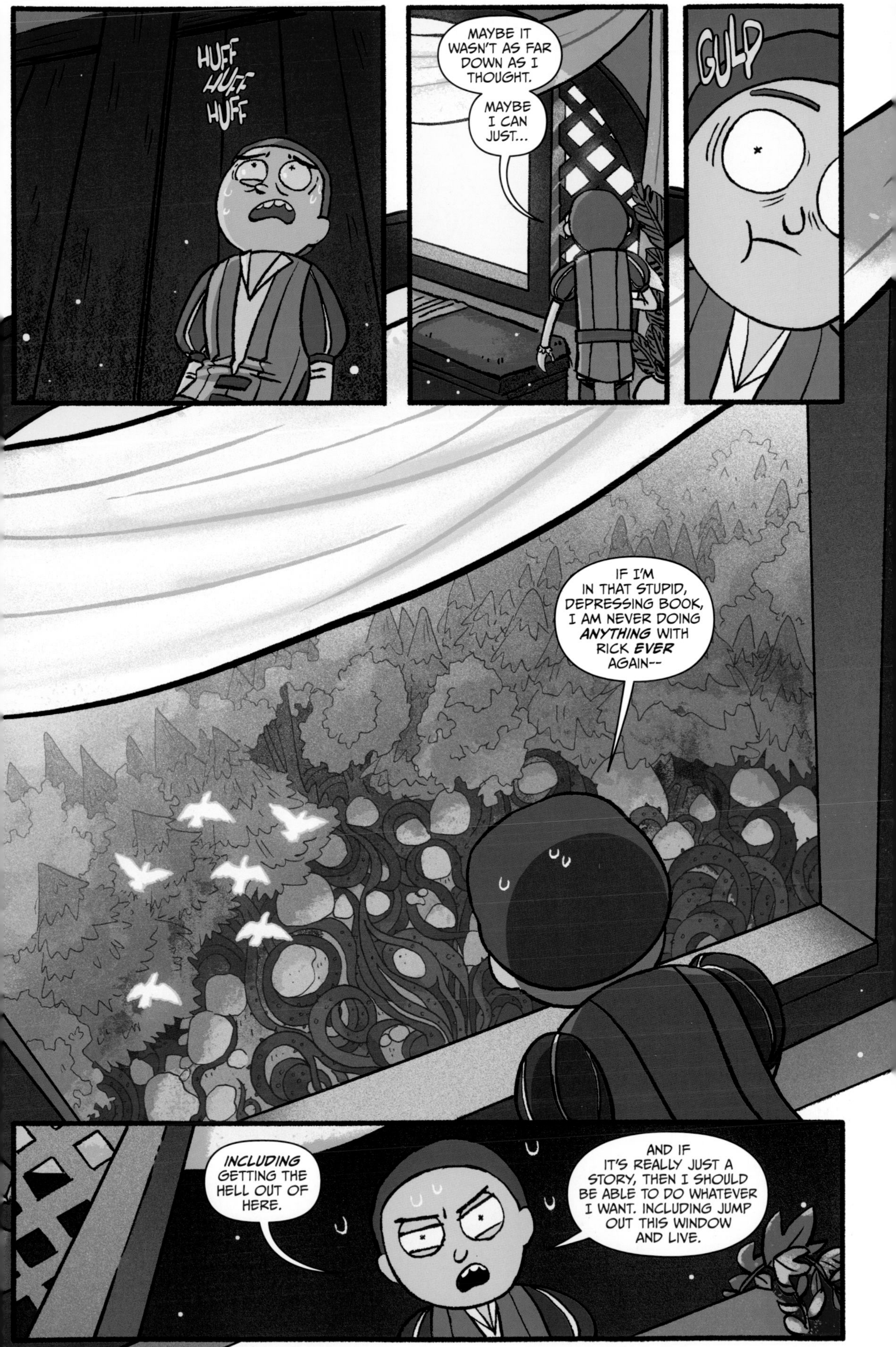
HUFF HUFF HUFF
MAYBE IT WASN'T AS FAR DOWN AS I THOUGHT.
MAYBE I CAN JUST...
GULP
IF I'M IN THAT STUPID, DEPRESSING BOOK, I AM NEVER DOING *ANYTHING* WITH RICK *EVER* AGAIN--
INCLUDING GETTING THE HELL OUT OF HERE.
AND IF IT'S REALLY JUST A STORY, THEN I SHOULD BE ABLE TO DO WHATEVER I WANT. INCLUDING JUMP OUT THIS WINDOW AND LIVE.

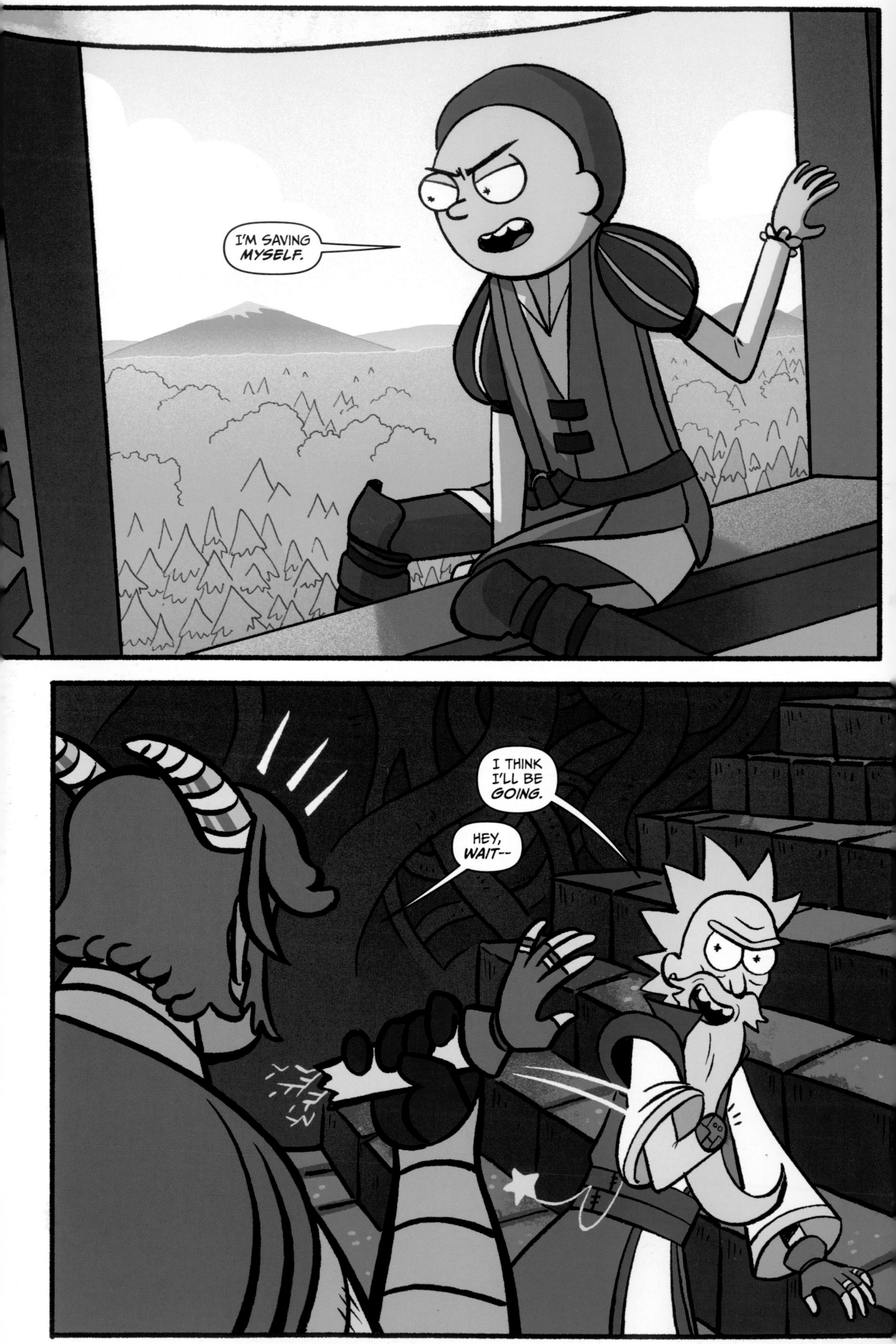
I'M SAVING *MYSELF.*
I THINK I'LL BE *GOING.*
HEY, *WAIT--*

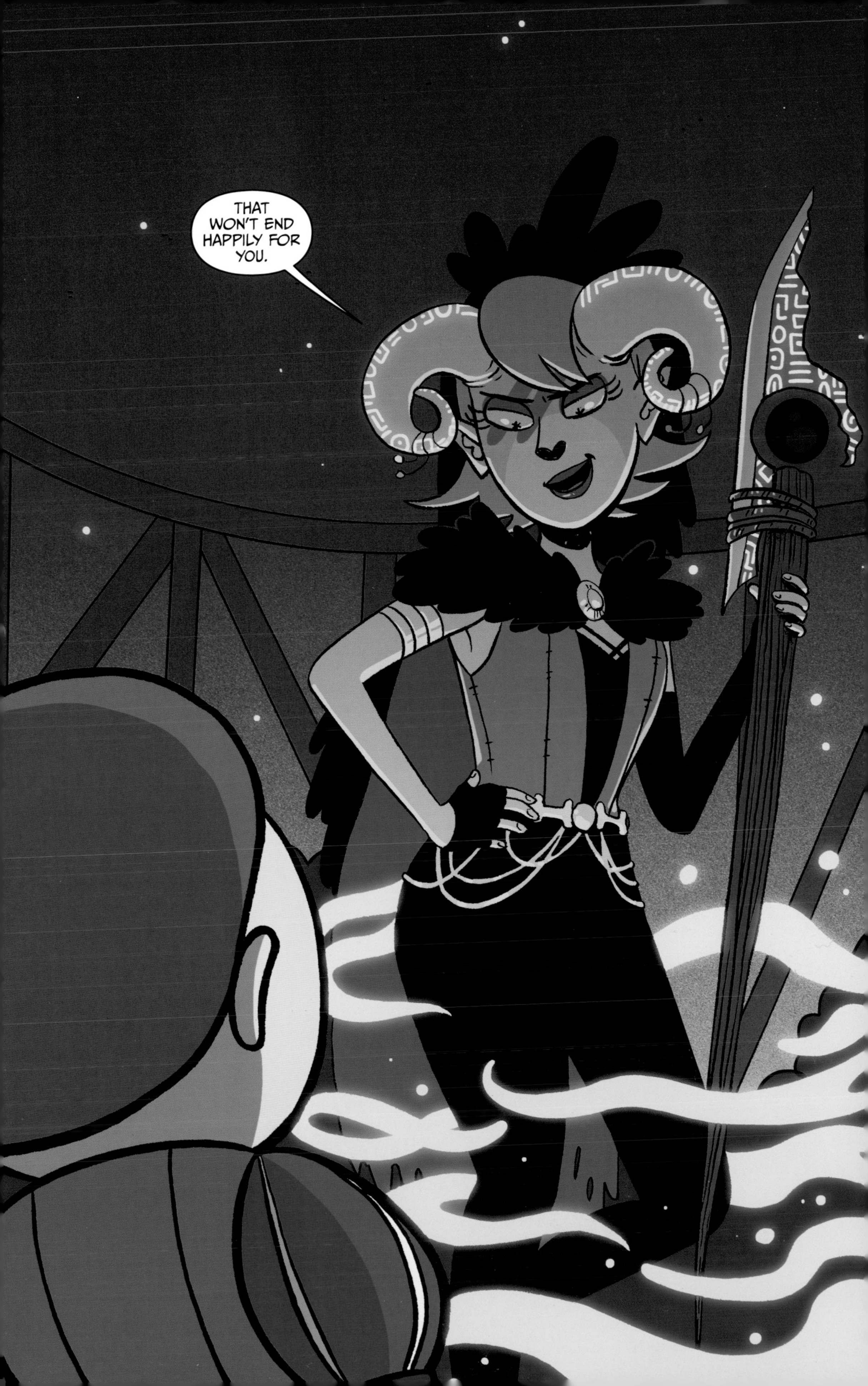
THAT WON'T END HAPPILY FOR YOU.

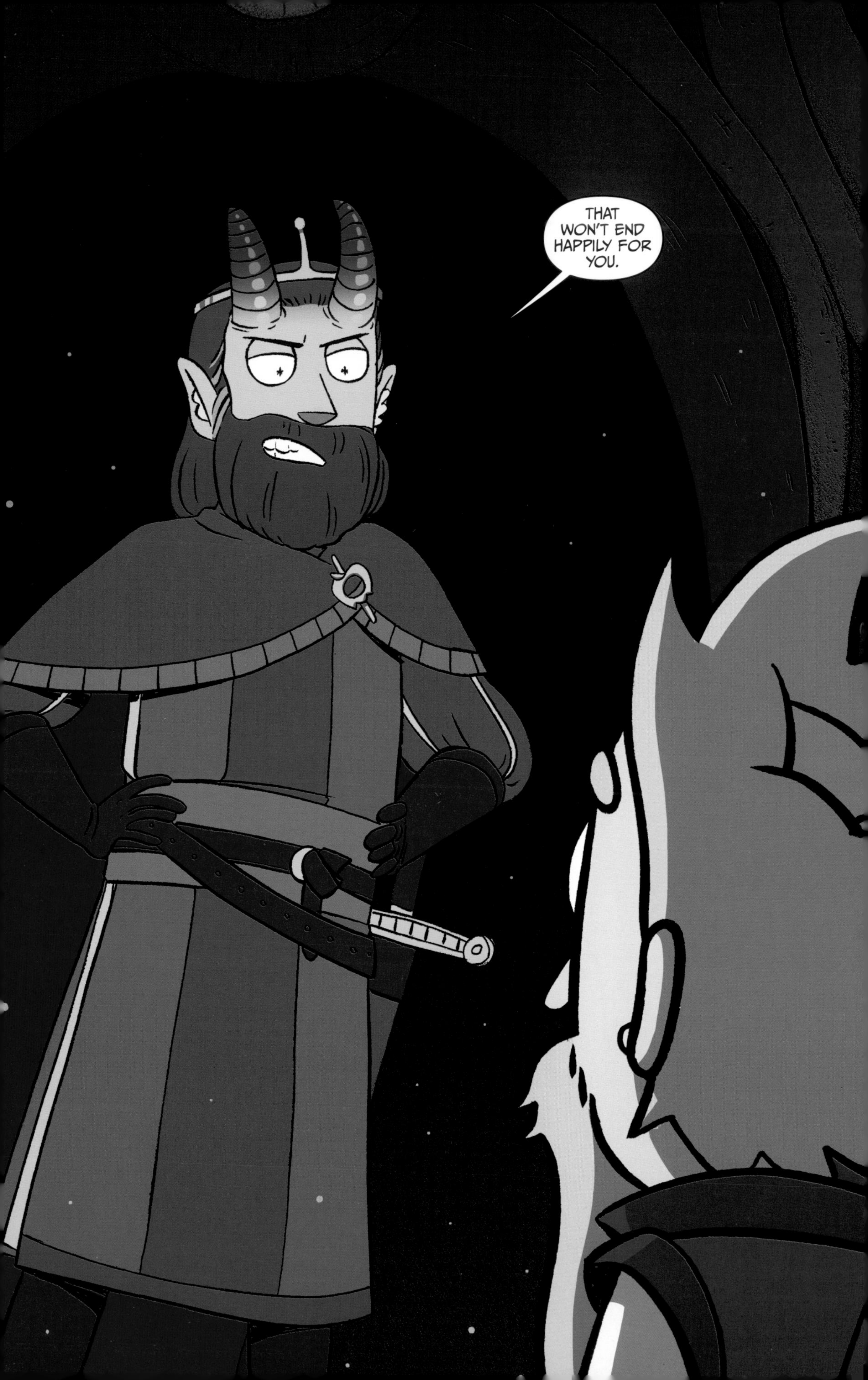
THAT WON'T END HAPPILY FOR YOU.

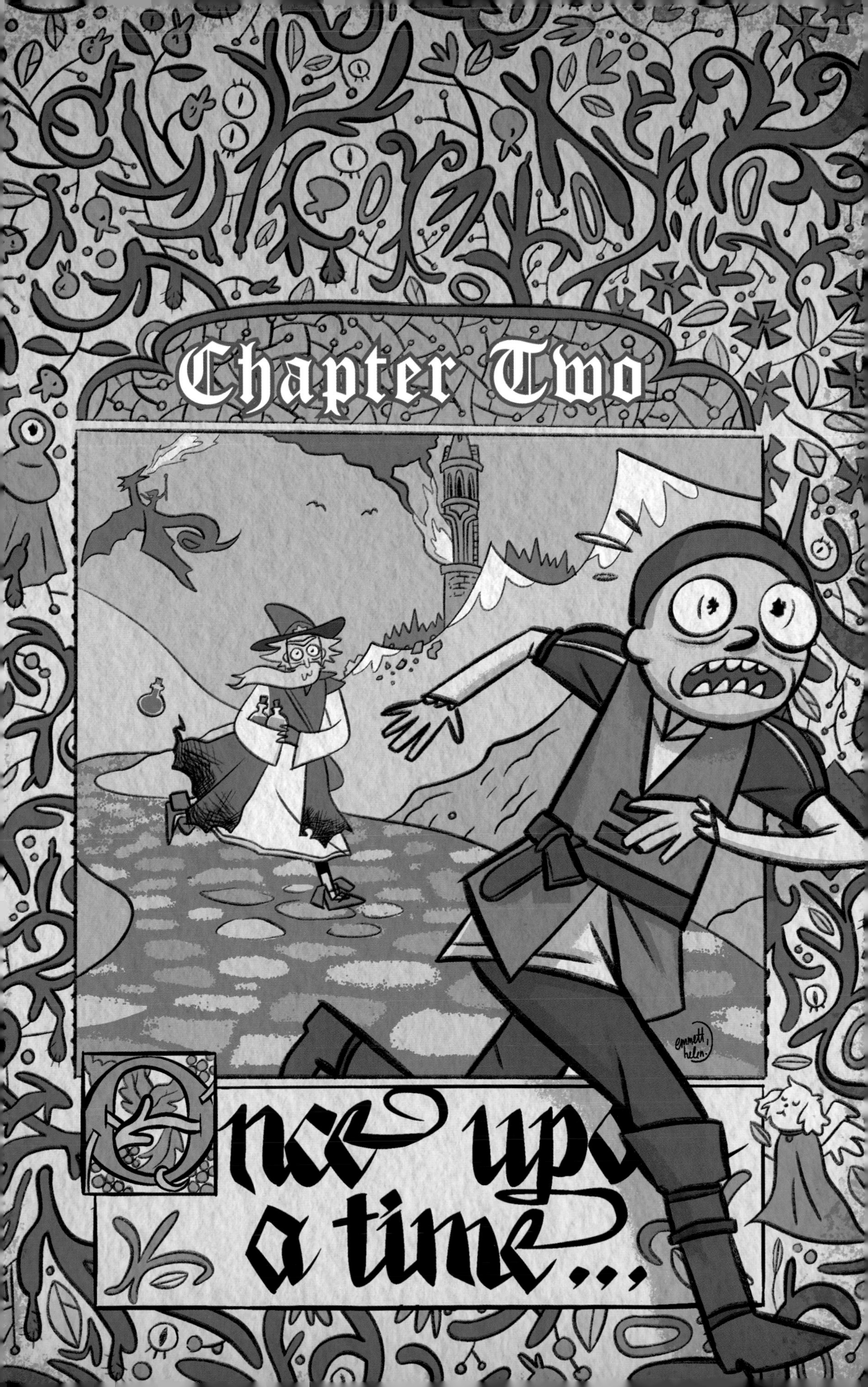
Chapter Two
Once upo
a time...
emmett, helen.

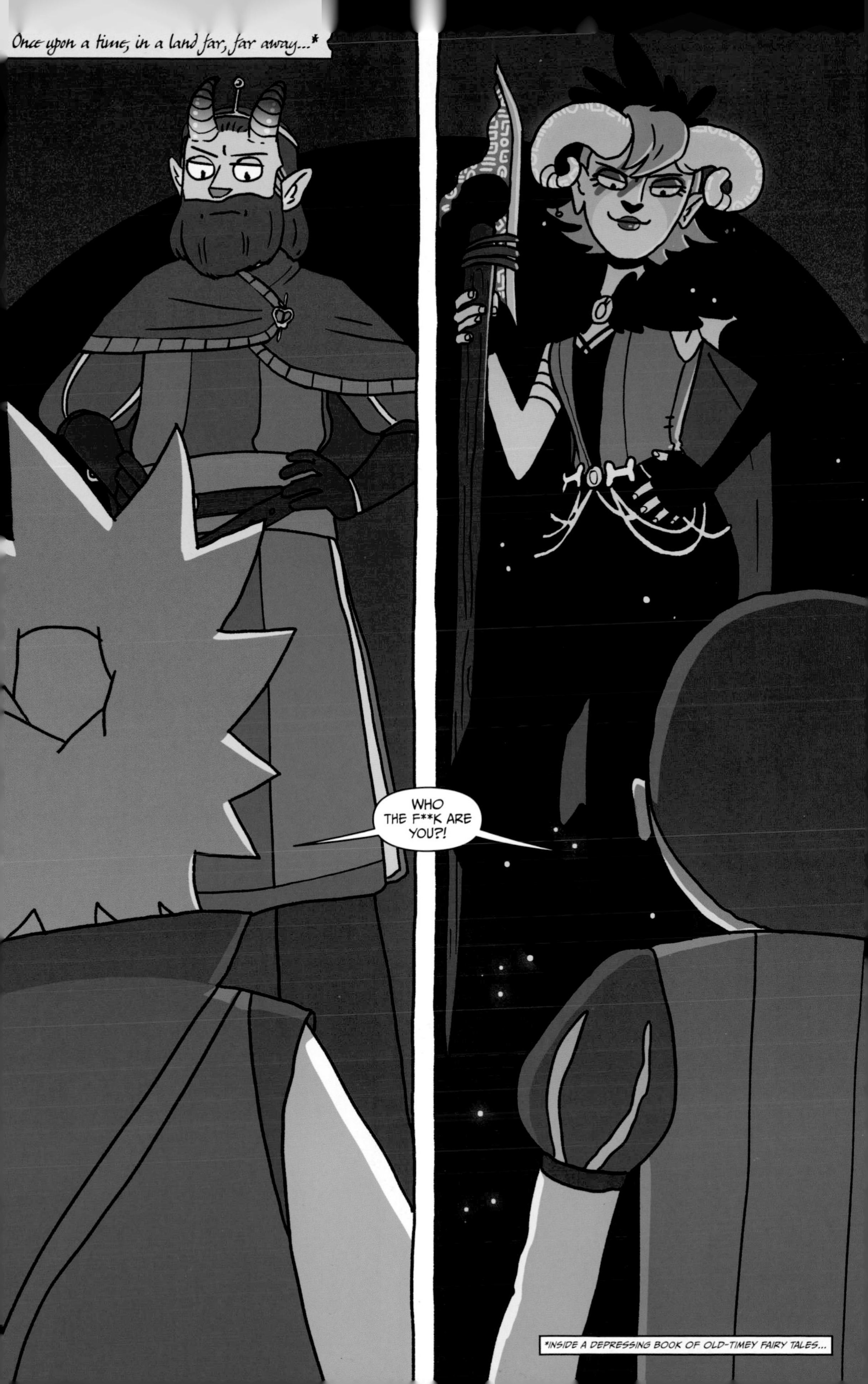
Once upon a time, in a land far, far away...*
WHO THE F**K ARE YOU?!
*INSIDE A DEPRESSING BOOK OF OLD-TIMEY FAIRY TALES...

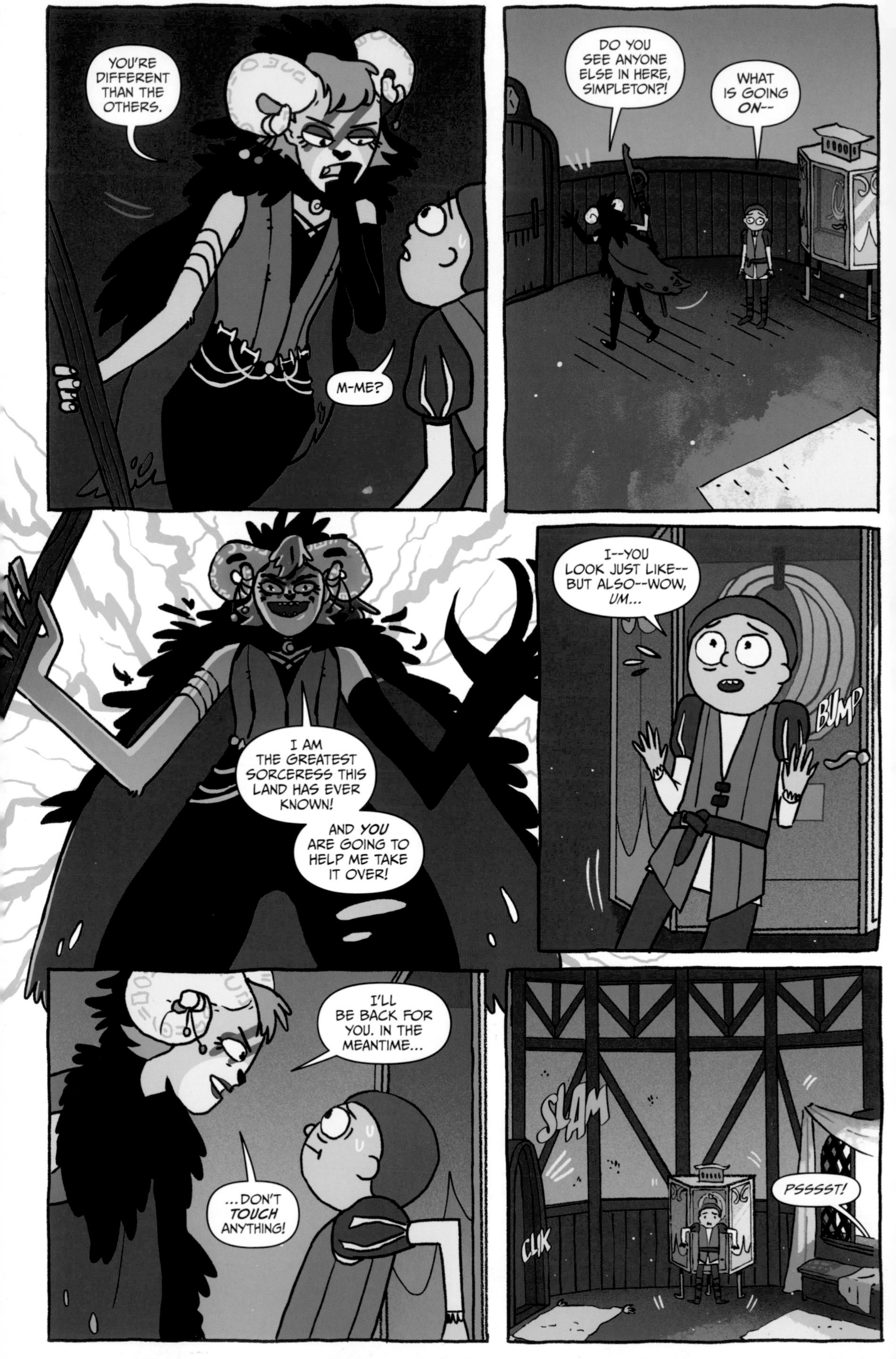

YOU'RE DIFFERENT THAN THE OTHERS.
M-ME?
DO YOU SEE ANYONE ELSE IN HERE, SIMPLETON?!
WHAT IS GOING ON--
I AM THE GREATEST SORCERESS THIS LAND HAS EVER KNOWN!
AND YOU ARE GOING TO HELP ME TAKE IT OVER!
I--YOU LOOK JUST LIKE-- BUT ALSO--WOW, UM...
BUMP
I'LL BE BACK FOR YOU. IN THE MEANTIME...
...DON'T TOUCH ANYTHING!
SLAM
CLIK
PSSSST!

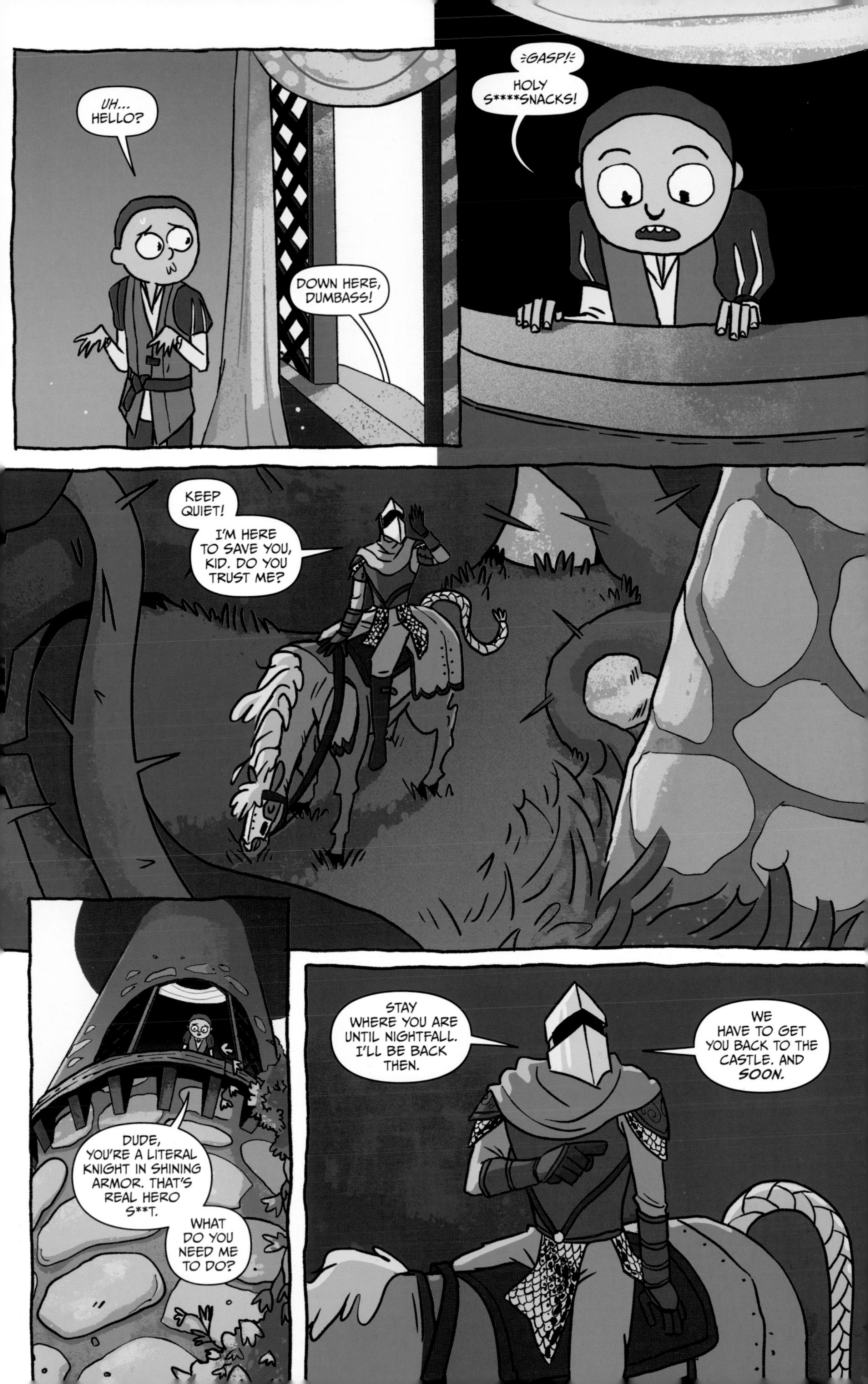
UH...
HELLO?
DOWN HERE, DUMBASS!
GASP!
HOLY S****SNACKS!
KEEP QUIET!
I'M HERE TO SAVE YOU, KID. DO YOU TRUST ME?
DUDE, YOU'RE A LITERAL KNIGHT IN SHINING ARMOR. THAT'S REAL HERO S**T.
WHAT DO YOU NEED ME TO DO?
STAY WHERE YOU ARE UNTIL NIGHTFALL. I'LL BE BACK THEN.
WE HAVE TO GET YOU BACK TO THE CASTLE. AND SOON.

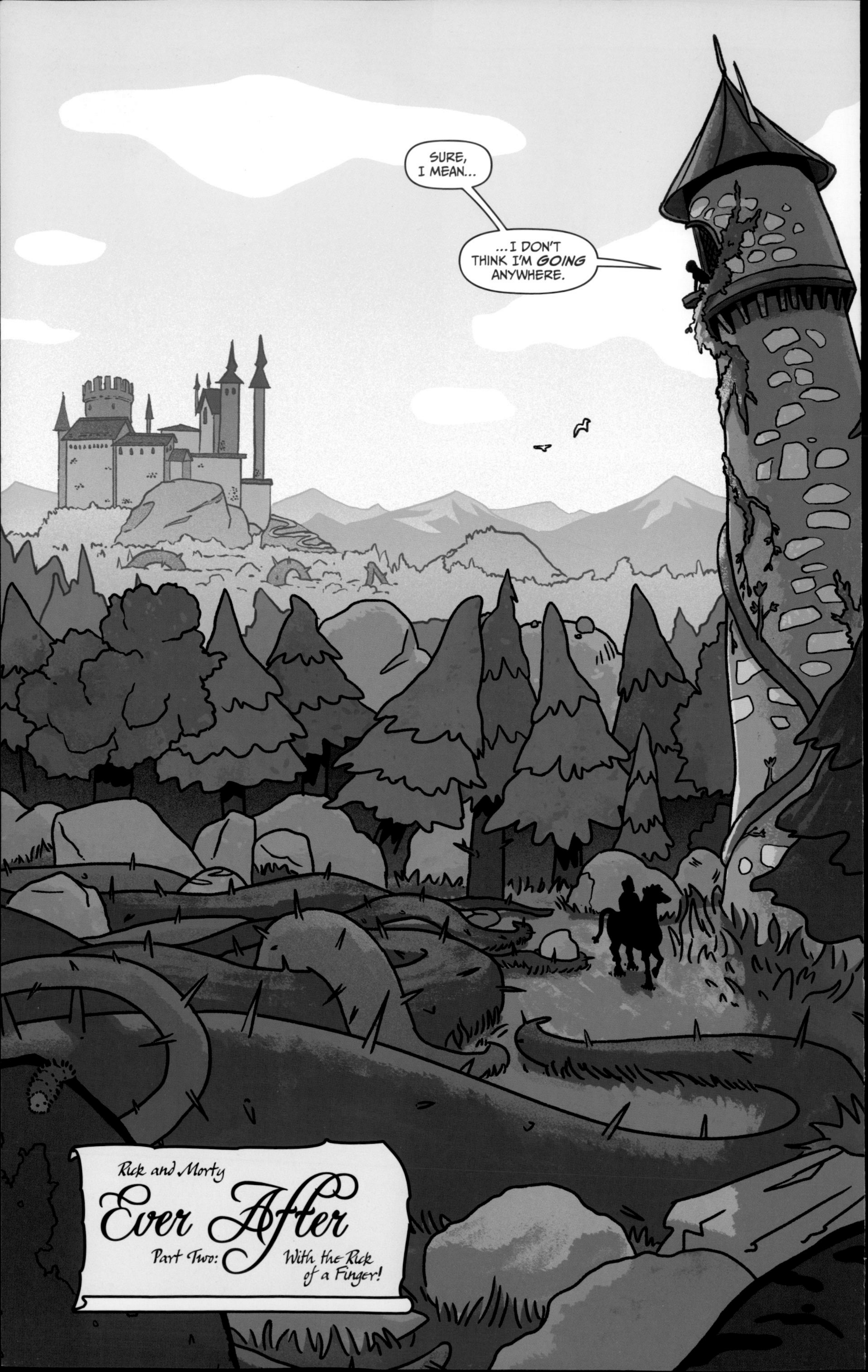
SURE, I MEAN...
...I DON'T THINK I'M GOING ANYWHERE.
Rick and Morty
Ever After
Part Two: With the Rick of a Finger!

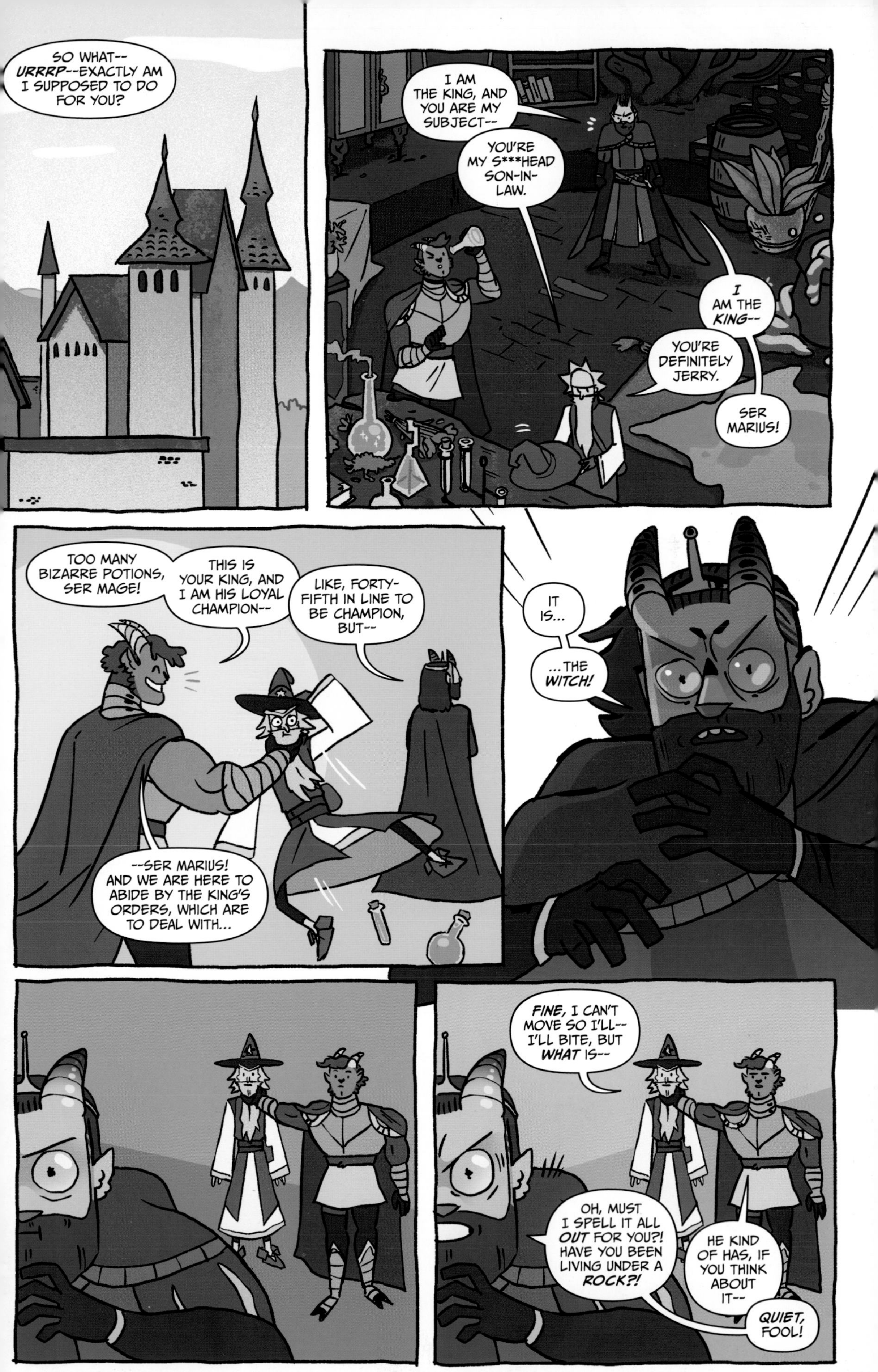
SO WHAT--URRRP--EXACTLY AM I SUPPOSED TO DO FOR YOU?
I AM THE KING, AND YOU ARE MY SUBJECT--
YOU'RE MY S***HEAD SON-IN-LAW.
I AM THE KING--
YOU'RE DEFINITELY JERRY.
SER MARIUS!
TOO MANY BIZARRE POTIONS, SER MAGE!
THIS IS YOUR KING, AND I AM HIS LOYAL CHAMPION--
LIKE, FORTY-FIFTH IN LINE TO BE CHAMPION, BUT--
--SER MARIUS! AND WE ARE HERE TO ABIDE BY THE KING'S ORDERS, WHICH ARE TO DEAL WITH...
IT IS...
...THE WITCH!
FINE, I CAN'T MOVE SO I'LL--I'LL BITE, BUT WHAT IS--
OH, MUST I SPELL IT ALL OUT FOR YOU?! HAVE YOU BEEN LIVING UNDER A ROCK?!
HE KIND OF HAS, IF YOU THINK ABOUT IT--
QUIET, FOOL!

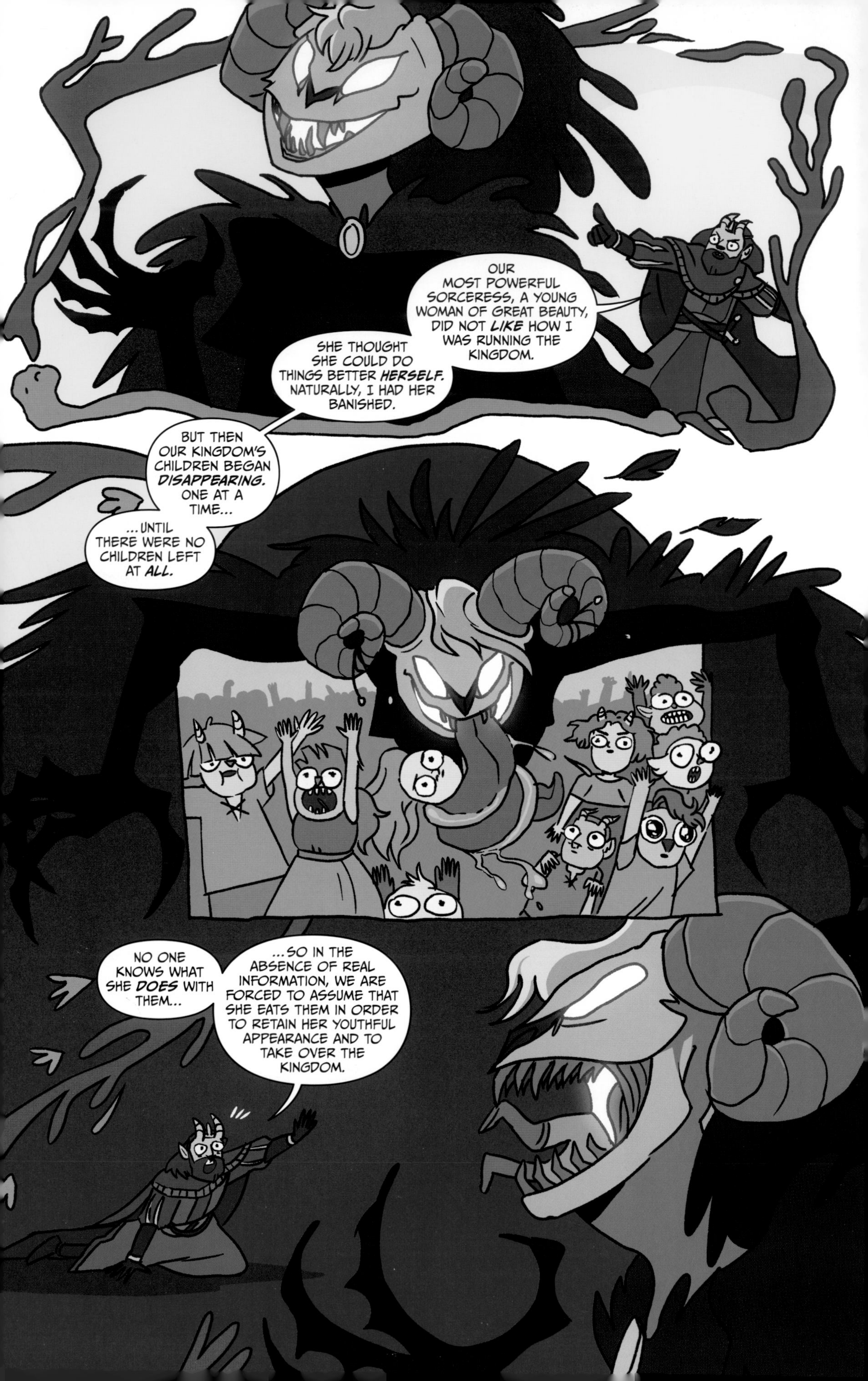
OUR MOST POWERFUL SORCERESS, A YOUNG WOMAN OF GREAT BEAUTY, DID NOT *LIKE* HOW I WAS RUNNING THE KINGDOM.
SHE THOUGHT SHE COULD DO THINGS BETTER *HERSELF.* NATURALLY, I HAD HER BANISHED.
BUT THEN OUR KINGDOM'S CHILDREN BEGAN *DISAPPEARING.* ONE AT A TIME...
...UNTIL THERE WERE NO CHILDREN LEFT AT *ALL.*
NO ONE KNOWS WHAT SHE *DOES* WITH THEM...
...SO IN THE ABSENCE OF REAL INFORMATION, WE ARE FORCED TO ASSUME THAT SHE EATS THEM IN ORDER TO RETAIN HER YOUTHFUL APPEARANCE AND TO TAKE OVER THE KINGDOM.

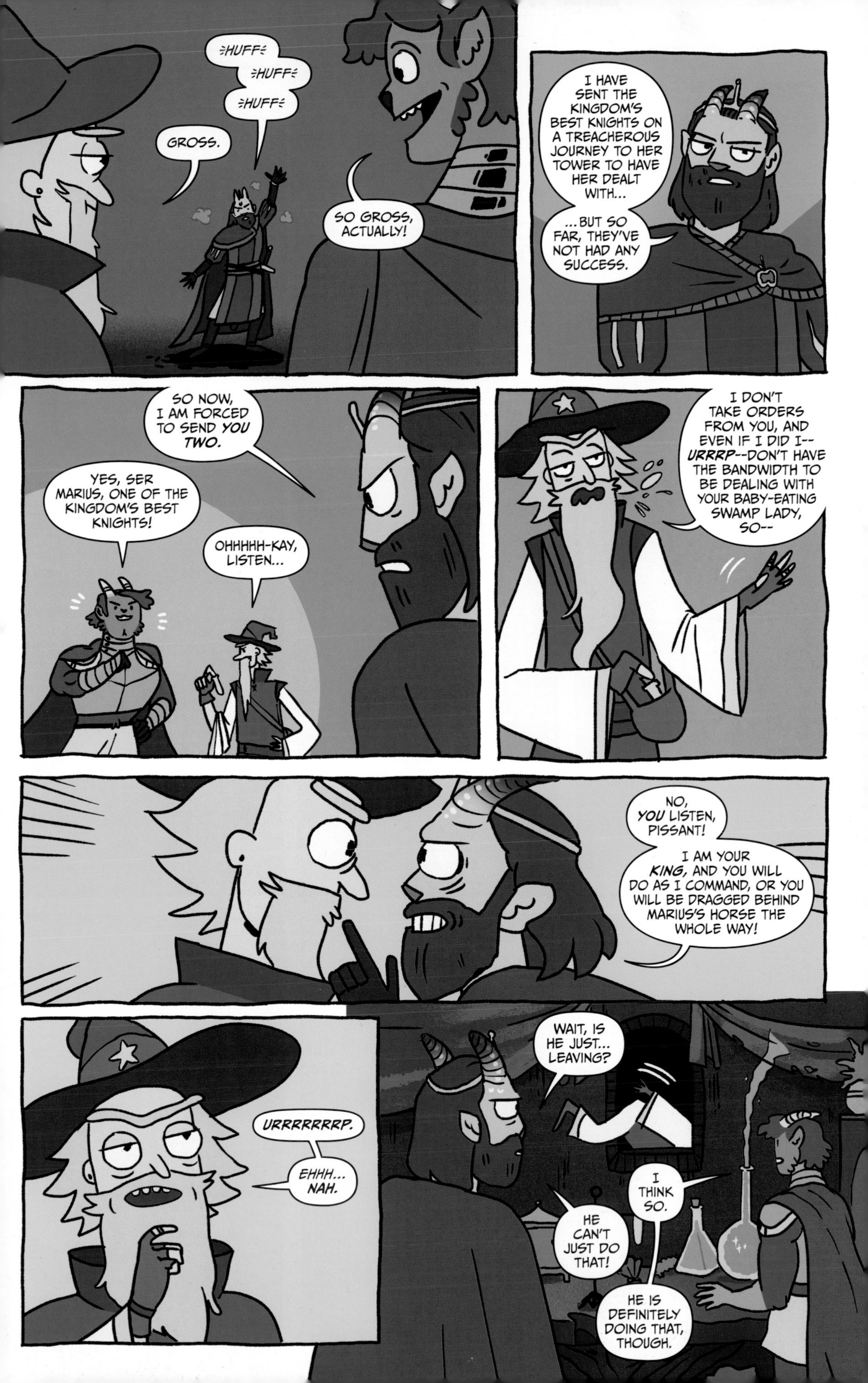

HUFF
HUFF
HUFF
GROSS.
SO GROSS, ACTUALLY!
I HAVE SENT THE KINGDOM'S BEST KNIGHTS ON A TREACHEROUS JOURNEY TO HER TOWER TO HAVE HER DEALT WITH...
...BUT SO FAR, THEY'VE NOT HAD ANY SUCCESS.
SO NOW, I AM FORCED TO SEND *YOU TWO.*
YES, SER MARIUS, ONE OF THE KINGDOM'S BEST KNIGHTS!
OHHHHH-KAY, LISTEN...
I DON'T TAKE ORDERS FROM YOU, AND EVEN IF I DID I-- *URRRP*--DON'T HAVE THE BANDWIDTH TO BE DEALING WITH YOUR BABY-EATING SWAMP LADY, SO--
NO, *YOU* LISTEN, PISSANT!
I AM YOUR *KING,* AND YOU WILL DO AS I COMMAND, OR YOU WILL BE DRAGGED BEHIND MARIUS'S HORSE THE WHOLE WAY!
URRRRRRRP.
EHHH... NAH.
WAIT, IS HE JUST... LEAVING?
I THINK SO.
HE CAN'T JUST DO THAT!
HE IS DEFINITELY DOING THAT, THOUGH.

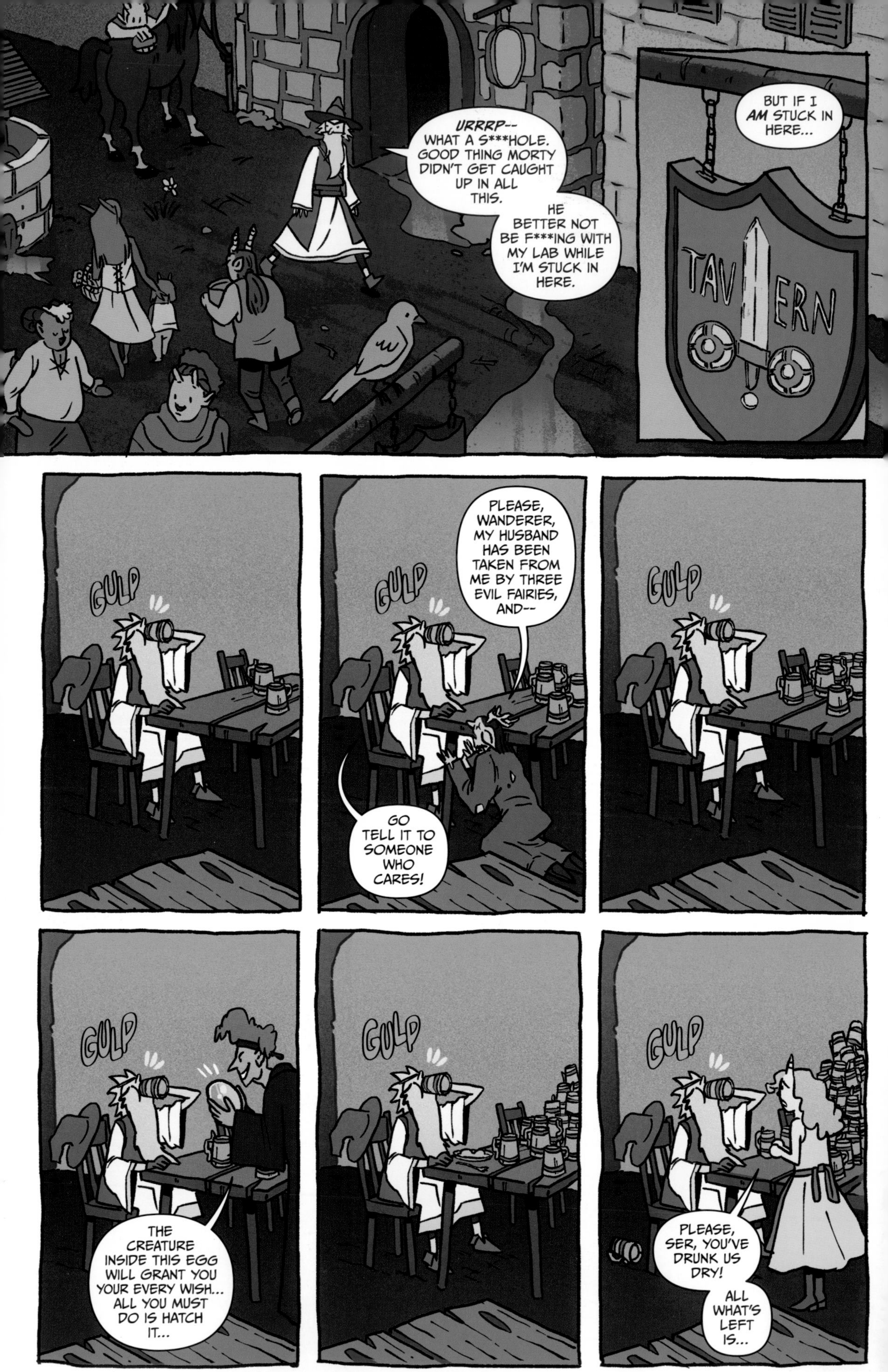
URRRP-- WHAT A S***HOLE. GOOD THING MORTY DIDN'T GET CAUGHT UP IN ALL THIS.
HE BETTER NOT BE F***ING WITH MY LAB WHILE I'M STUCK IN HERE.
BUT IF I AM STUCK IN HERE...
TAVERN
GULP
GULP
PLEASE, WANDERER, MY HUSBAND HAS BEEN TAKEN FROM ME BY THREE EVIL FAIRIES, AND--
GO TELL IT TO SOMEONE WHO CARES!
GULP
GULP
THE CREATURE INSIDE THIS EGG WILL GRANT YOU YOUR EVERY WISH... ALL YOU MUST DO IS HATCH IT...
GULP
GULP
PLEASE, SER, YOU'VE DRUNK US DRY!
ALL WHAT'S LEFT IS...

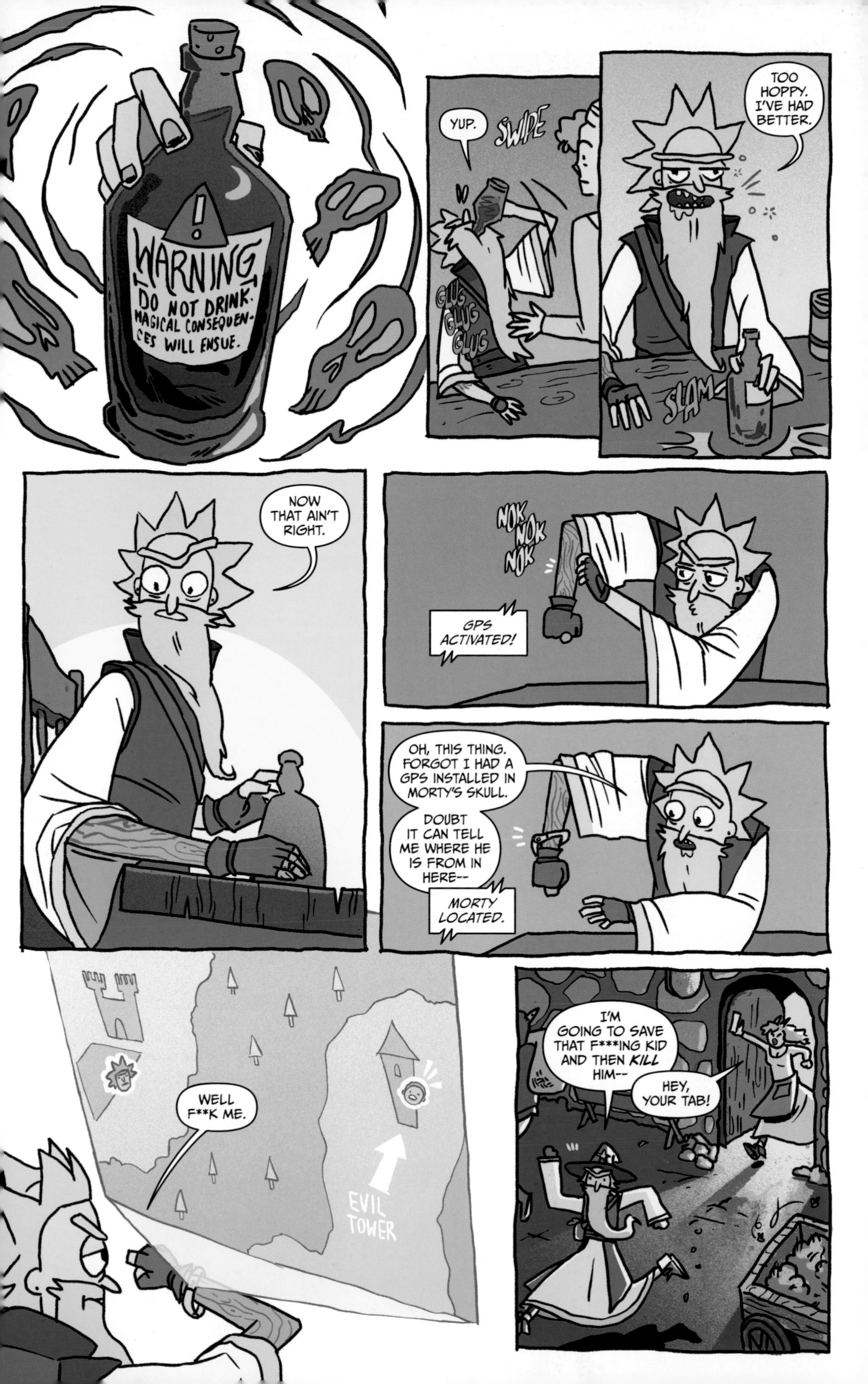
WARNING
DO NOT DRINK.
MAGICAL CONSEQUENCES WILL ENSUE.
YUP.
SWIPE
GLUG GLUG GLUG
TOO HOPPY. I'VE HAD BETTER.
SLAM
NOW THAT AIN'T RIGHT.
NOK NOK NOK
GPS ACTIVATED!
OH, THIS THING. FORGOT I HAD A GPS INSTALLED IN MORTY'S SKULL.
DOUBT IT CAN TELL ME WHERE HE IS FROM IN HERE--
MORTY LOCATED.
WELL F**K ME.
EVIL TOWER
I'M GOING TO SAVE THAT F***ING KID AND THEN KILL HIM--
HEY, YOUR TAB!

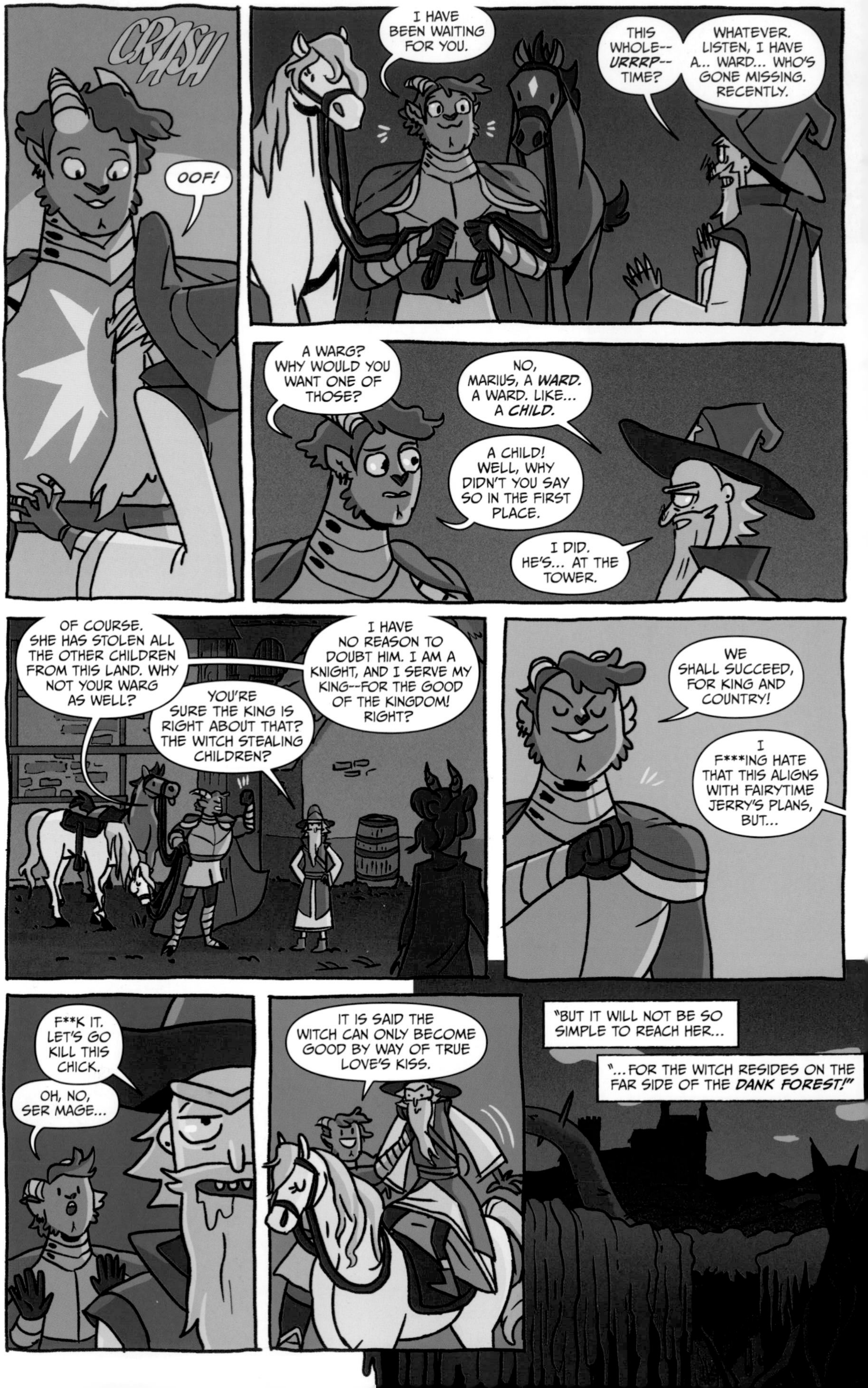
CRASH
OOF!
I HAVE BEEN WAITING FOR YOU.
THIS WHOLE-- URRRP-- TIME?
WHATEVER. LISTEN, I HAVE A... WARD... WHO'S GONE MISSING. RECENTLY.
A WARG? WHY WOULD YOU WANT ONE OF THOSE?
NO, MARIUS, A WARD. A WARD. LIKE... A CHILD.
A CHILD! WELL, WHY DIDN'T YOU SAY SO IN THE FIRST PLACE.
I DID. HE'S... AT THE TOWER.
OF COURSE. SHE HAS STOLEN ALL THE OTHER CHILDREN FROM THIS LAND. WHY NOT YOUR WARG AS WELL?
YOU'RE SURE THE KING IS RIGHT ABOUT THAT? THE WITCH STEALING CHILDREN?
I HAVE NO REASON TO DOUBT HIM. I AM A KNIGHT, AND I SERVE MY KING--FOR THE GOOD OF THE KINGDOM! RIGHT?
WE SHALL SUCCEED, FOR KING AND COUNTRY!
I F***ING HATE THAT THIS ALIGNS WITH FAIRYTIME JERRY'S PLANS, BUT...
F**K IT. LET'S GO KILL THIS CHICK.
OH, NO, SER MAGE...
IT IS SAID THE WITCH CAN ONLY BECOME GOOD BY WAY OF TRUE LOVE'S KISS.
"BUT IT WILL NOT BE SO SIMPLE TO REACH HER...
"...FOR THE WITCH RESIDES ON THE FAR SIDE OF THE DANK FOREST!"

HEY, KID! I'M BACK!

OKAY, LET'S DO THIS.

TOSS IT DOWN.

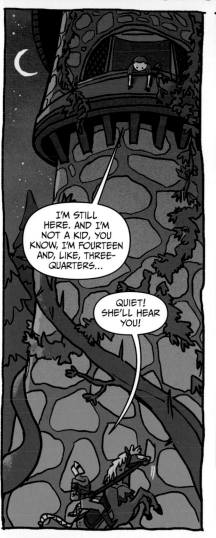

I'M STILL HERE. AND I'M NOT A KID, YOU KNOW, I'M FOURTEEN AND, LIKE, THREE-QUARTERS...

QUIET! SHE'LL HEAR YOU!

C'MON. TOSS DOWN THE HAIR. LET'S GO.

THIS IS MY HAIR. THIS IS ALL OF IT.

YOU'RE SEEING ALL OF IT.

WHAT ELSE HAVE YOU BEEN DOING UP THERE?!

I HAVEN'T BEEN UP HERE VERY LONG!

WELL, I CAN TELL THAT NOW!

OKAY!

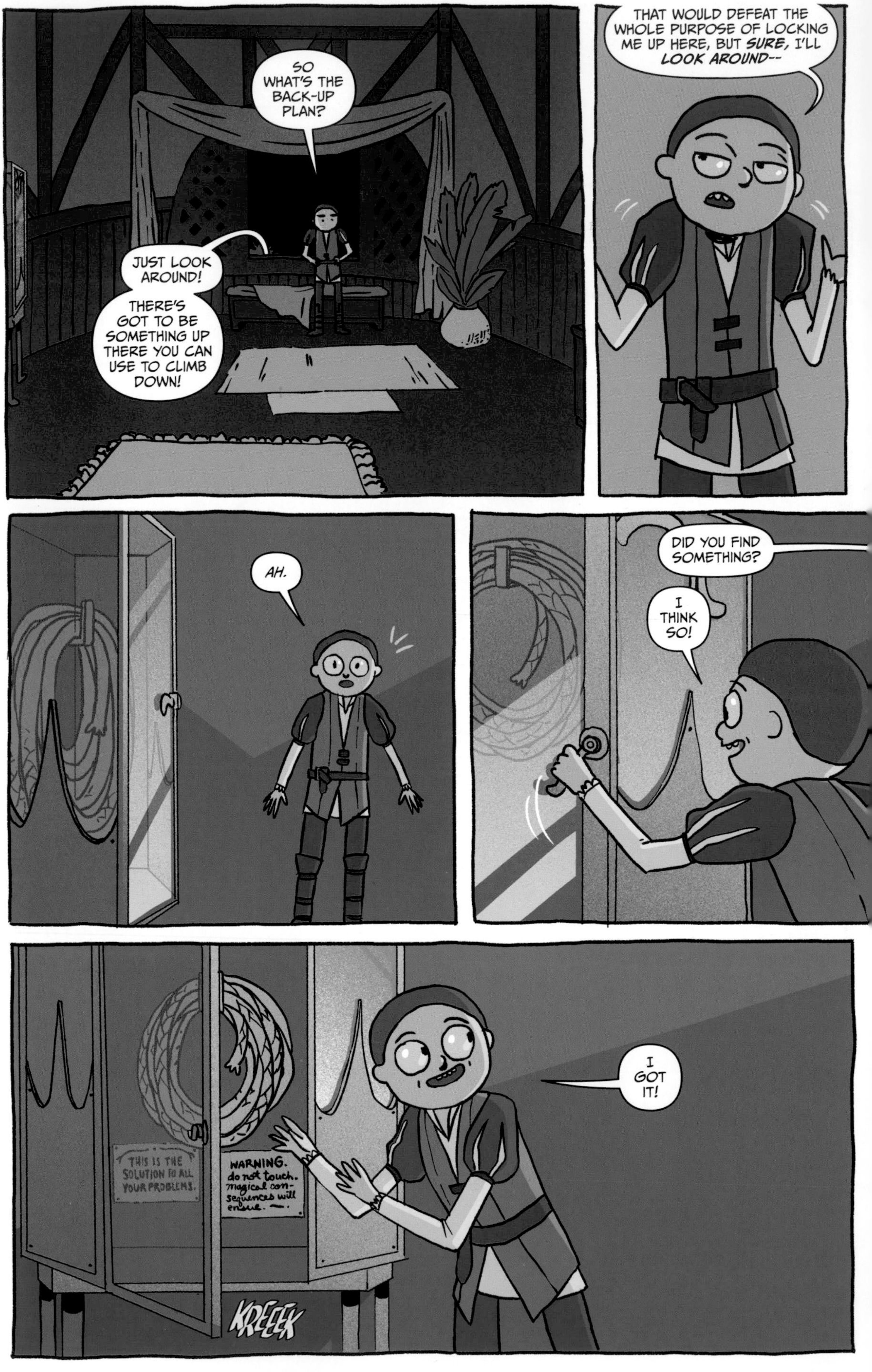
SO WHAT'S THE BACK-UP PLAN?
JUST LOOK AROUND!
THERE'S GOT TO BE SOMETHING UP THERE YOU CAN USE TO CLIMB DOWN!
THAT WOULD DEFEAT THE WHOLE PURPOSE OF LOCKING ME UP HERE, BUT *SURE*, I'LL *LOOK AROUND--*
AH.
DID YOU FIND SOMETHING?
I THINK SO!
THIS IS THE SOLUTION TO ALL YOUR PROBLEMS.
WARNING. do not touch. magical consequences will ensue.
KREEEK
I GOT IT!

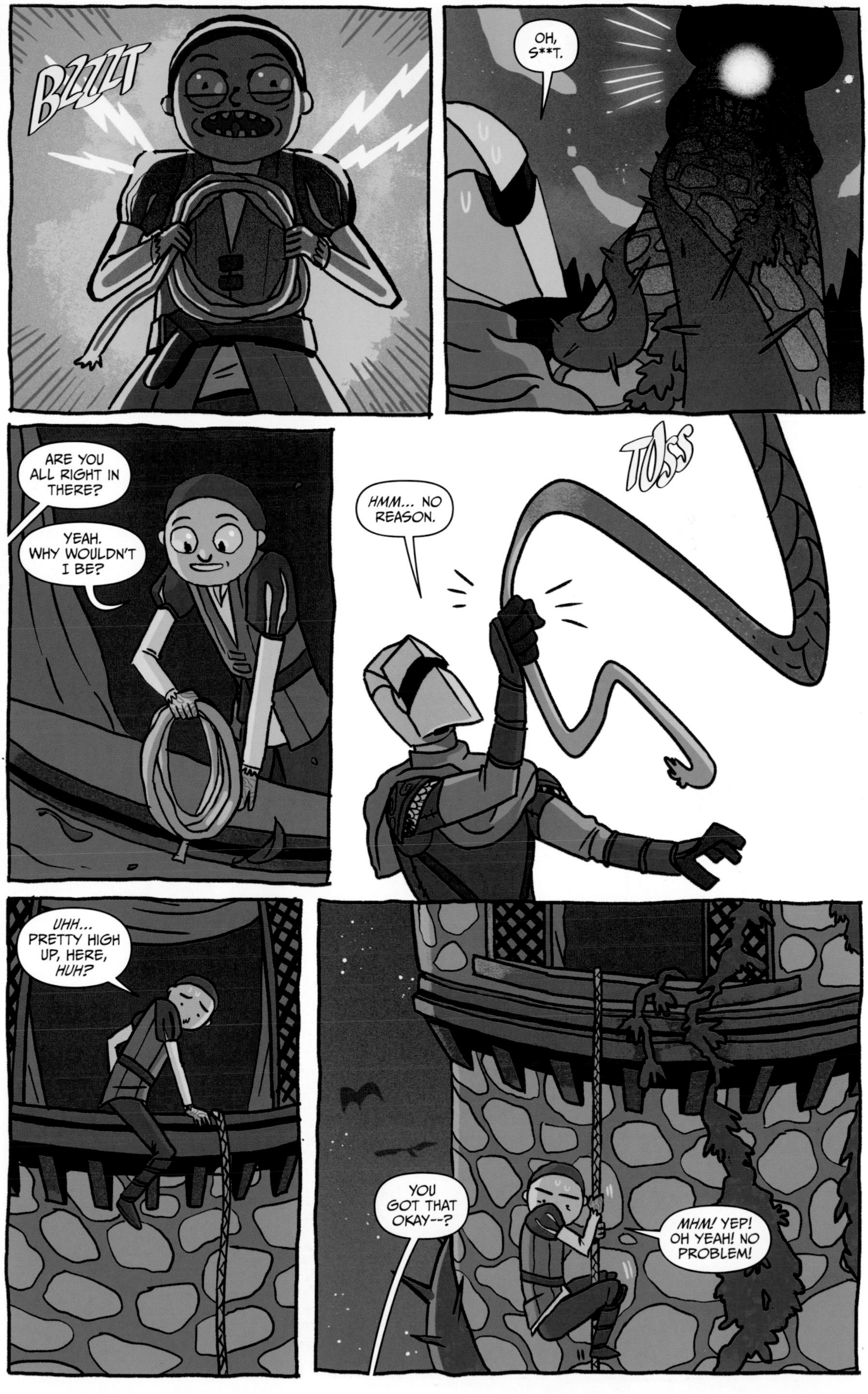

BZZZZT
OH, S**T.
ARE YOU ALL RIGHT IN THERE?
YEAH. WHY WOULDN'T I BE?
HMM... NO REASON.
TOSS
UHH... PRETTY HIGH UP, HERE, HUH?
YOU GOT THAT OKAY--?
MHM! YEP! OH YEAH! NO PROBLEM!

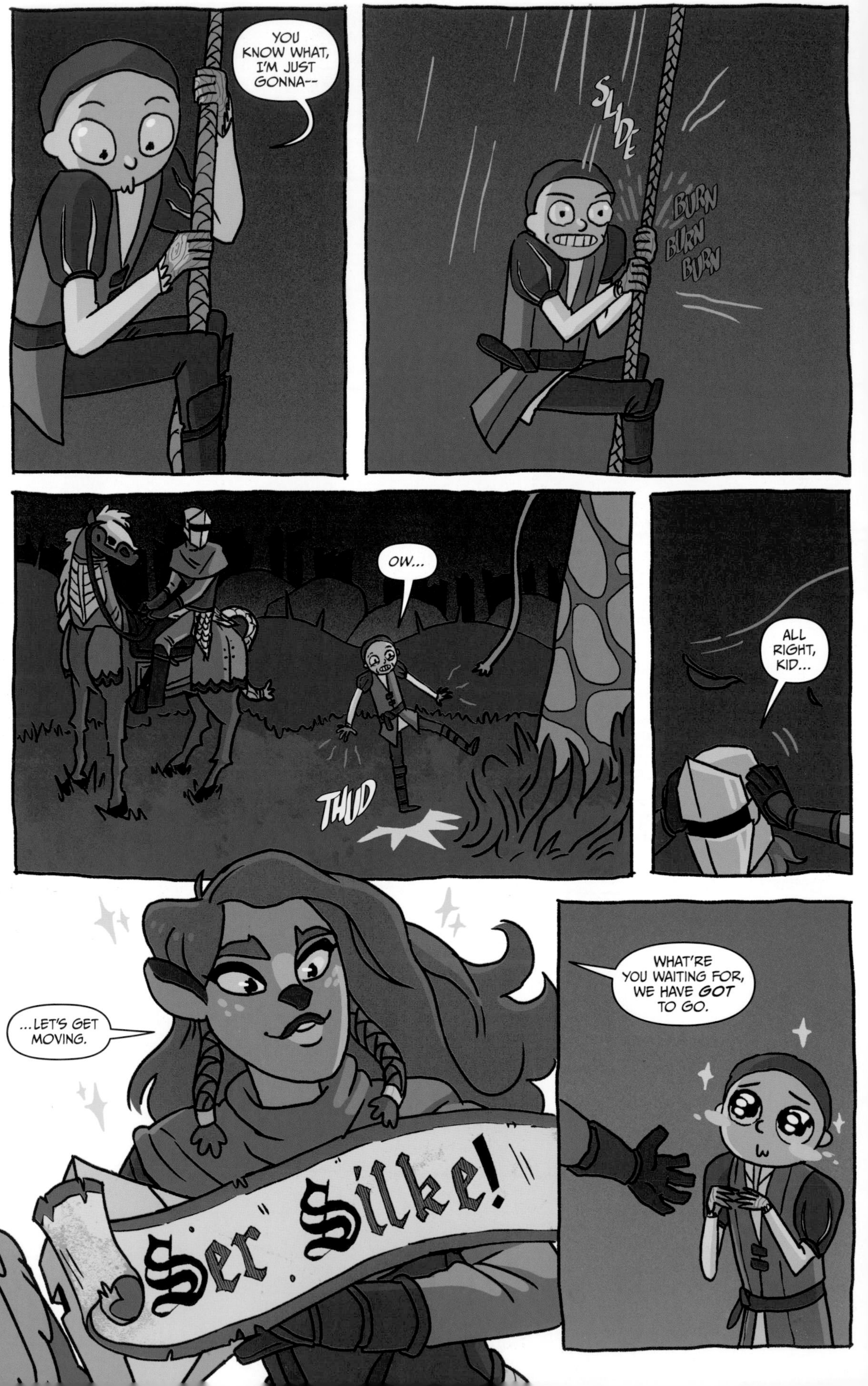
YOU KNOW WHAT, I'M JUST GONNA--
SLIDE
BURN BURN BURN
OW...
THUD
ALL RIGHT, KID...
...LET'S GET MOVING.
Ser Silke!
WHAT'RE YOU WAITING FOR, WE HAVE GOT TO GO.

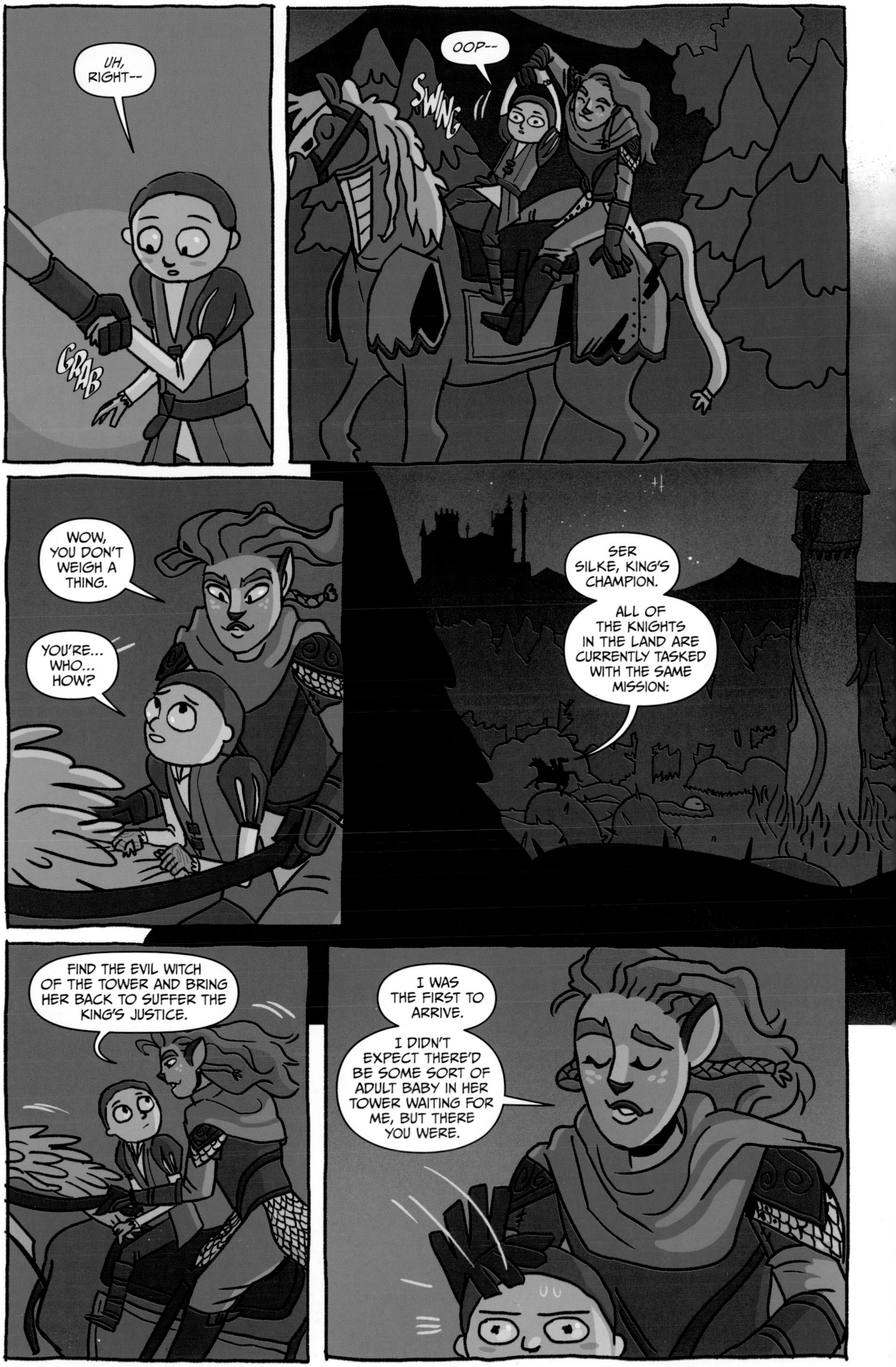
UH, RIGHT--
GRAB
OOP--
SWING
WOW, YOU DON'T WEIGH A THING.
YOU'RE... WHO... HOW?
SER SILKE, KING'S CHAMPION.
ALL OF THE KNIGHTS IN THE LAND ARE CURRENTLY TASKED WITH THE SAME MISSION:
FIND THE EVIL WITCH OF THE TOWER AND BRING HER BACK TO SUFFER THE KING'S JUSTICE.
I WAS THE FIRST TO ARRIVE.
I DIDN'T EXPECT THERE'D BE SOME SORT OF ADULT BABY IN HER TOWER WAITING FOR ME, BUT THERE YOU WERE.

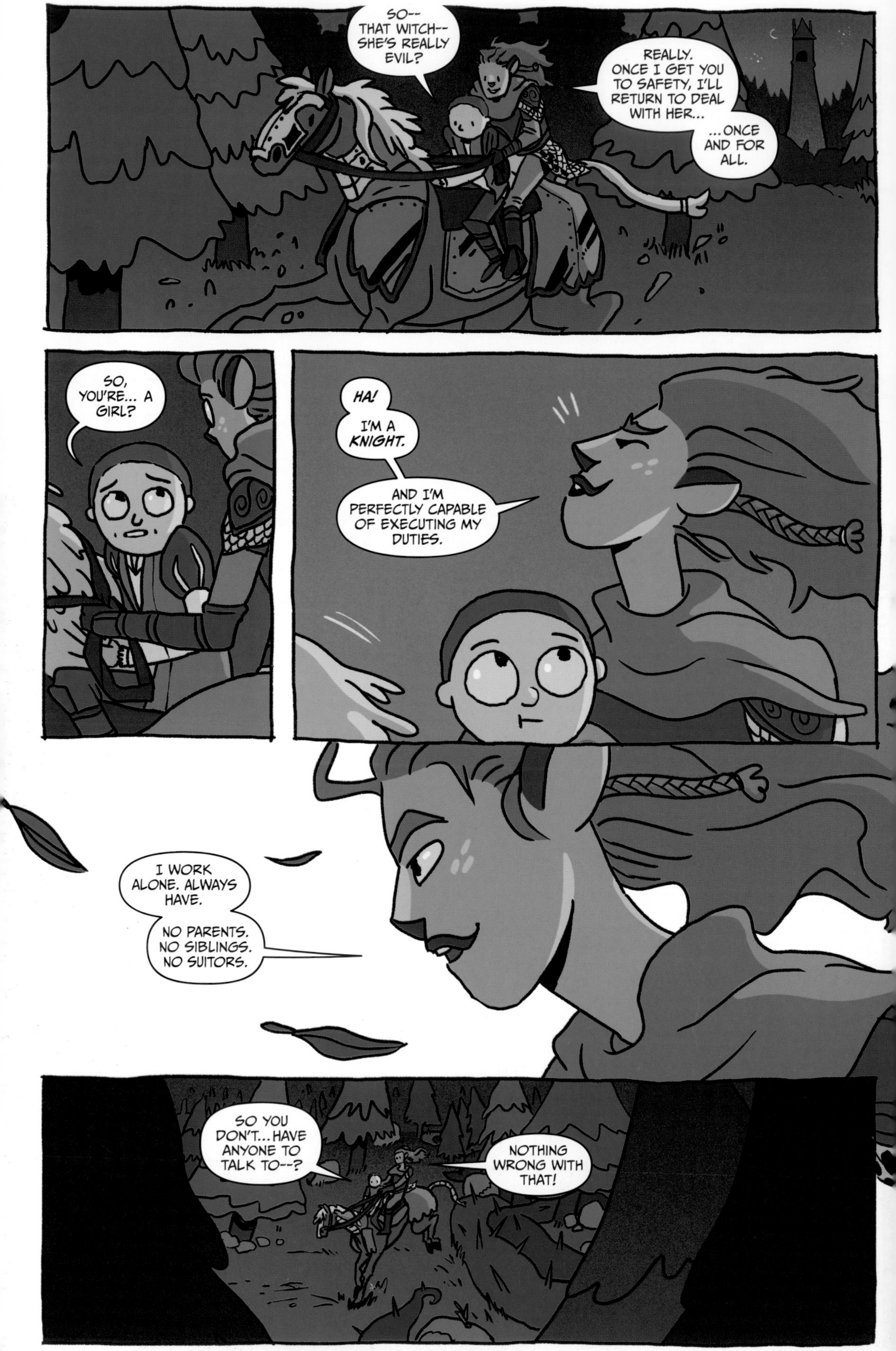
SO-- THAT WITCH-- SHE'S REALLY EVIL?
REALLY. ONCE I GET YOU TO SAFETY, I'LL RETURN TO DEAL WITH HER...
...ONCE AND FOR ALL.
SO, YOU'RE... A GIRL?
HA!
I'M A KNIGHT.
AND I'M PERFECTLY CAPABLE OF EXECUTING MY DUTIES.
I WORK ALONE. ALWAYS HAVE.
NO PARENTS. NO SIBLINGS. NO SUITORS.
SO YOU DON'T...HAVE ANYONE TO TALK TO--?
NOTHING WRONG WITH THAT!

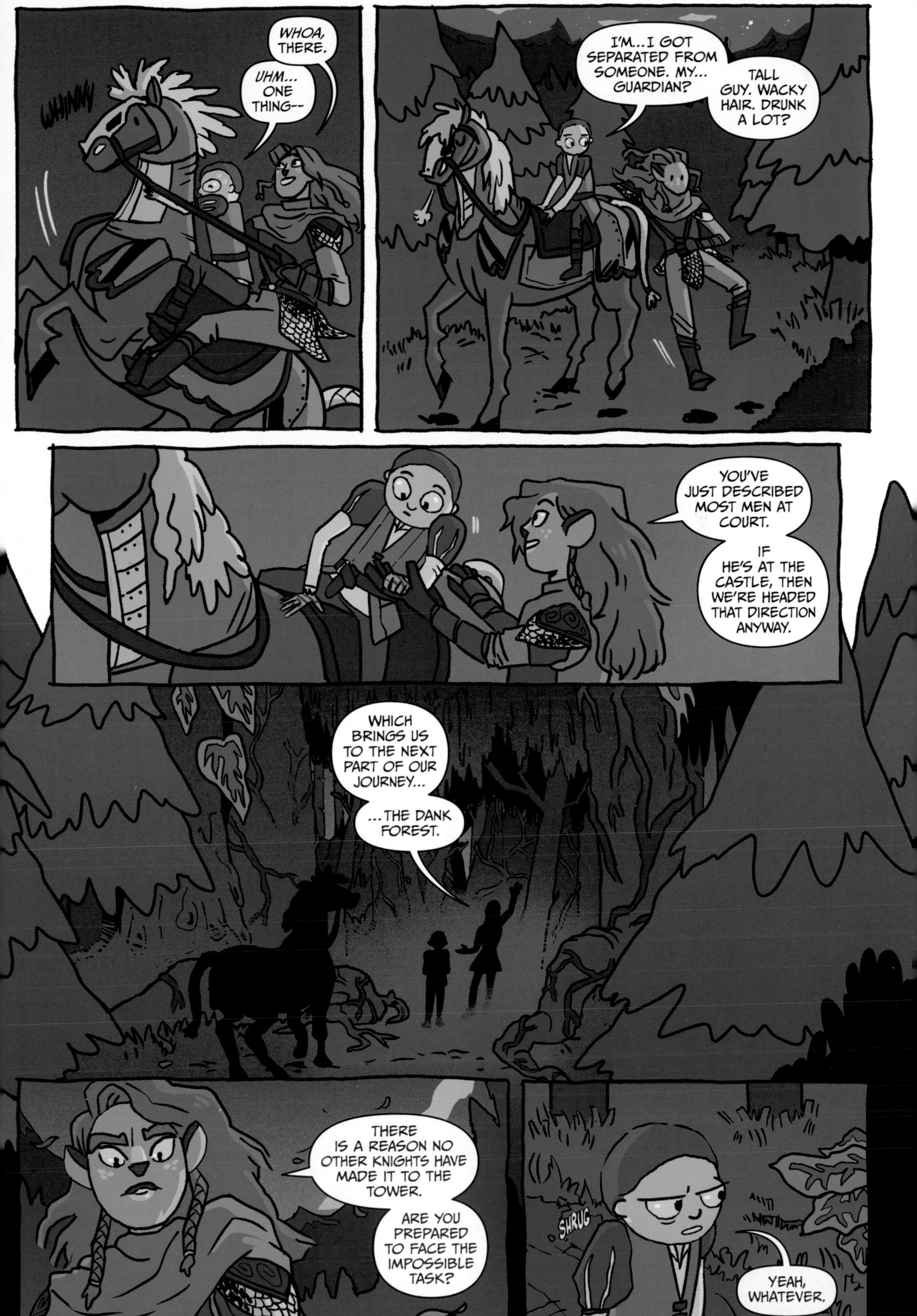
WHINNY
WHOA, THERE.
UHM... ONE THING--
I'M...I GOT SEPARATED FROM SOMEONE. MY... GUARDIAN?
TALL GUY. WACKY HAIR. DRUNK A LOT?
YOU'VE JUST DESCRIBED MOST MEN AT COURT.
IF HE'S AT THE CASTLE, THEN WE'RE HEADED THAT DIRECTION ANYWAY.
WHICH BRINGS US TO THE NEXT PART OF OUR JOURNEY...
...THE DANK FOREST.
THERE IS A REASON NO OTHER KNIGHTS HAVE MADE IT TO THE TOWER.
ARE YOU PREPARED TO FACE THE IMPOSSIBLE TASK?
SHRUG
YEAH, WHATEVER.

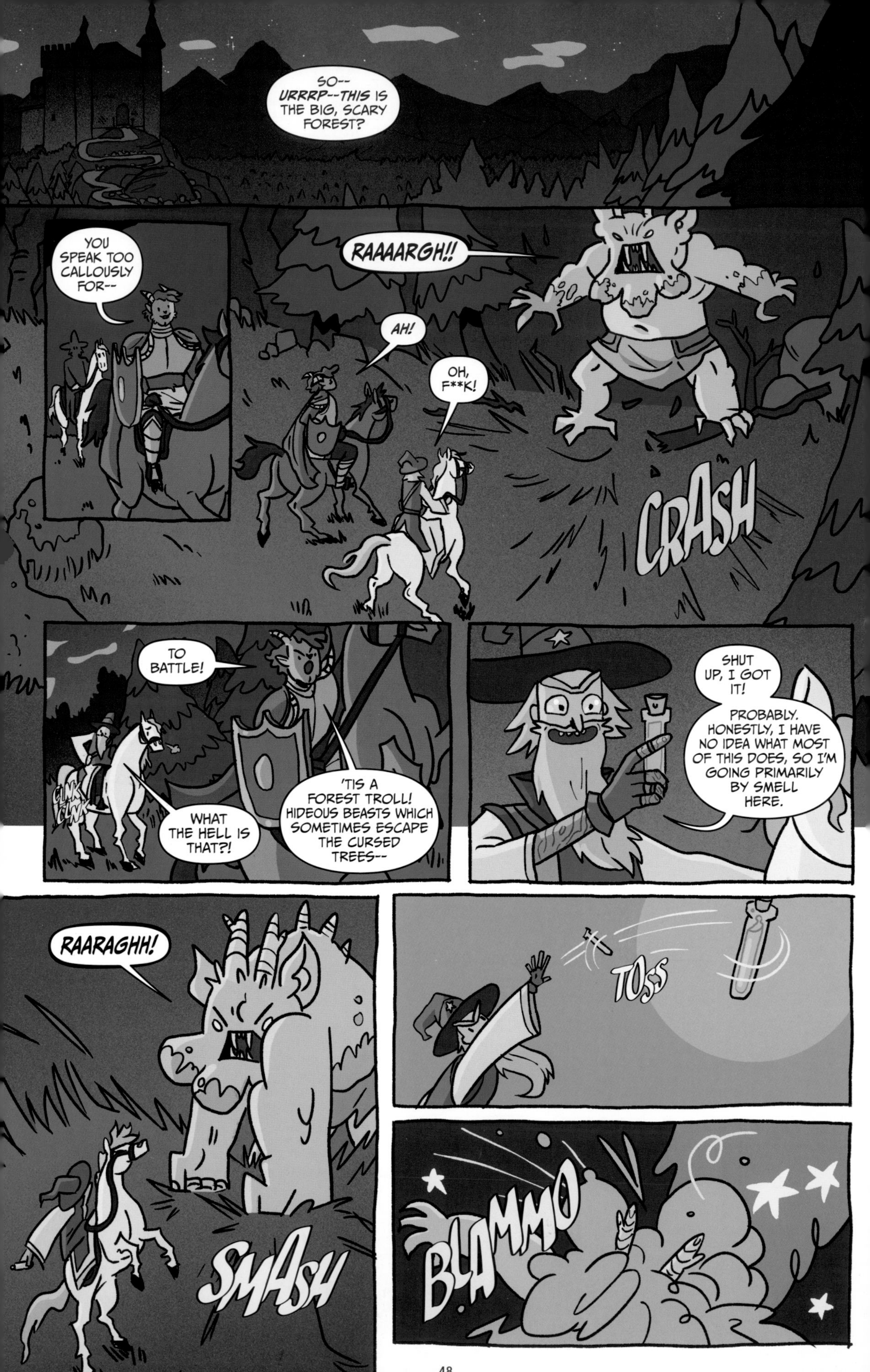
SO-- URRRP--THIS IS THE BIG, SCARY FOREST?
YOU SPEAK TOO CALLOUSLY FOR--
RAAAARGH!!
AH!
OH, F**K!
CRASH
TO BATTLE!
CLNK CLNK
WHAT THE HELL IS THAT?!
'TIS A FOREST TROLL! HIDEOUS BEASTS WHICH SOMETIMES ESCAPE THE CURSED TREES--
SHUT UP, I GOT IT!
PROBABLY. HONESTLY, I HAVE NO IDEA WHAT MOST OF THIS DOES, SO I'M GOING PRIMARILY BY SMELL HERE.
RAARAGHH!
SMASH
TOSS
BLAMMO

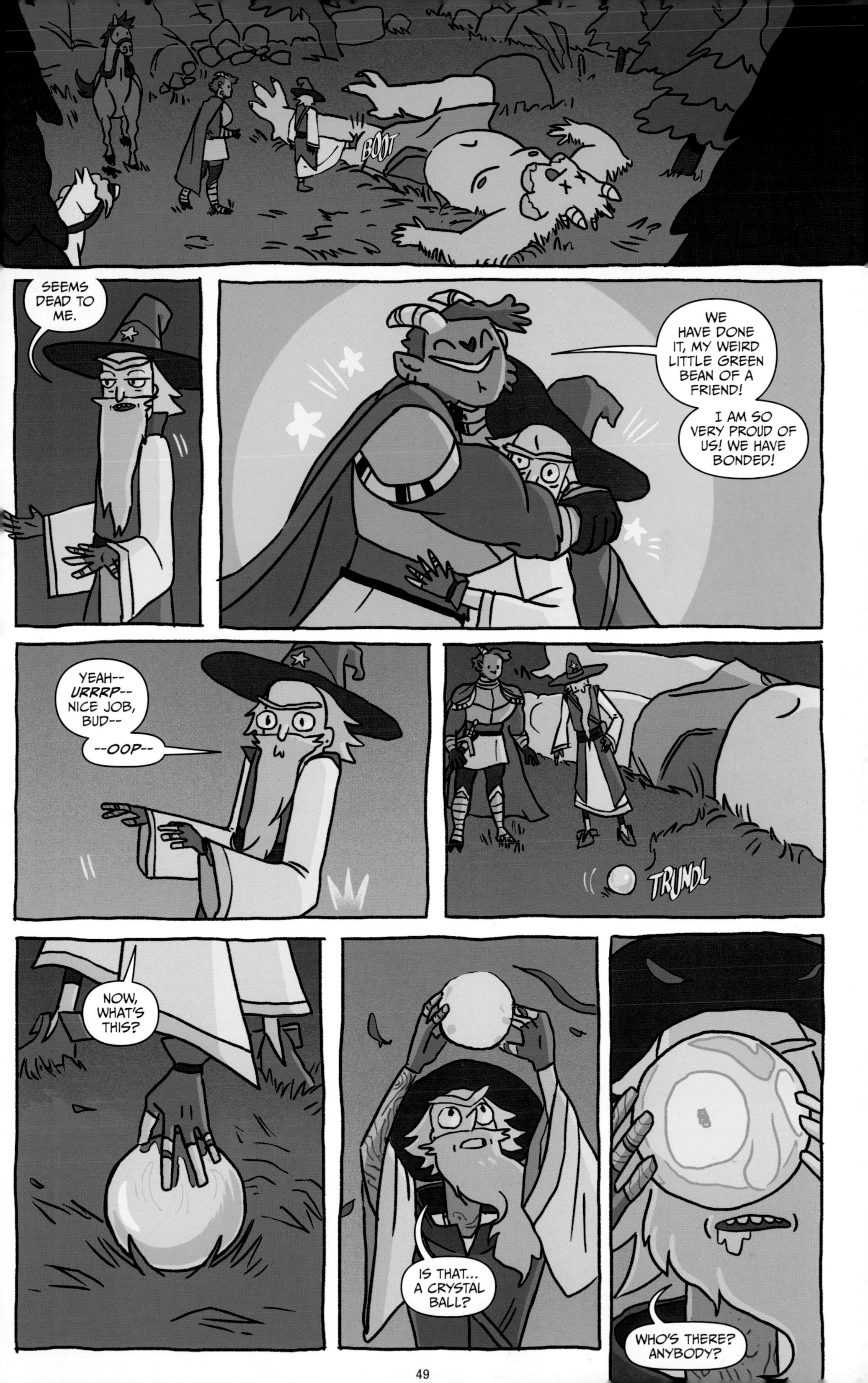
BOOT
SEEMS DEAD TO ME.
WE HAVE DONE IT, MY WEIRD LITTLE GREEN BEAN OF A FRIEND!
I AM SO VERY PROUD OF US! WE HAVE BONDED!
YEAH-- URRRP-- NICE JOB, BUD--
--OOP--
TRUNDL
NOW, WHAT'S THIS?
IS THAT... A CRYSTAL BALL?
WHO'S THERE? ANYBODY?

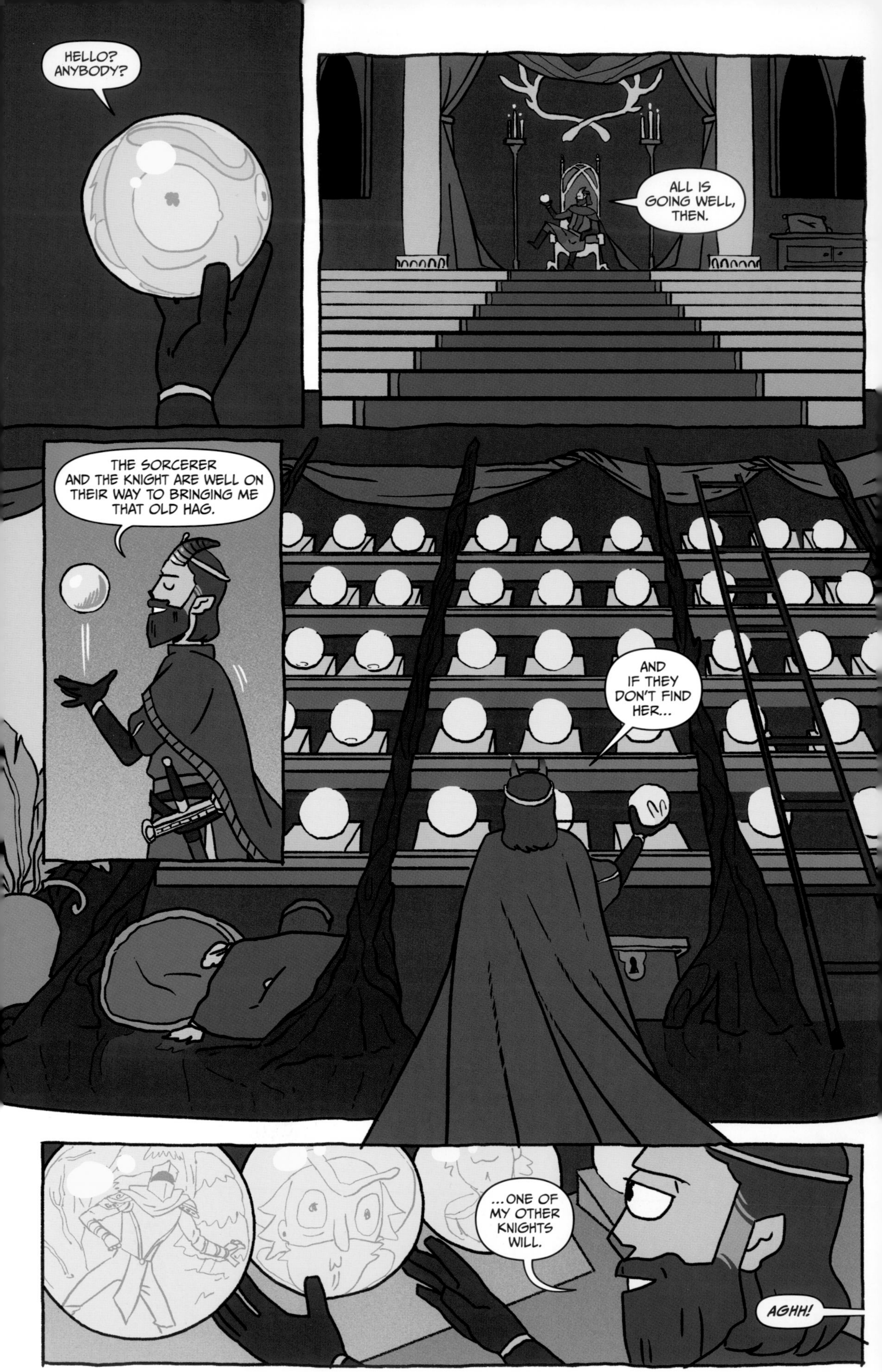
HELLO? ANYBODY?
ALL IS GOING WELL, THEN.
THE SORCERER AND THE KNIGHT ARE WELL ON THEIR WAY TO BRINGING ME THAT OLD HAG.
AND IF THEY DON'T FIND HER...
...ONE OF MY OTHER KNIGHTS WILL.
AGHH!

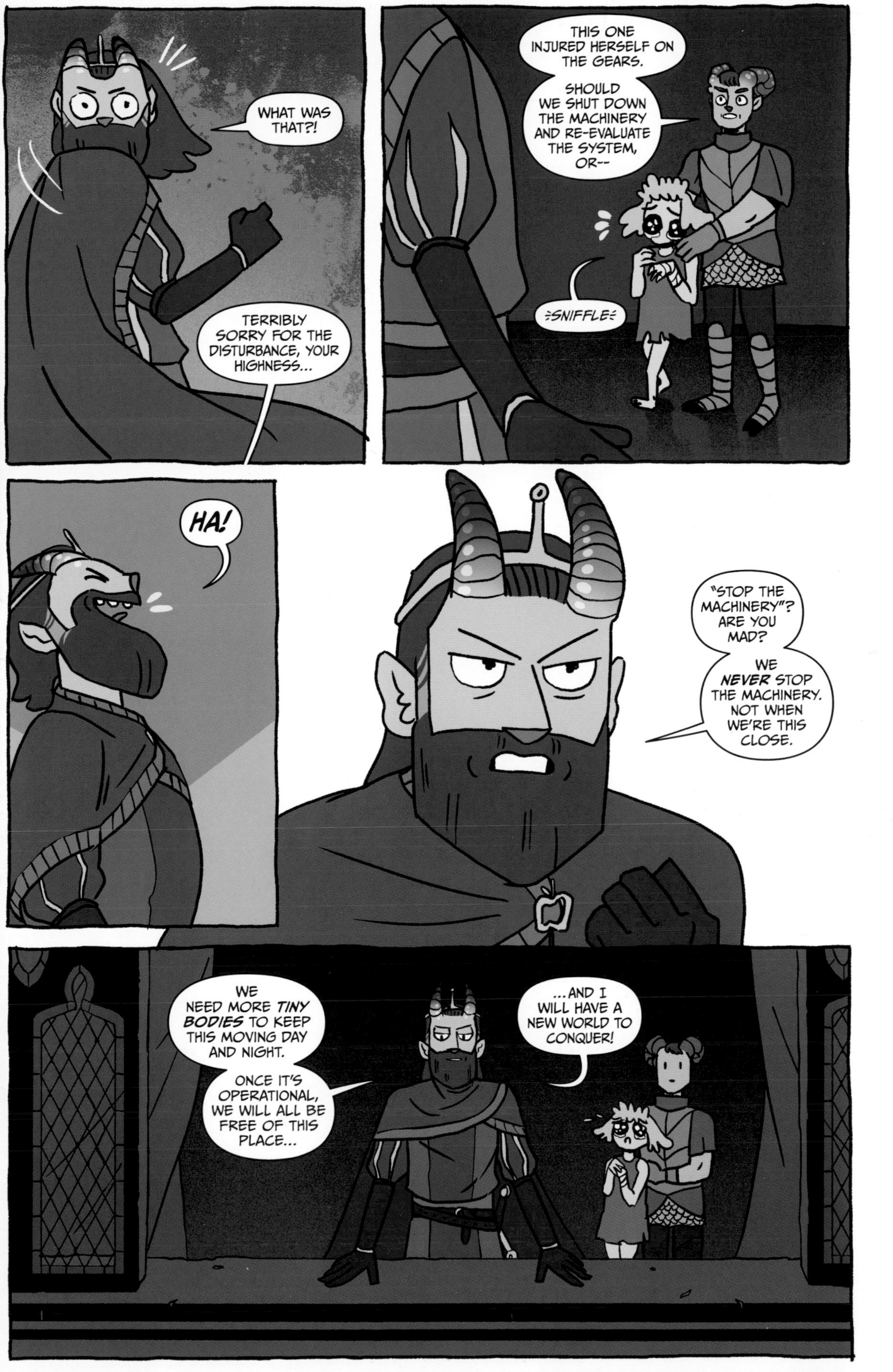
WHAT WAS THAT?!
TERRIBLY SORRY FOR THE DISTURBANCE, YOUR HIGHNESS...
THIS ONE INJURED HERSELF ON THE GEARS.
SHOULD WE SHUT DOWN THE MACHINERY AND RE-EVALUATE THE SYSTEM, OR--
≈SNIFFLE≈
HA!
"STOP THE MACHINERY"? ARE YOU MAD?
WE NEVER STOP THE MACHINERY. NOT WHEN WE'RE THIS CLOSE.
WE NEED MORE TINY BODIES TO KEEP THIS MOVING DAY AND NIGHT.
ONCE IT'S OPERATIONAL, WE WILL ALL BE FREE OF THIS PLACE...
...AND I WILL HAVE A NEW WORLD TO CONQUER!

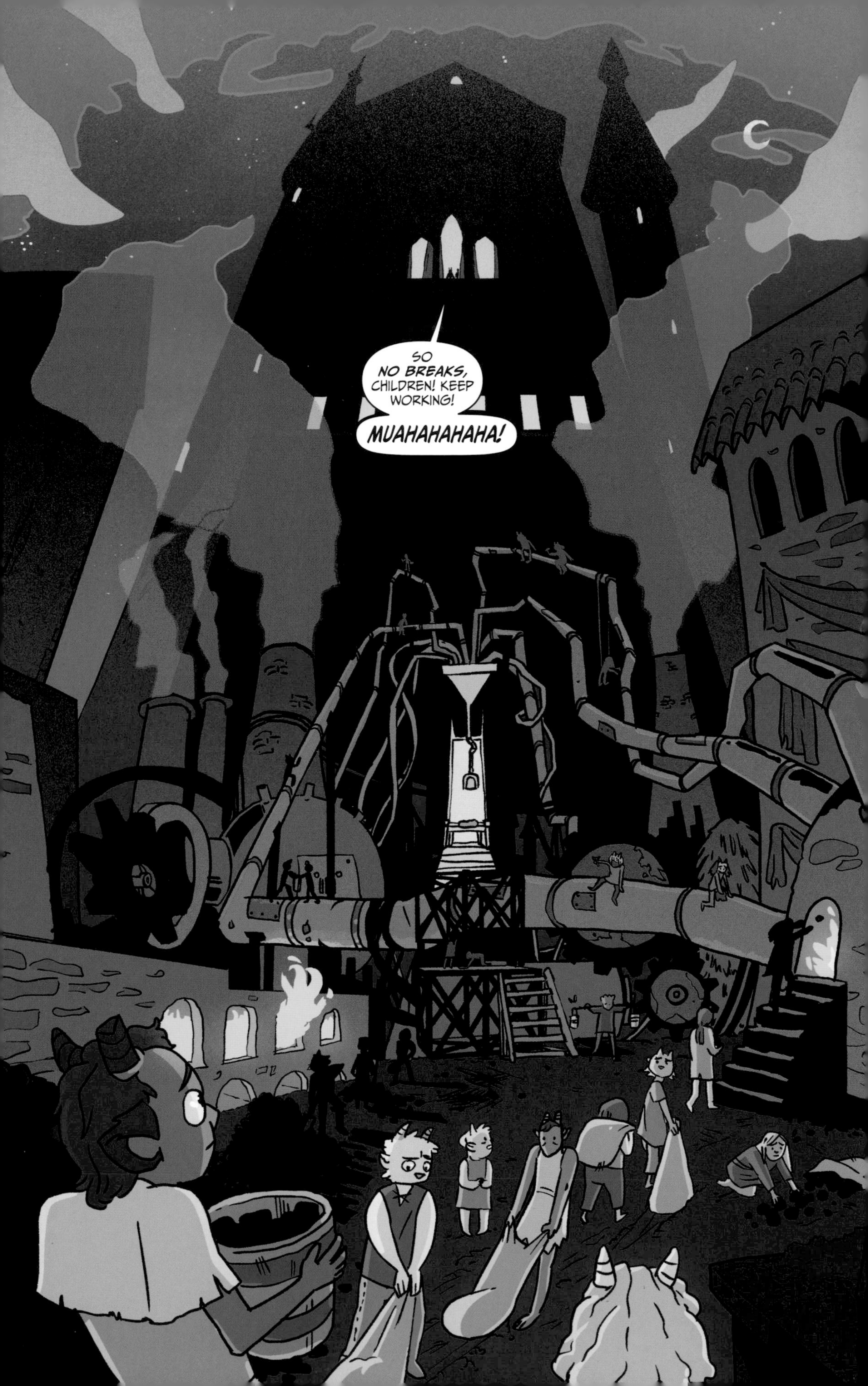
SO NO BREAKS, CHILDREN! KEEP WORKING!
MUAHAHAHAHA!

Chapter Three

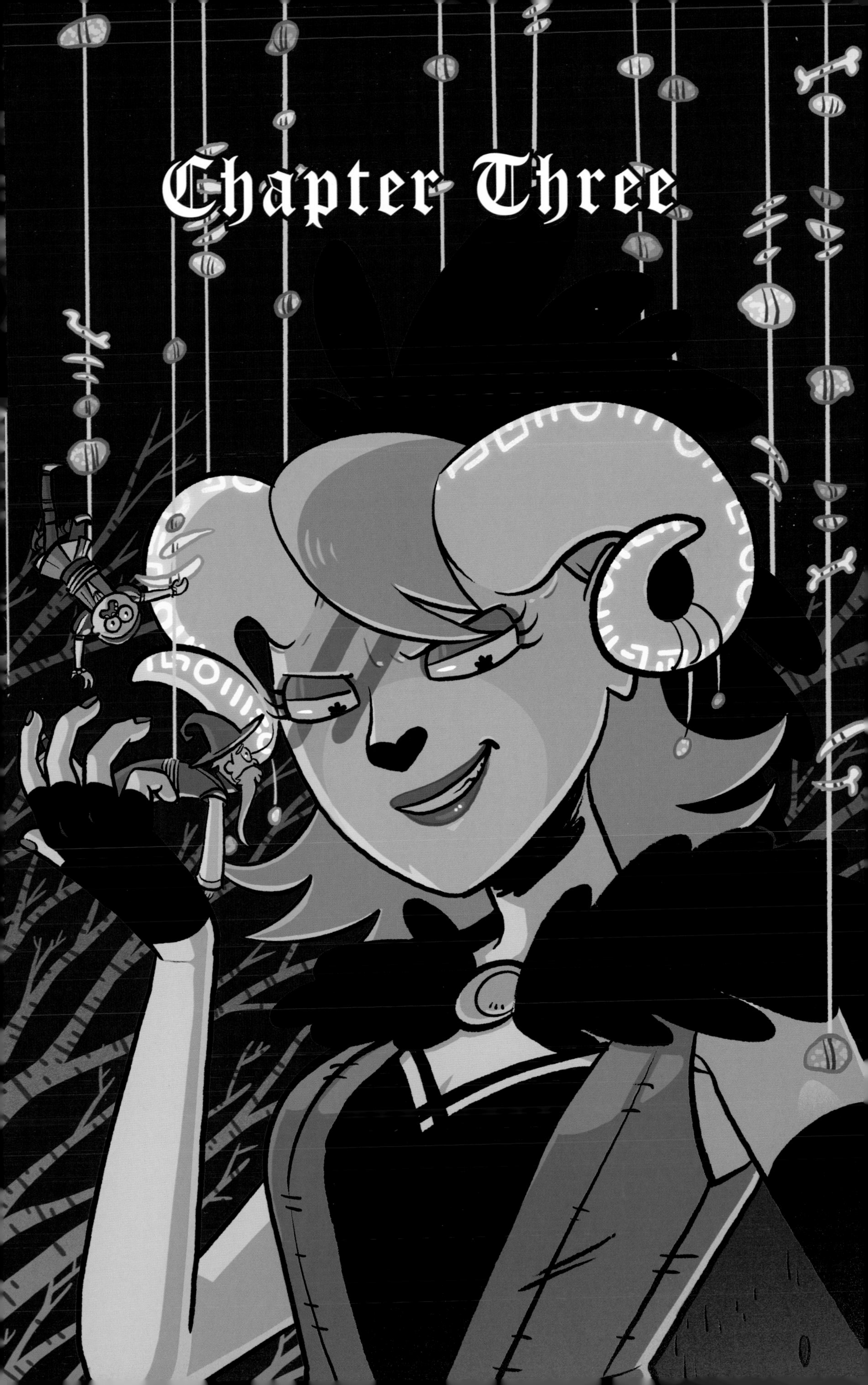

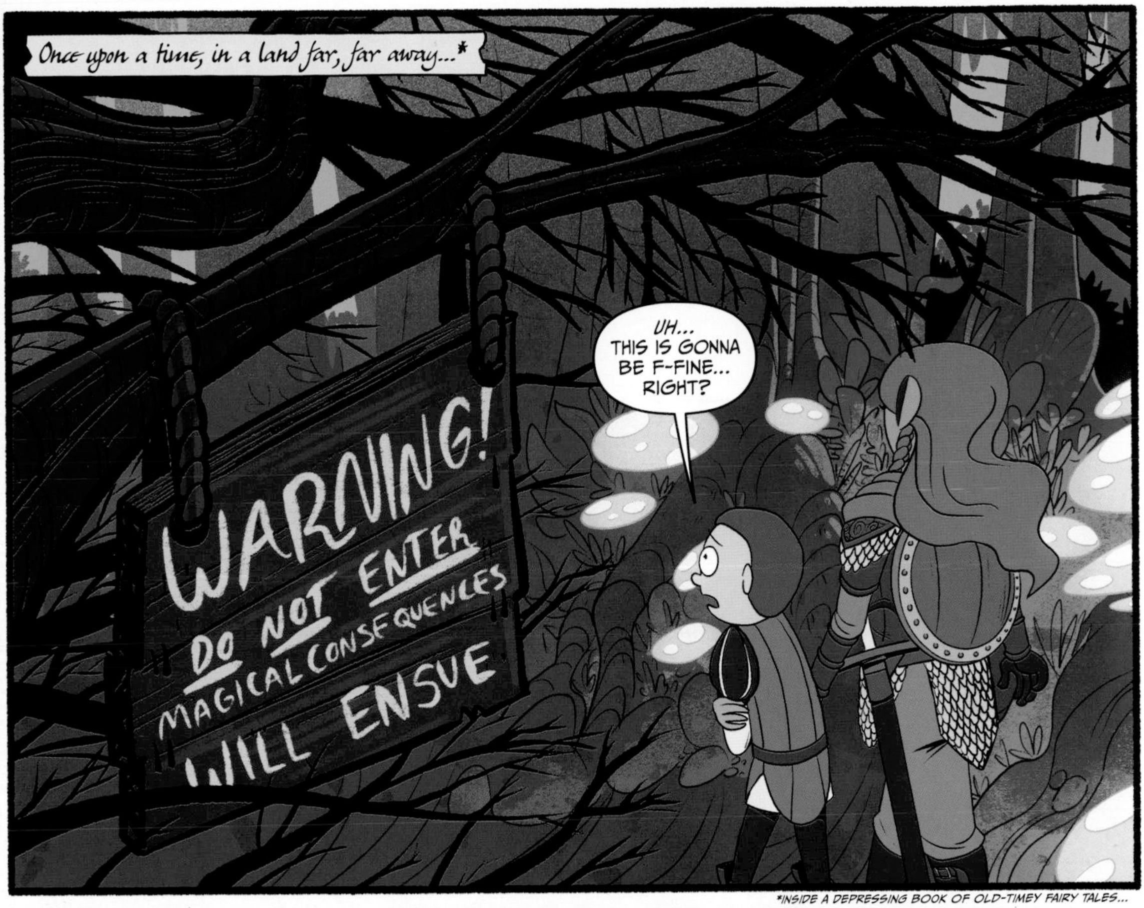
Once upon a time, in a land far, far away...*
WARNING! DO NOT ENTER MAGICAL CONSEQUENCES WILL ENSUE
UH... THIS IS GONNA BE F-FINE... RIGHT?

*INSIDE A DEPRESSING BOOK OF OLD-TIMEY FAIRY TALES...

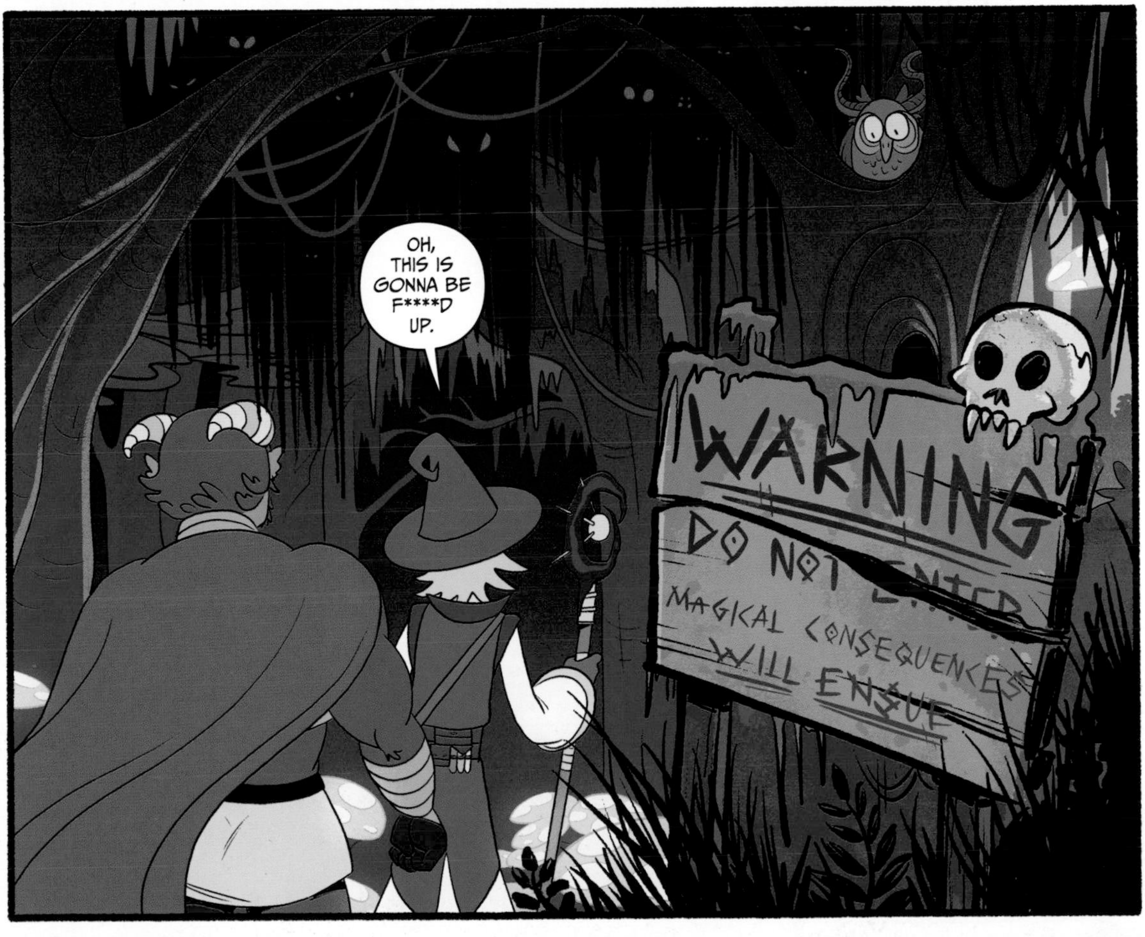
OH, THIS IS GONNA BE F****D UP.
WARNING
DO NOT
MAGICAL CONSEQUENCES
WILL ENSUE

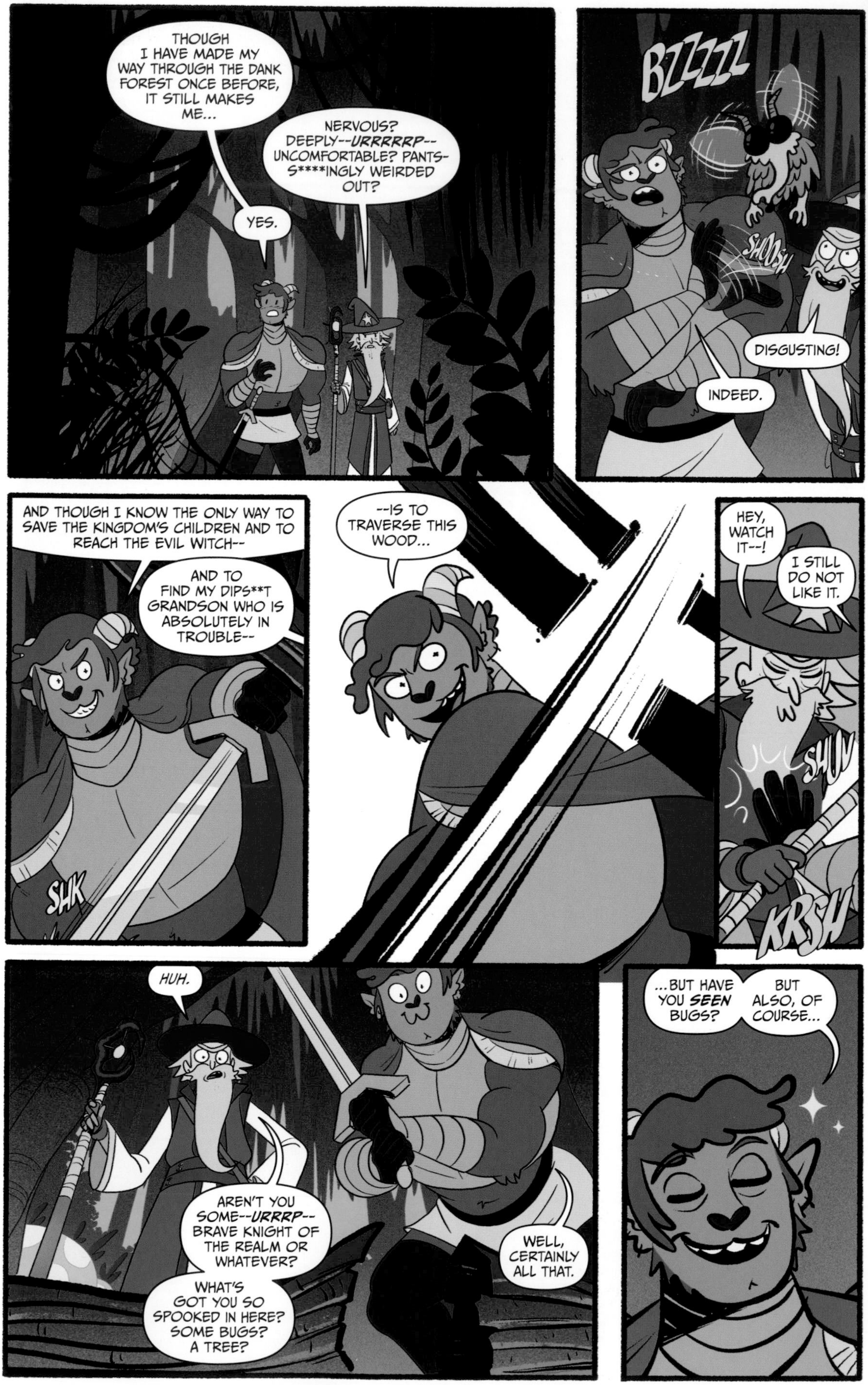
THOUGH I HAVE MADE MY WAY THROUGH THE DANK FOREST ONCE BEFORE, IT STILL MAKES ME...
NERVOUS? DEEPLY--URRRRRP--UNCOMFORTABLE? PANTS-S****INGLY WEIRDED OUT?
YES.
BZZZZZ
SHOOSH
DISGUSTING!
INDEED.
AND THOUGH I KNOW THE ONLY WAY TO SAVE THE KINGDOM'S CHILDREN AND TO REACH THE EVIL WITCH--
AND TO FIND MY DIPS**T GRANDSON WHO IS ABSOLUTELY IN TROUBLE--
SHK
--IS TO TRAVERSE THIS WOOD...
HEY, WATCH IT--!
I STILL DO NOT LIKE IT.
SHUN
KRSH
HUH.
AREN'T YOU SOME--URRRP--BRAVE KNIGHT OF THE REALM OR WHATEVER?
WHAT'S GOT YOU SO SPOOKED IN HERE? SOME BUGS? A TREE?
WELL, CERTAINLY ALL THAT.
BUT ALSO, OF COURSE...
...BUT HAVE YOU SEEN BUGS?

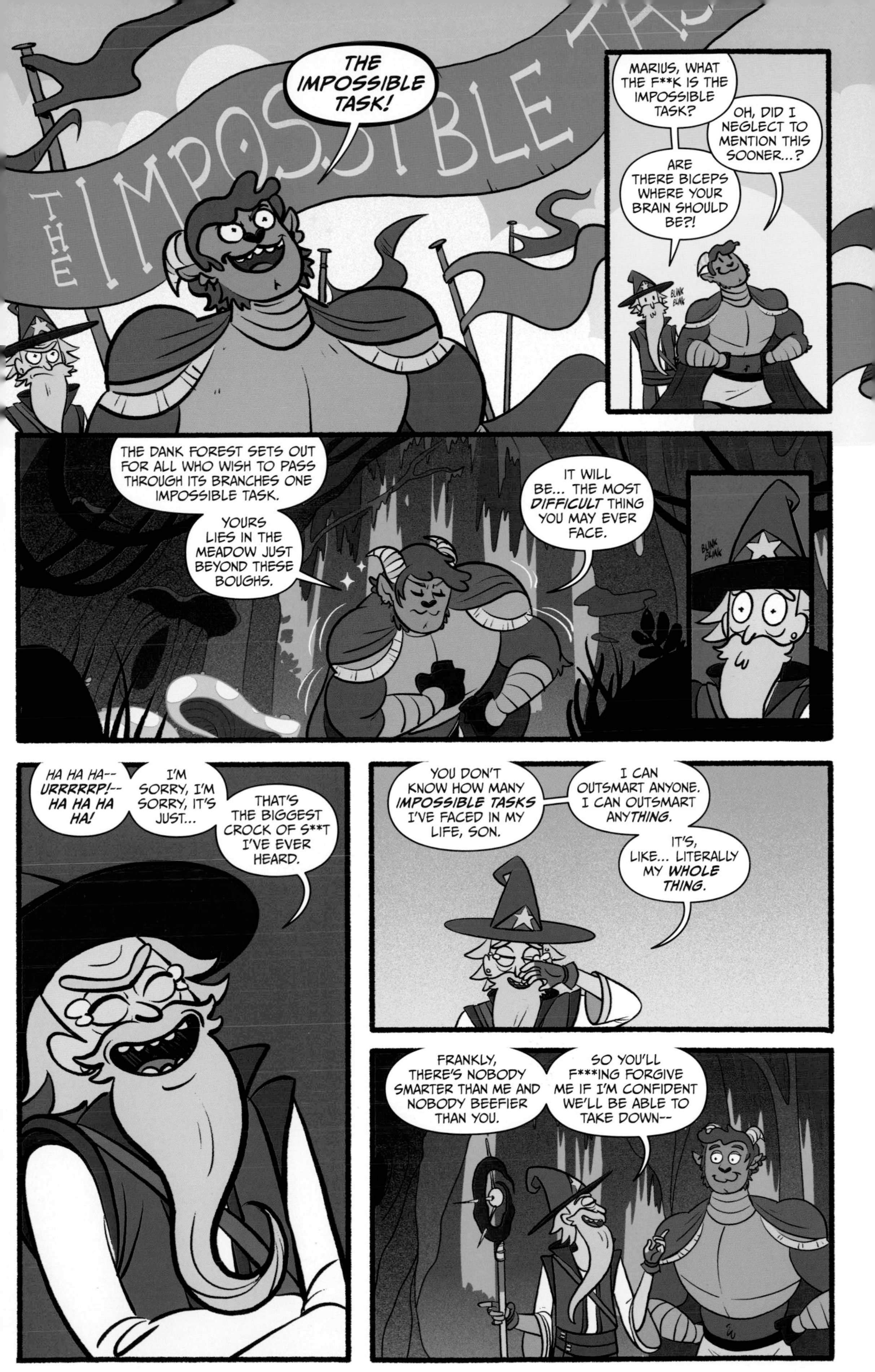
THE IMPOSSIBLE TASK
THE IMPOSSIBLE TASK!
MARIUS, WHAT THE F**K IS THE IMPOSSIBLE TASK?
ARE THERE BICEPS WHERE YOUR BRAIN SHOULD BE?!
OH, DID I NEGLECT TO MENTION THIS SOONER...?
BLINK BLINK
THE DANK FOREST SETS OUT FOR ALL WHO WISH TO PASS THROUGH ITS BRANCHES ONE IMPOSSIBLE TASK.
YOURS LIES IN THE MEADOW JUST BEYOND THESE BOUGHS.
IT WILL BE... THE MOST DIFFICULT THING YOU MAY EVER FACE.
BLINK BLINK
HA HA HA--URRRRRP!--HA HA HA HA!
I'M SORRY, I'M SORRY, IT'S JUST...
THAT'S THE BIGGEST CROCK OF S**T I'VE EVER HEARD.
YOU DON'T KNOW HOW MANY IMPOSSIBLE TASKS I'VE FACED IN MY LIFE, SON.
I CAN OUTSMART ANYONE. I CAN OUTSMART ANYTHING.
IT'S, LIKE... LITERALLY MY WHOLE THING.
FRANKLY, THERE'S NOBODY SMARTER THAN ME AND NOBODY BEEFIER THAN YOU.
SO YOU'LL F***ING FORGIVE ME IF I'M CONFIDENT WE'LL BE ABLE TO TAKE DOWN--

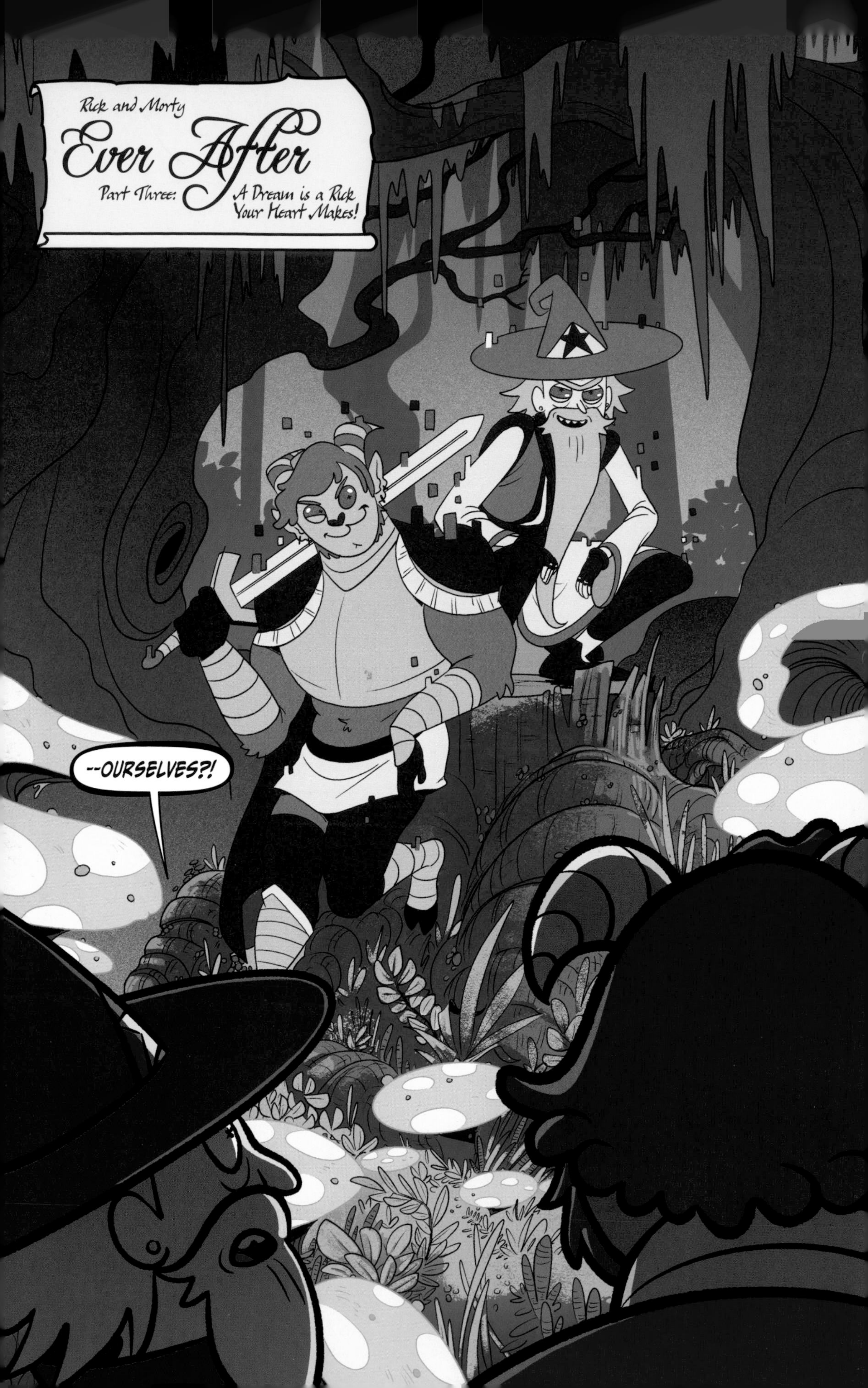
Rick and Morty
Ever After
Part Three: A Dream is a Rick Your Heart Makes!
--OURSELVES?!

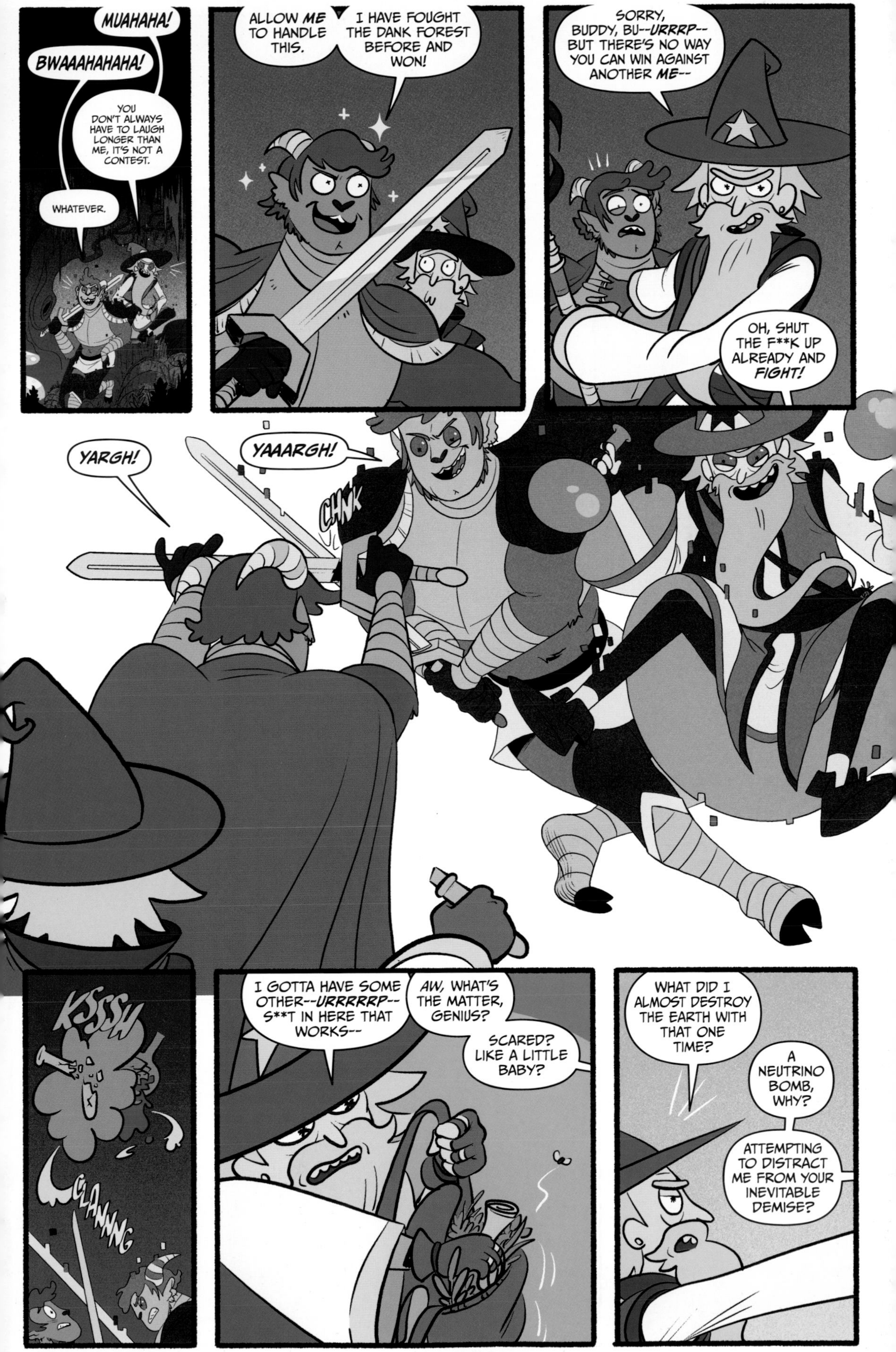

MUAHAHA!
BWAAAHAHAHA!
YOU DON'T ALWAYS HAVE TO LAUGH LONGER THAN ME, IT'S NOT A CONTEST.
WHATEVER.
ALLOW ME TO HANDLE THIS.
I HAVE FOUGHT THE DANK FOREST BEFORE AND WON!
SORRY, BUDDY, BU--URRRP-- BUT THERE'S NO WAY YOU CAN WIN AGAINST ANOTHER ME--
OH, SHUT THE F**K UP ALREADY AND FIGHT!
YARGH!
YAAARGH!
CHNK
KSSSH
CLANNNG
I GOTTA HAVE SOME OTHER--URRRRRP-- S**T IN HERE THAT WORKS--
AW, WHAT'S THE MATTER, GENIUS?
SCARED? LIKE A LITTLE BABY?
WHAT DID I ALMOST DESTROY THE EARTH WITH THAT ONE TIME?
A NEUTRINO BOMB, WHY?
ATTEMPTING TO DISTRACT ME FROM YOUR INEVITABLE DEMISE?

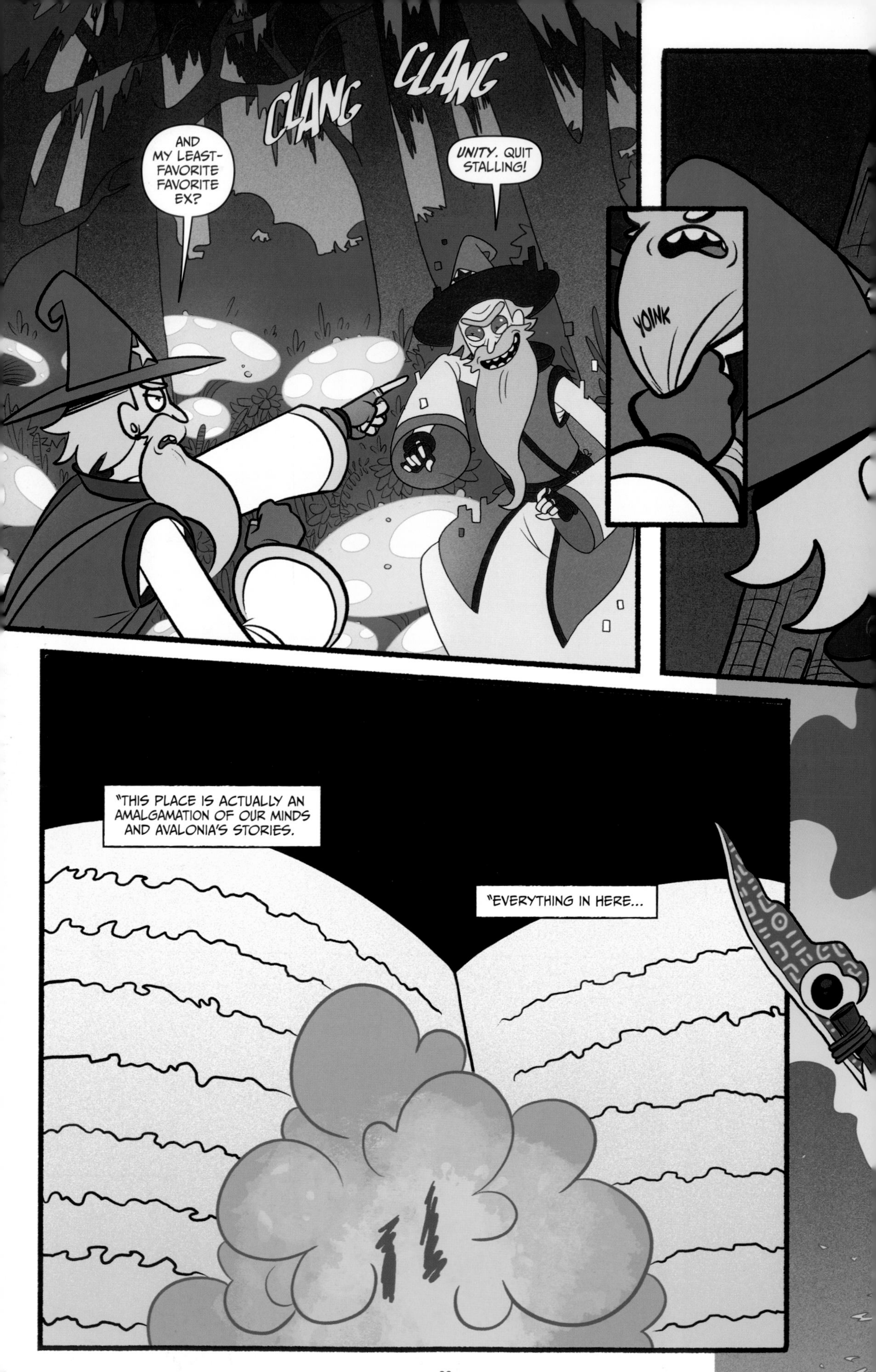
CLANG
CLANG
AND MY LEAST-FAVORITE FAVORITE EX?
UNITY. QUIT STALLING!
YOINK
"THIS PLACE IS ACTUALLY AN AMALGAMATION OF OUR MINDS AND AVALONIA'S STORIES.
"EVERYTHING IN HERE...

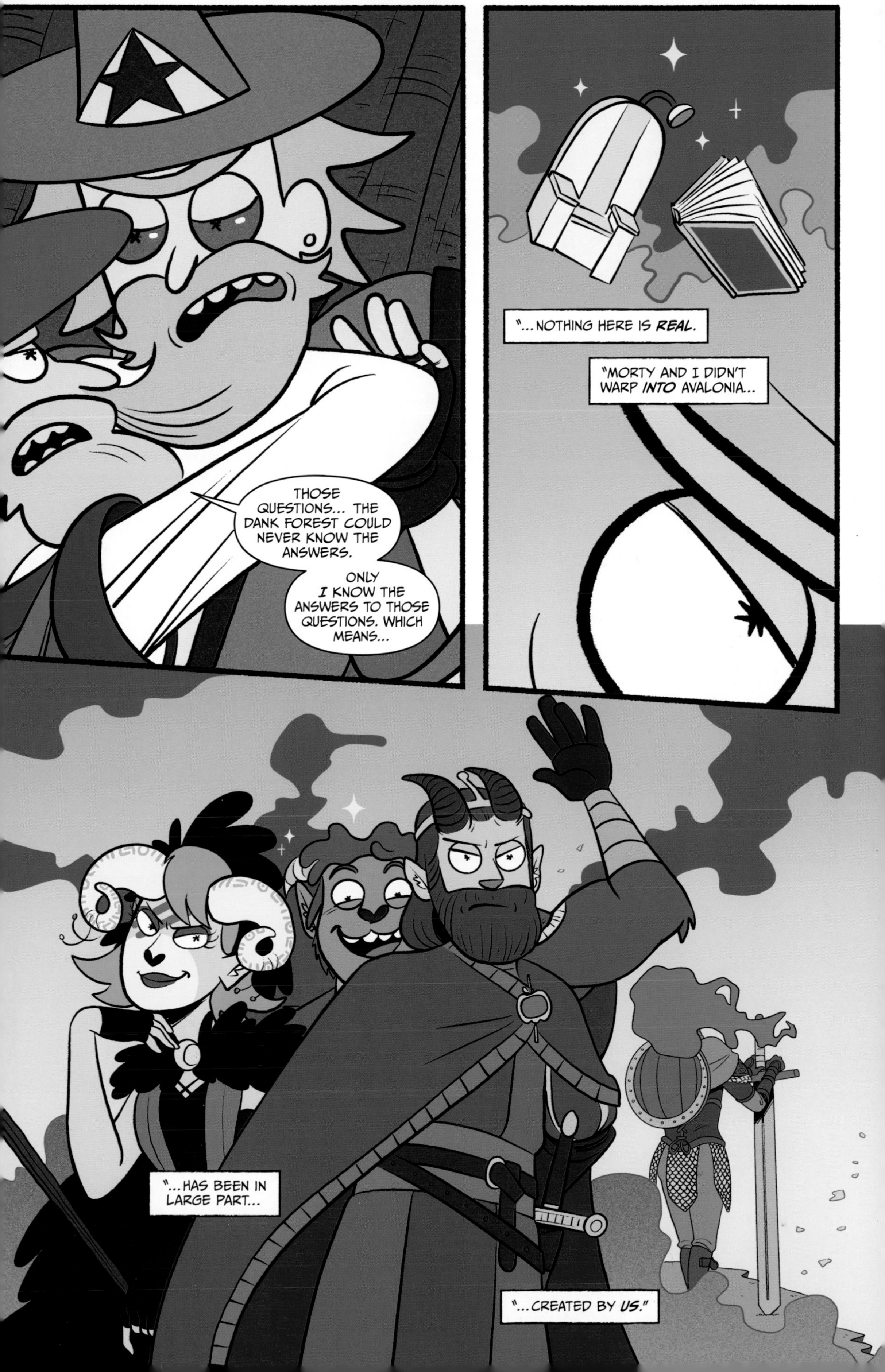
THOSE QUESTIONS... THE DANK FOREST COULD NEVER KNOW THE ANSWERS.
ONLY *I* KNOW THE ANSWERS TO THOSE QUESTIONS. WHICH MEANS...
"...NOTHING HERE IS ***REAL***.
"MORTY AND I DIDN'T WARP ***INTO*** AVALONIA...
"...HAS BEEN IN LARGE PART...
"...CREATED BY ***US***."

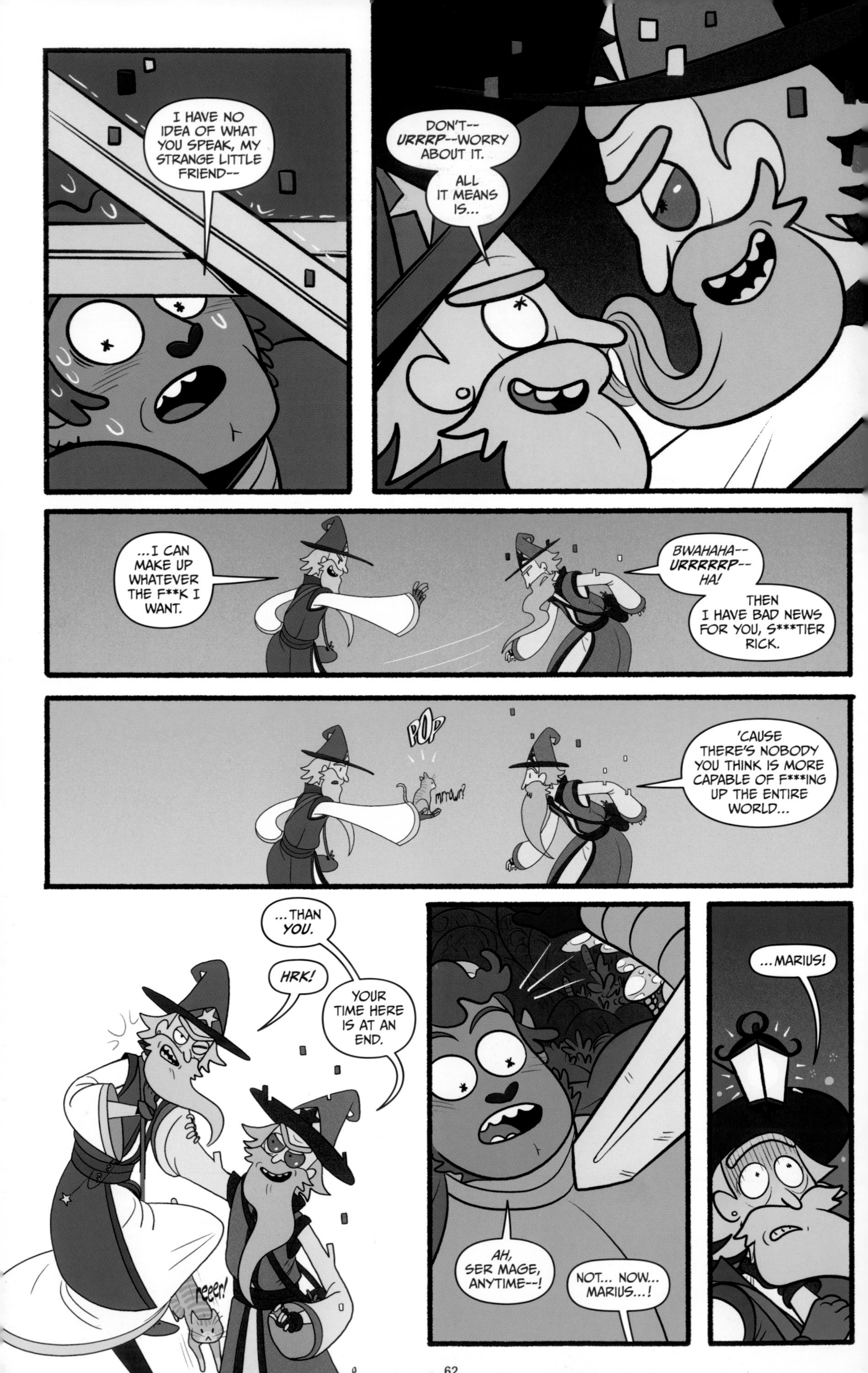

I HAVE NO IDEA OF WHAT YOU SPEAK, MY STRANGE LITTLE FRIEND--
DON'T-- URRRP--WORRY ABOUT IT.
ALL IT MEANS IS...
...I CAN MAKE UP WHATEVER THE F**K I WANT.
BWAHAHA-- URRRRRP-- HA!
THEN I HAVE BAD NEWS FOR YOU, S***TIER RICK.
POP
mrrrow?
'CAUSE THERE'S NOBODY YOU THINK IS MORE CAPABLE OF F***ING UP THE ENTIRE WORLD...
...THAN YOU.
HRK!
YOUR TIME HERE IS AT AN END.
reeer!
AH, SER MAGE, ANYTIME--!
NOT... NOW... MARIUS...!
...MARIUS!

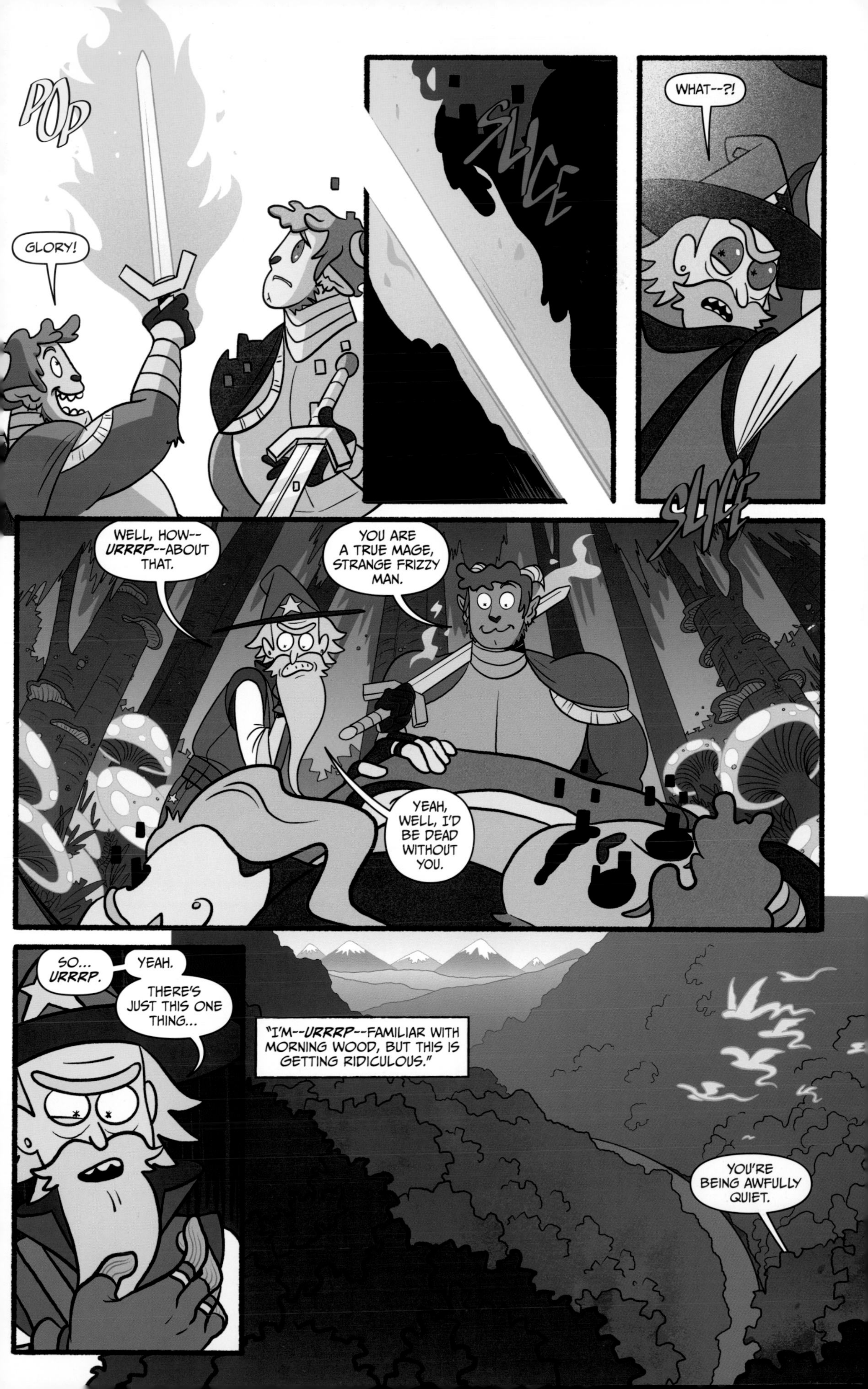
POP
GLORY!
SLICE
WHAT--?!
SLICE
WELL, HOW--URRRP--ABOUT THAT.
YOU ARE A TRUE MAGE, STRANGE FRIZZY MAN.
YEAH, WELL, I'D BE DEAD WITHOUT YOU.
SO... URRRP.
YEAH.
THERE'S JUST THIS ONE THING...
"I'M--URRRP--FAMILIAR WITH MORNING WOOD, BUT THIS IS GETTING RIDICULOUS."
YOU'RE BEING AWFULLY QUIET.

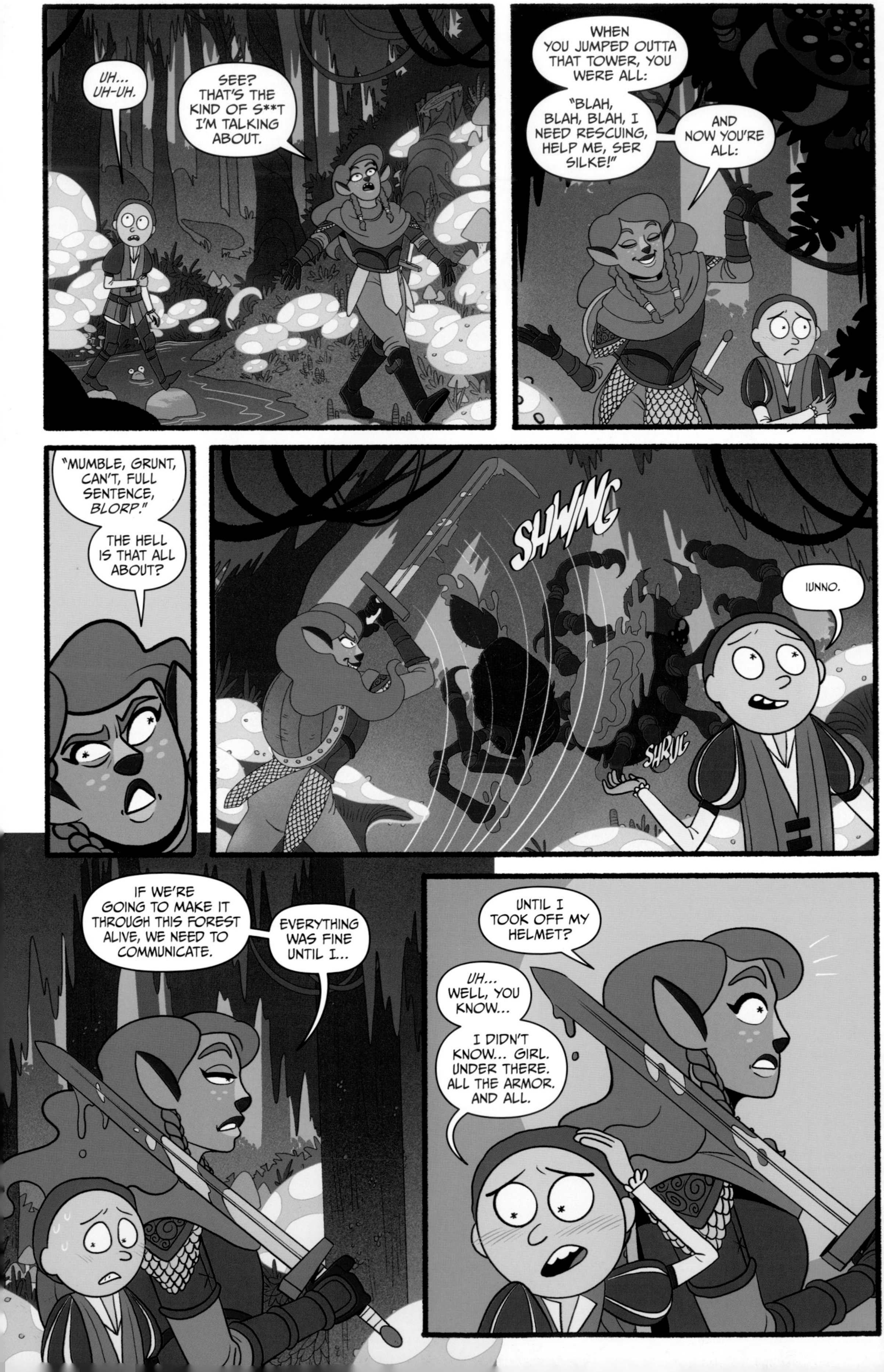
UH... UH-UH.
SEE? THAT'S THE KIND OF S**T I'M TALKING ABOUT.
WHEN YOU JUMPED OUTTA THAT TOWER, YOU WERE ALL:
"BLAH, BLAH, BLAH, I NEED RESCUING, HELP ME, SER SILKE!"
AND NOW YOU'RE ALL:
"MUMBLE, GRUNT, CAN'T, FULL SENTENCE, BLORP."
THE HELL IS THAT ALL ABOUT?
SHWING
IUNNO.
SHRUG
IF WE'RE GOING TO MAKE IT THROUGH THIS FOREST ALIVE, WE NEED TO COMMUNICATE.
EVERYTHING WAS FINE UNTIL I...
UNTIL I TOOK OFF MY HELMET?
UH... WELL, YOU KNOW...
I DIDN'T KNOW... GIRL. UNDER THERE. ALL THE ARMOR. AND ALL.

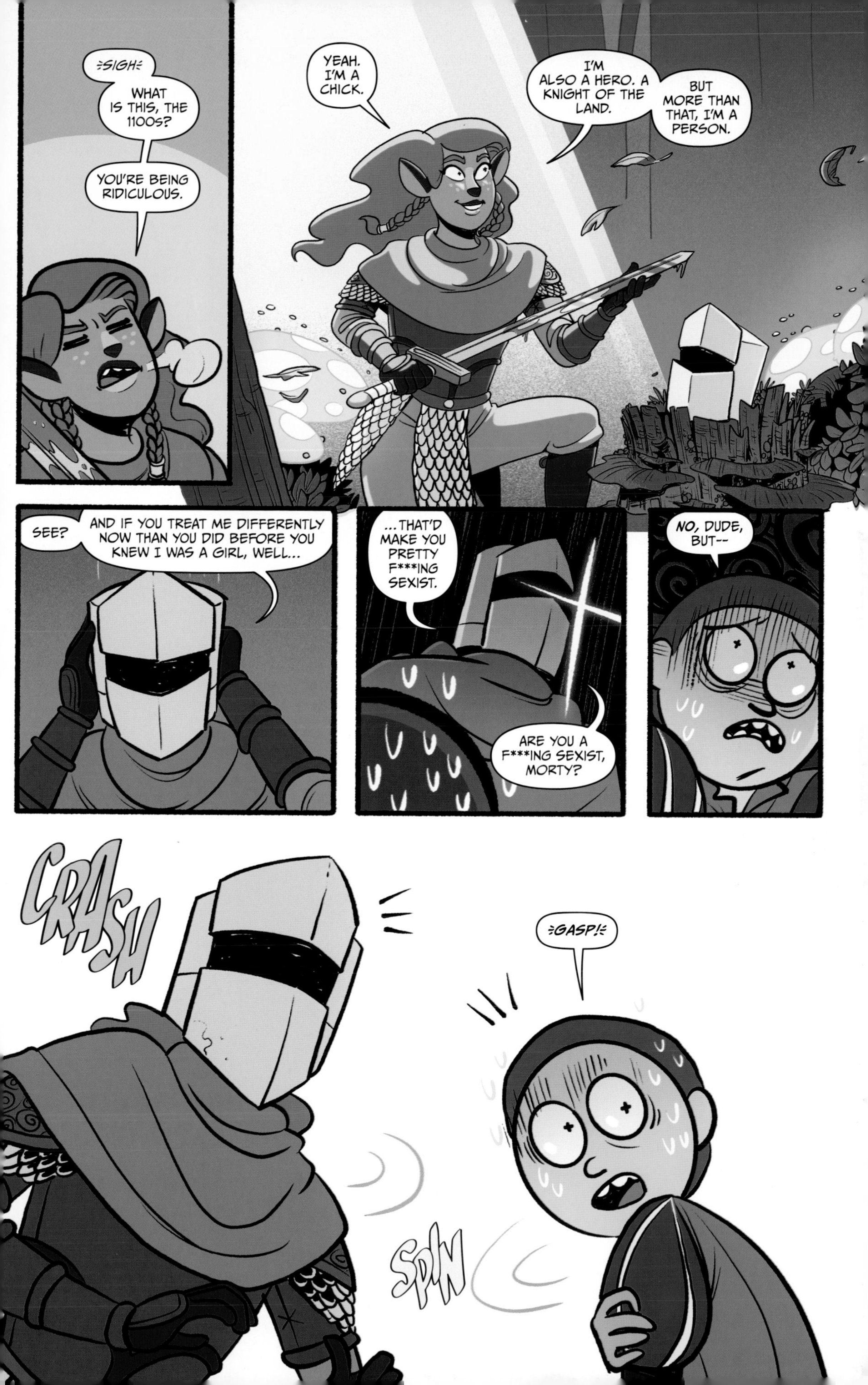

=SIGH=
WHAT IS THIS, THE 1100s?
YOU'RE BEING RIDICULOUS.
YEAH. I'M A CHICK.
I'M ALSO A HERO. A KNIGHT OF THE LAND.
BUT MORE THAN THAT, I'M A PERSON.
SEE?
AND IF YOU TREAT ME DIFFERENTLY NOW THAN YOU DID BEFORE YOU KNEW I WAS A GIRL, WELL...
...THAT'D MAKE YOU PRETTY F***ING SEXIST.
ARE YOU A F***ING SEXIST, MORTY?
NO, DUDE, BUT--
CRASH
=GASP!=
SPIN

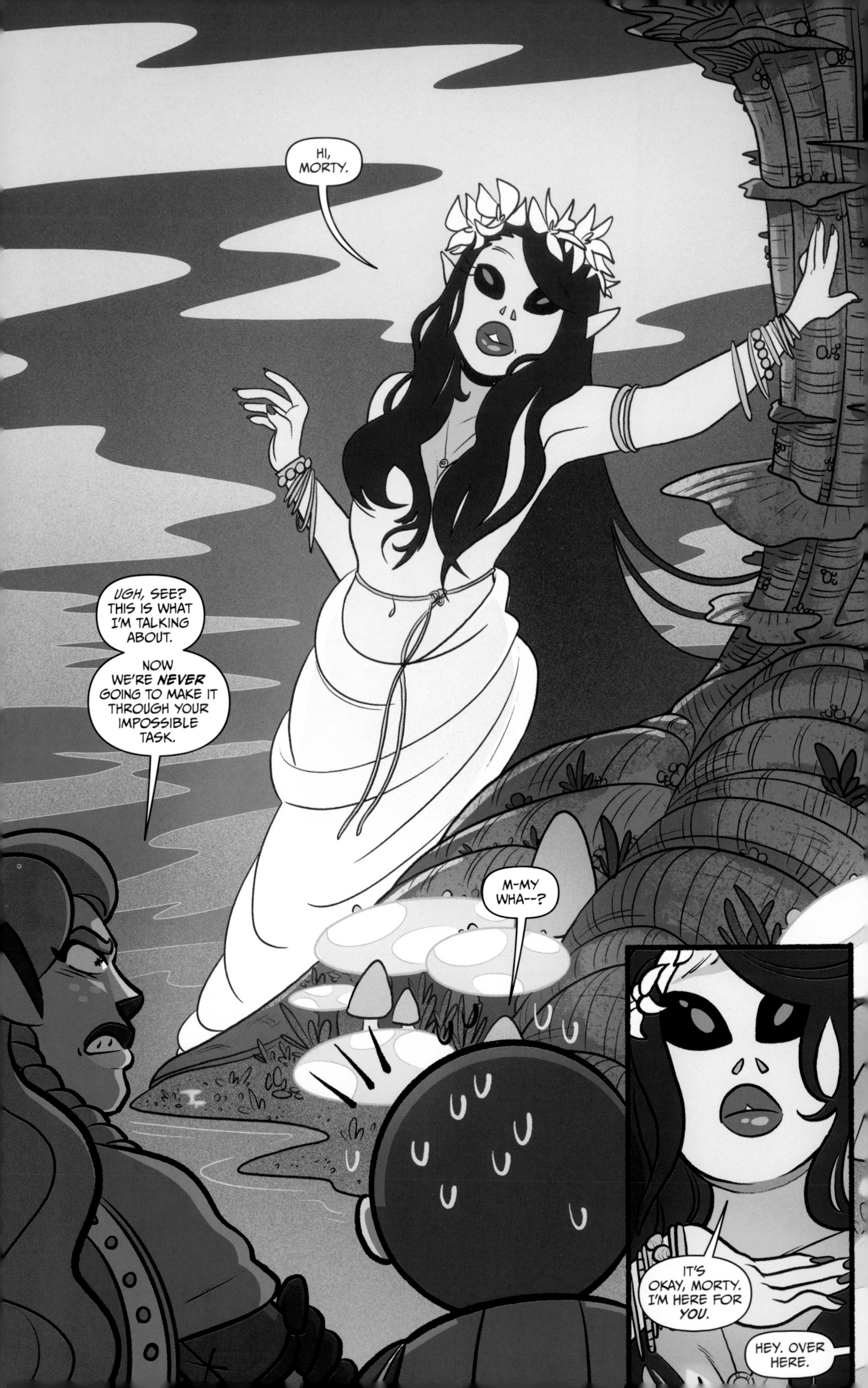
HI, MORTY.
UGH, SEE? THIS IS WHAT I'M TALKING ABOUT.
NOW WE'RE NEVER GOING TO MAKE IT THROUGH YOUR IMPOSSIBLE TASK.
M-MY WHA--?
IT'S OKAY, MORTY. I'M HERE FOR YOU.
HEY. OVER HERE.

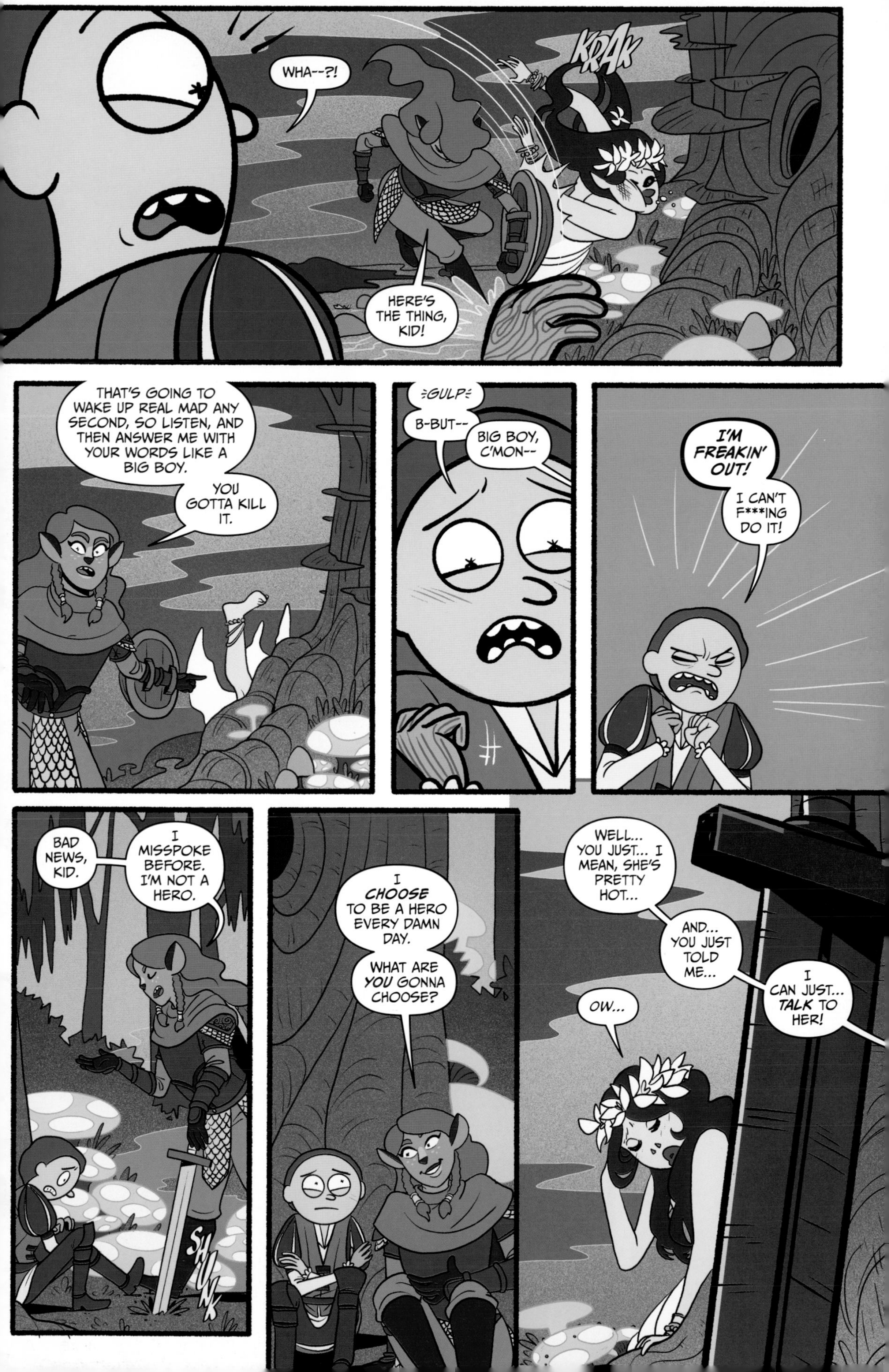
WHA--?!
KRAK
HERE'S THE THING, KID!
THAT'S GOING TO WAKE UP REAL MAD ANY SECOND, SO LISTEN, AND THEN ANSWER ME WITH YOUR WORDS LIKE A BIG BOY.
YOU GOTTA KILL IT.
GULP
B-BUT--
BIG BOY, C'MON--
I'M FREAKIN' OUT!
I CAN'T F***ING DO IT!
BAD NEWS, KID.
I MISSPOKE BEFORE. I'M NOT A HERO.
SHUNK
I CHOOSE TO BE A HERO EVERY DAMN DAY.
WHAT ARE YOU GONNA CHOOSE?
WELL... YOU JUST... I MEAN, SHE'S PRETTY HOT...
AND... YOU JUST TOLD ME...
I CAN JUST... TALK TO HER!
OW...

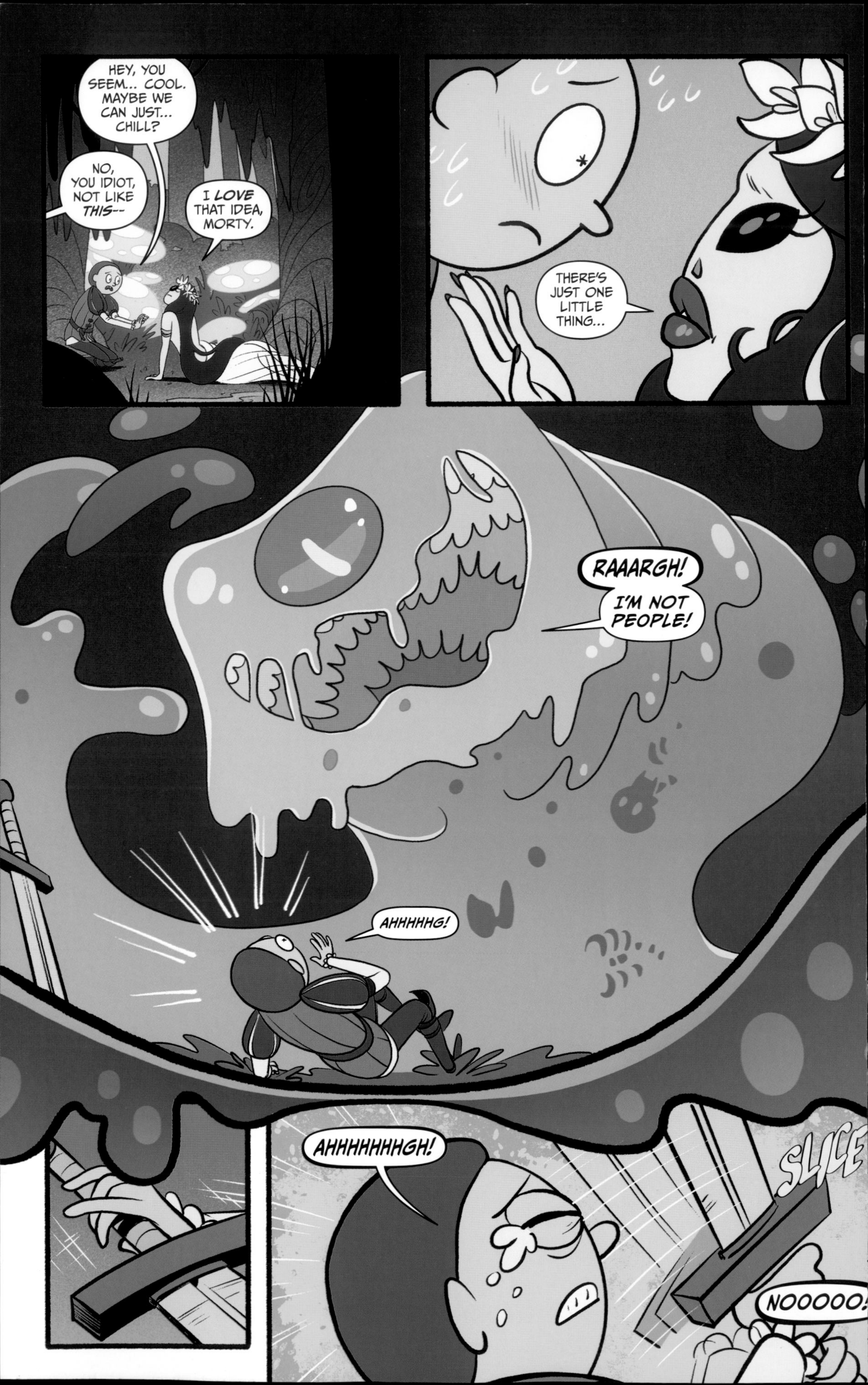
HEY, YOU SEEM... COOL. MAYBE WE CAN JUST... CHILL?
NO, YOU IDIOT, NOT LIKE THIS--
I LOVE THAT IDEA, MORTY.
THERE'S JUST ONE LITTLE THING...
RAAARGH!
I'M NOT PEOPLE!
AHHHHHG!
AHHHHHHHGH!
SLICE
NOOOOO!

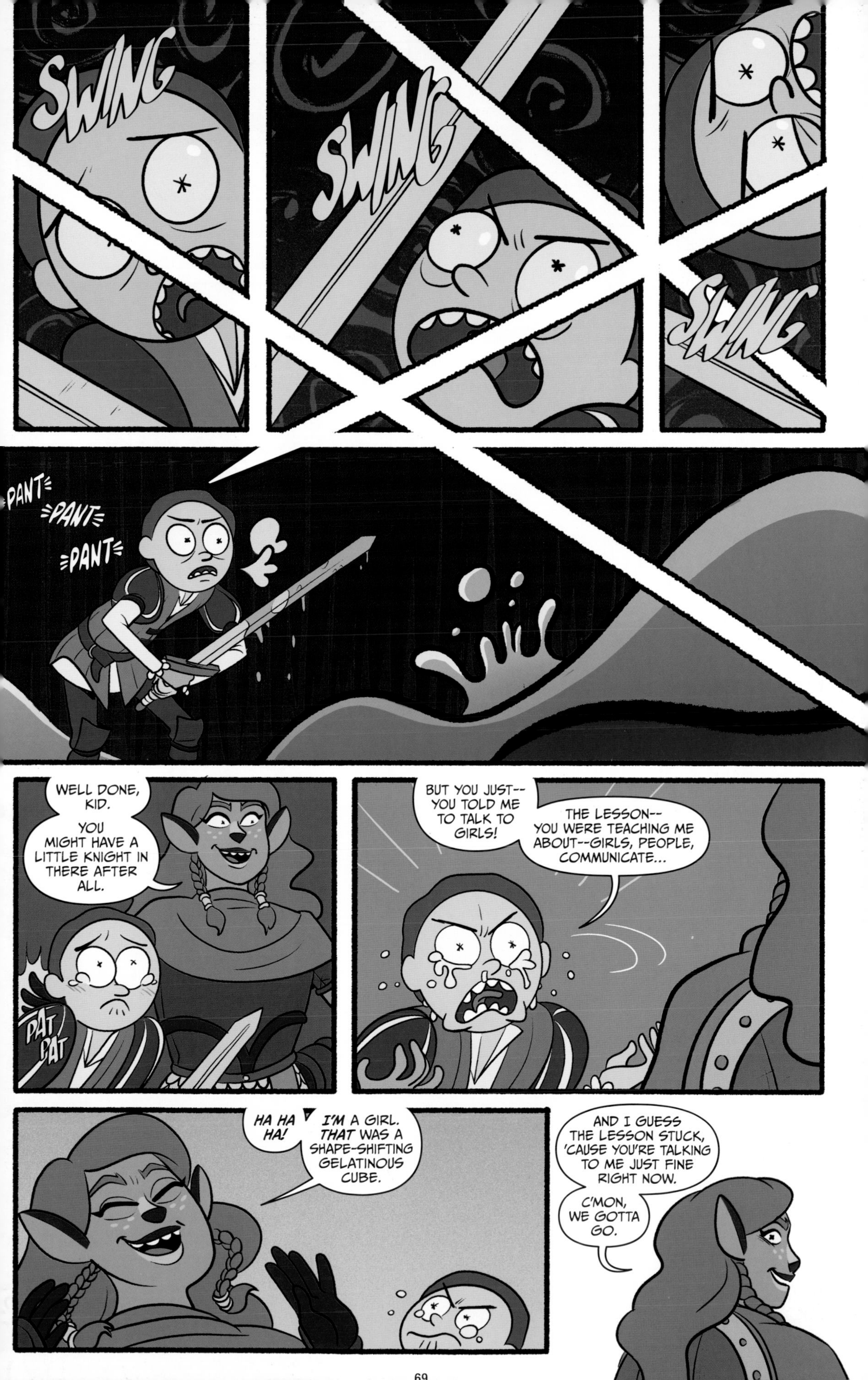
SWING
SWING
SWING
PANT PANT PANT
WELL DONE, KID.
YOU MIGHT HAVE A LITTLE KNIGHT IN THERE AFTER ALL.
PAT PAT
BUT YOU JUST-- YOU TOLD ME TO TALK TO GIRLS!
THE LESSON-- YOU WERE TEACHING ME ABOUT--GIRLS, PEOPLE, COMMUNICATE...
HA HA HA!
I'M A GIRL. THAT WAS A SHAPE-SHIFTING GELATINOUS CUBE.
AND I GUESS THE LESSON STUCK, 'CAUSE YOU'RE TALKING TO ME JUST FINE RIGHT NOW.
C'MON, WE GOTTA GO.

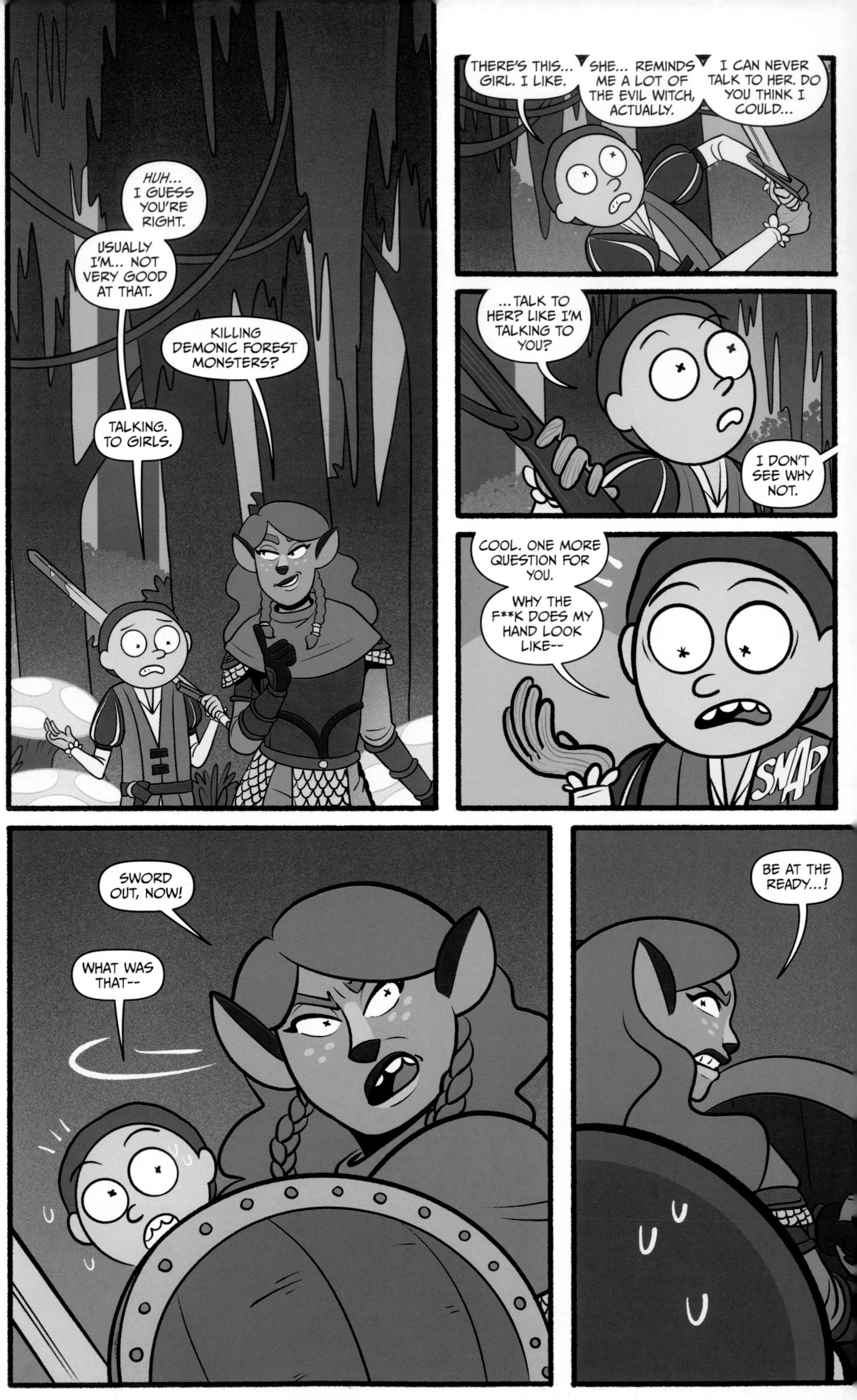
HUH... I GUESS YOU'RE RIGHT.
USUALLY I'M... NOT VERY GOOD AT THAT.
KILLING DEMONIC FOREST MONSTERS?
TALKING. TO GIRLS.
THERE'S THIS... GIRL. I LIKE.
SHE... REMINDS ME A LOT OF THE EVIL WITCH, ACTUALLY.
I CAN NEVER TALK TO HER. DO YOU THINK I COULD...
...TALK TO HER? LIKE I'M TALKING TO YOU?
I DON'T SEE WHY NOT.
COOL. ONE MORE QUESTION FOR YOU.
WHY THE F**K DOES MY HAND LOOK LIKE--
SNAP
SWORD OUT, NOW!
WHAT WAS THAT--
BE AT THE READY...!

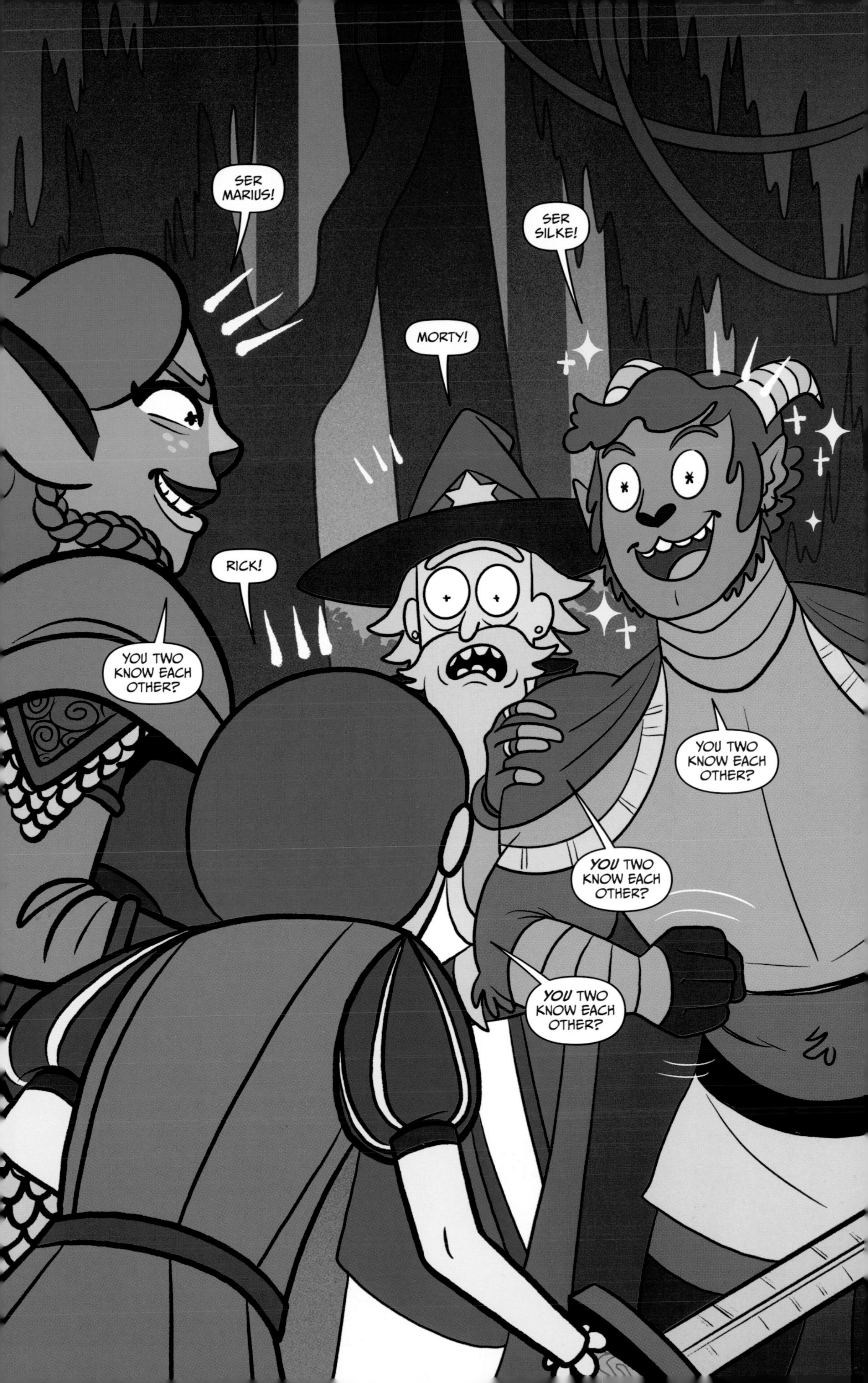
SER MARIUS!
SER SILKE!
MORTY!
RICK!
YOU TWO KNOW EACH OTHER?
YOU TWO KNOW EACH OTHER?
YOU TWO KNOW EACH OTHER?
YOU TWO KNOW EACH OTHER?

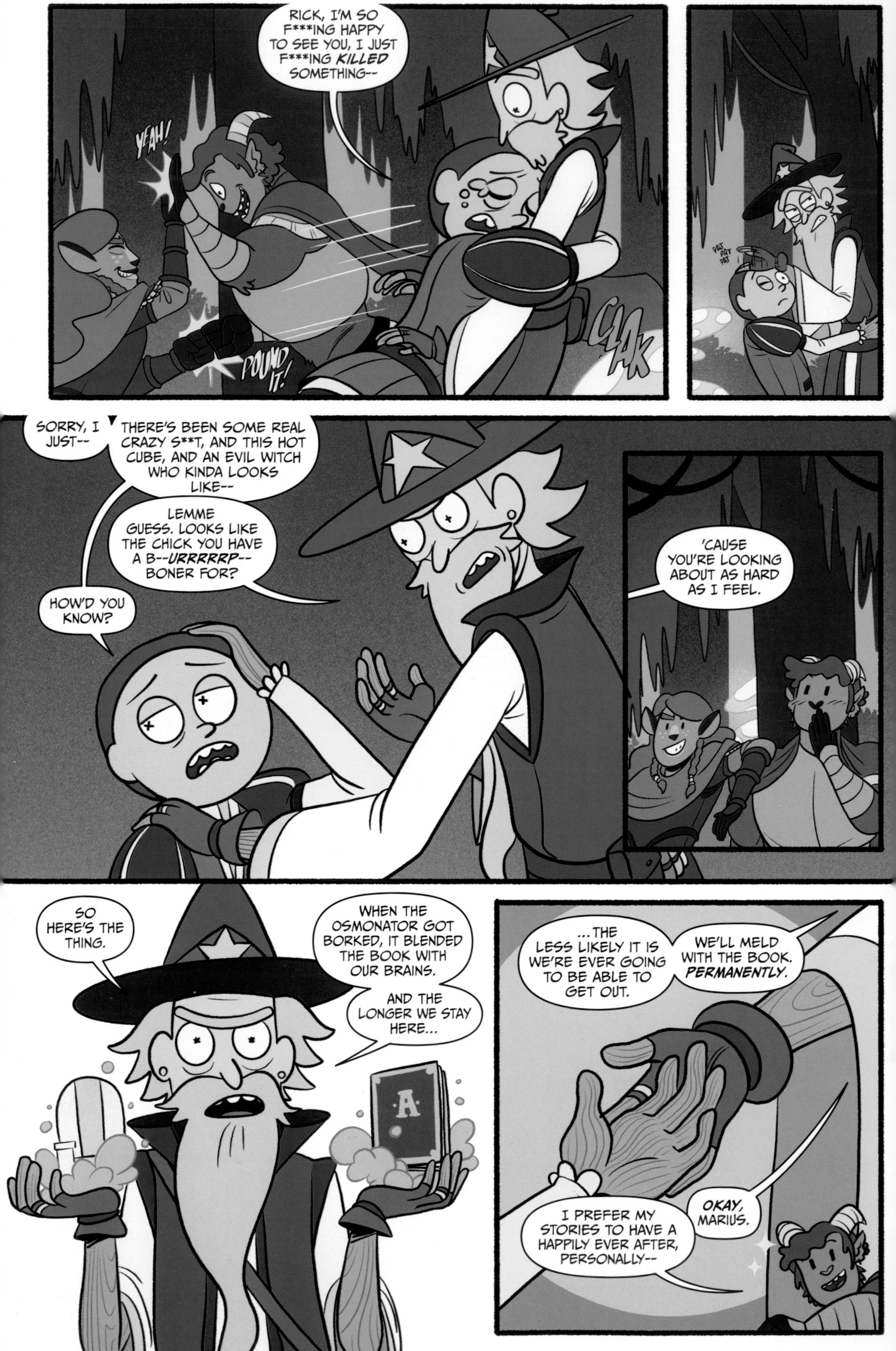

RICK, I'M SO F***ING HAPPY TO SEE YOU, I JUST F***ING KILLED SOMETHING--
YEAH!
POUND IT!
CLAK
PAT PAT PAT
SORRY, I JUST--
THERE'S BEEN SOME REAL CRAZY S**T, AND THIS HOT CUBE, AND AN EVIL WITCH WHO KINDA LOOKS LIKE--
LEMME GUESS. LOOKS LIKE THE CHICK YOU HAVE A B--URRRRRP--BONER FOR?
HOW'D YOU KNOW?
'CAUSE YOU'RE LOOKING ABOUT AS HARD AS I FEEL.
SO HERE'S THE THING.
WHEN THE OSMONATOR GOT BORKED, IT BLENDED THE BOOK WITH OUR BRAINS.
AND THE LONGER WE STAY HERE...
...THE LESS LIKELY IT IS WE'RE EVER GOING TO BE ABLE TO GET OUT.
WE'LL MELD WITH THE BOOK. PERMANENTLY.
I PREFER MY STORIES TO HAVE A HAPPILY EVER AFTER, PERSONALLY--
OKAY, MARIUS.

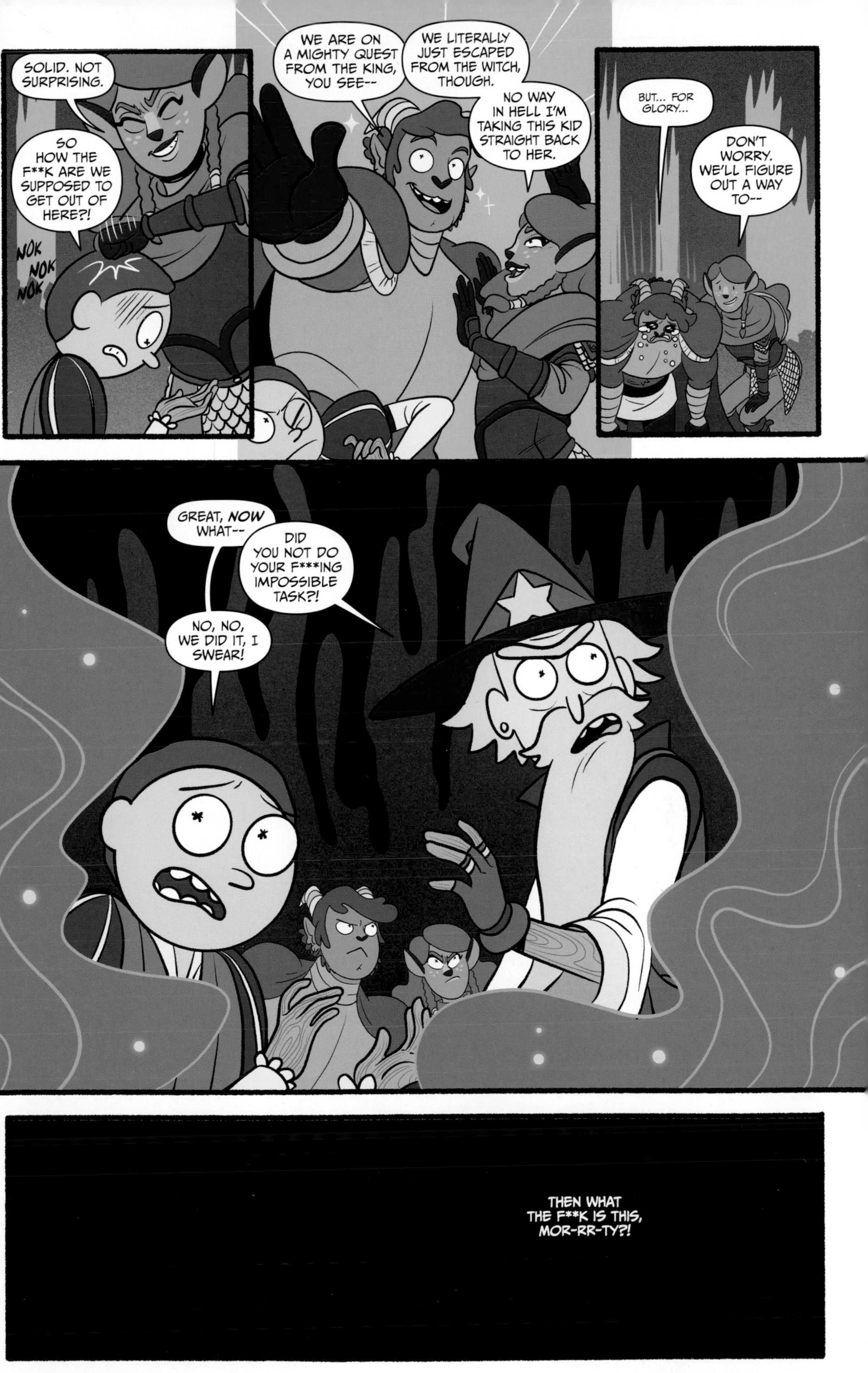
SOLID. NOT SURPRISING.
SO HOW THE F**K ARE WE SUPPOSED TO GET OUT OF HERE?!
NOK NOK NOK
WE ARE ON A MIGHTY QUEST FROM THE KING, YOU SEE--
WE LITERALLY JUST ESCAPED FROM THE WITCH, THOUGH.
NO WAY IN HELL I'M TAKING THIS KID STRAIGHT BACK TO HER.
BUT... FOR GLORY...
DON'T WORRY. WE'LL FIGURE OUT A WAY TO--
GREAT, *NOW* WHAT--
DID YOU NOT DO YOUR F***ING IMPOSSIBLE TASK?!
NO, NO, WE DID IT, I SWEAR!
THEN WHAT THE F**K IS THIS, MOR-RR-TY?!

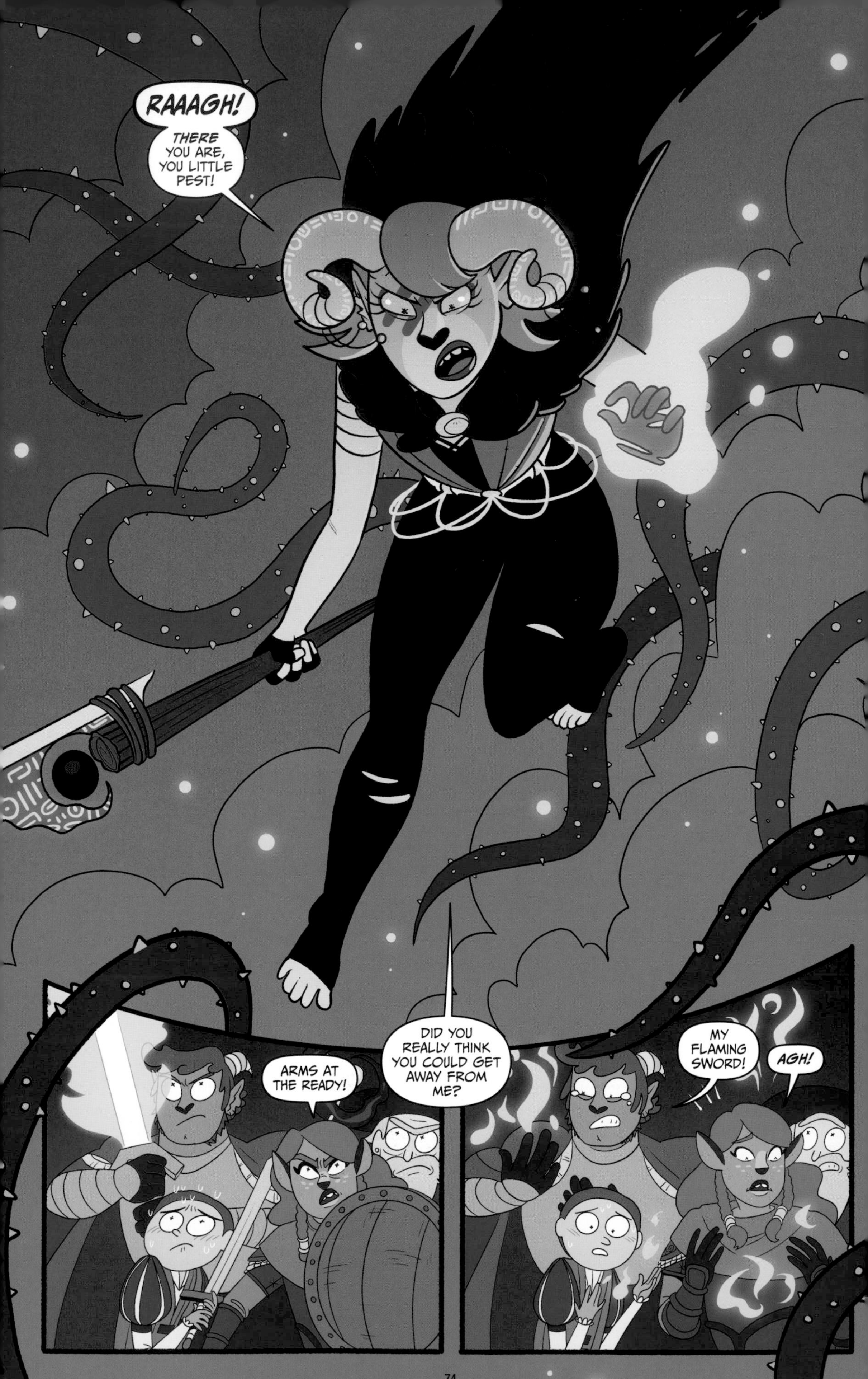
RAAAGH!
THERE YOU ARE, YOU LITTLE PEST!
ARMS AT THE READY!
DID YOU REALLY THINK YOU COULD GET AWAY FROM ME?
MY FLAMING SWORD!
AGH!

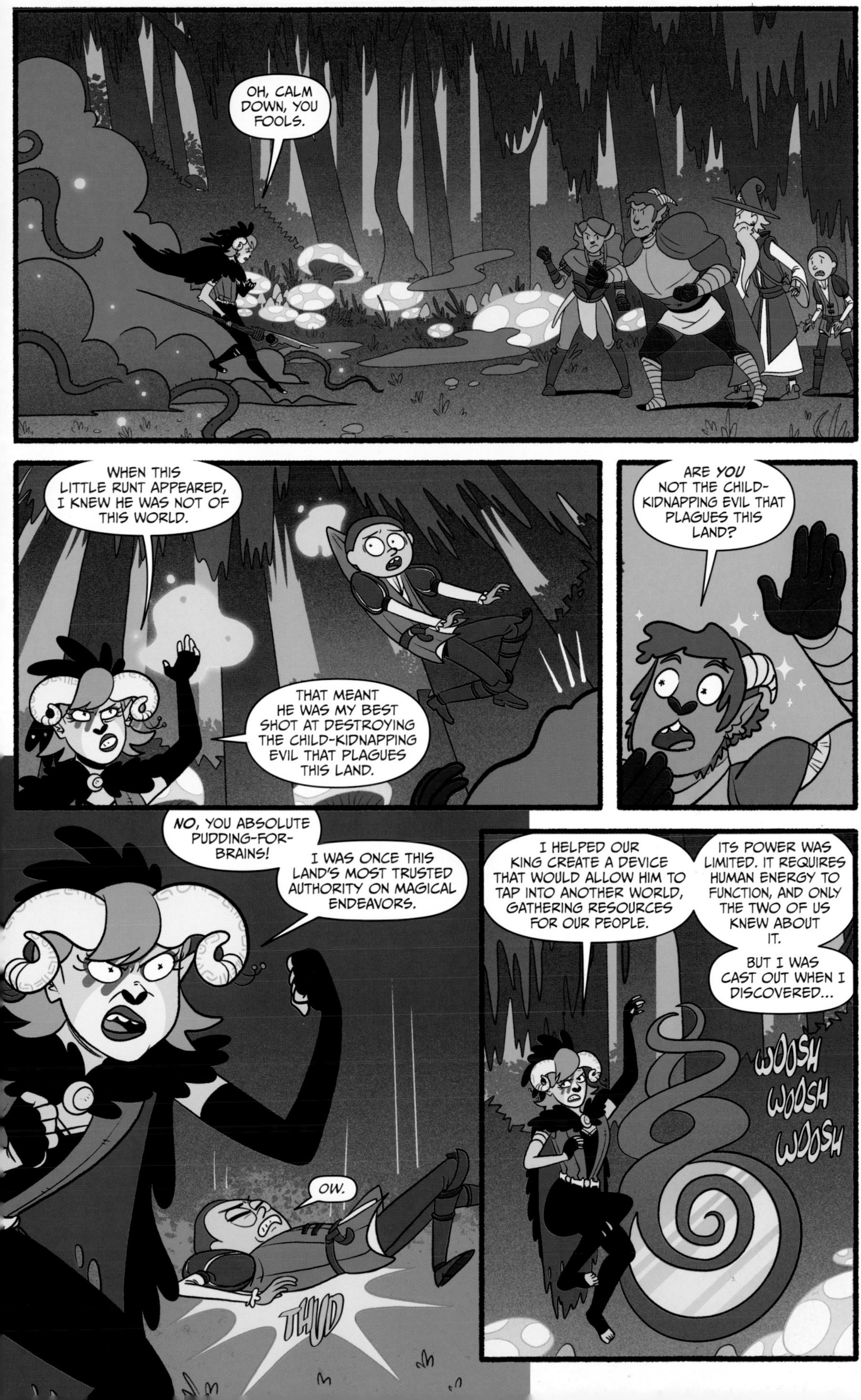

OH, CALM DOWN, YOU FOOLS.
WHEN THIS LITTLE RUNT APPEARED, I KNEW HE WAS NOT OF THIS WORLD.
THAT MEANT HE WAS MY BEST SHOT AT DESTROYING THE CHILD-KIDNAPPING EVIL THAT PLAGUES THIS LAND.
ARE *YOU* NOT THE CHILD-KIDNAPPING EVIL THAT PLAGUES THIS LAND?
NO, YOU ABSOLUTE PUDDING-FOR-BRAINS!
I WAS ONCE THIS LAND'S MOST TRUSTED AUTHORITY ON MAGICAL ENDEAVORS.
OW.
THUD
I HELPED OUR KING CREATE A DEVICE THAT WOULD ALLOW HIM TO TAP INTO ANOTHER WORLD, GATHERING RESOURCES FOR OUR PEOPLE.
ITS POWER WAS LIMITED. IT REQUIRES HUMAN ENERGY TO FUNCTION, AND ONLY THE TWO OF US KNEW ABOUT IT.
BUT I WAS CAST OUT WHEN I DISCOVERED...
WOOSH WOOSH WOOSH

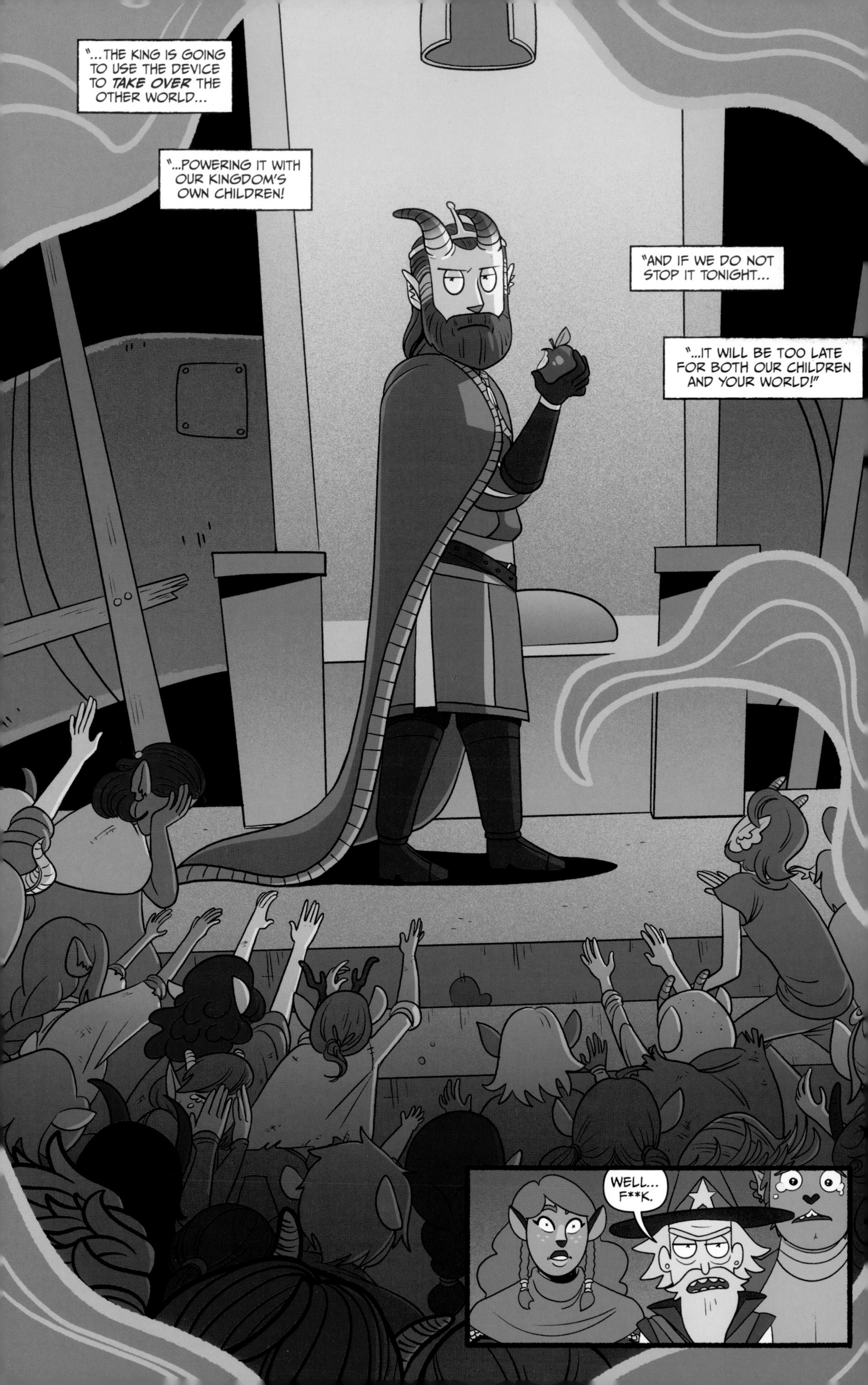
"...THE KING IS GOING TO USE THE DEVICE TO TAKE OVER THE OTHER WORLD...
"...POWERING IT WITH OUR KINGDOM'S OWN CHILDREN!
"AND IF WE DO NOT STOP IT TONIGHT...
"...IT WILL BE TOO LATE FOR BOTH OUR CHILDREN AND YOUR WORLD!"
WELL... F**K.

Chapter Four

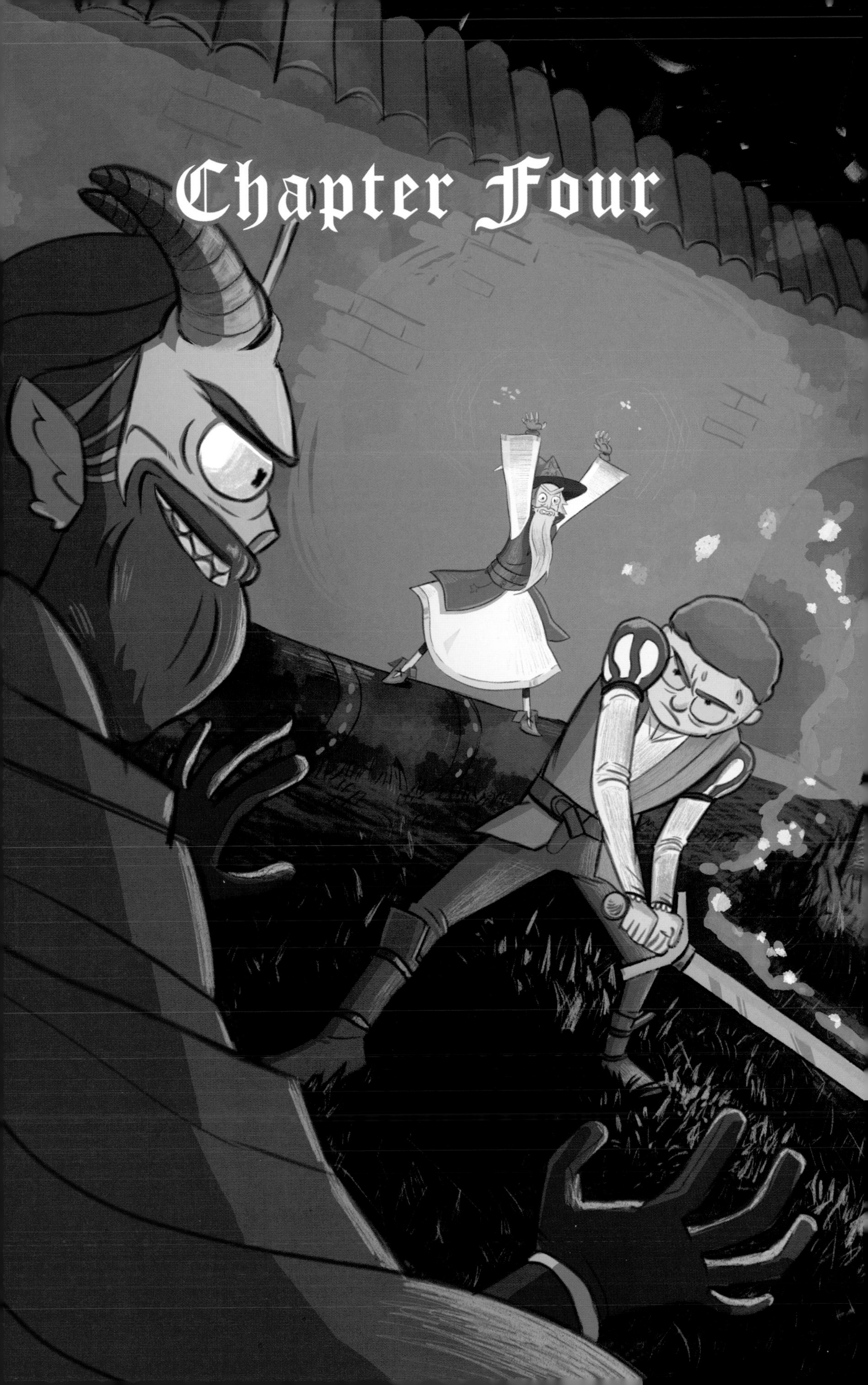

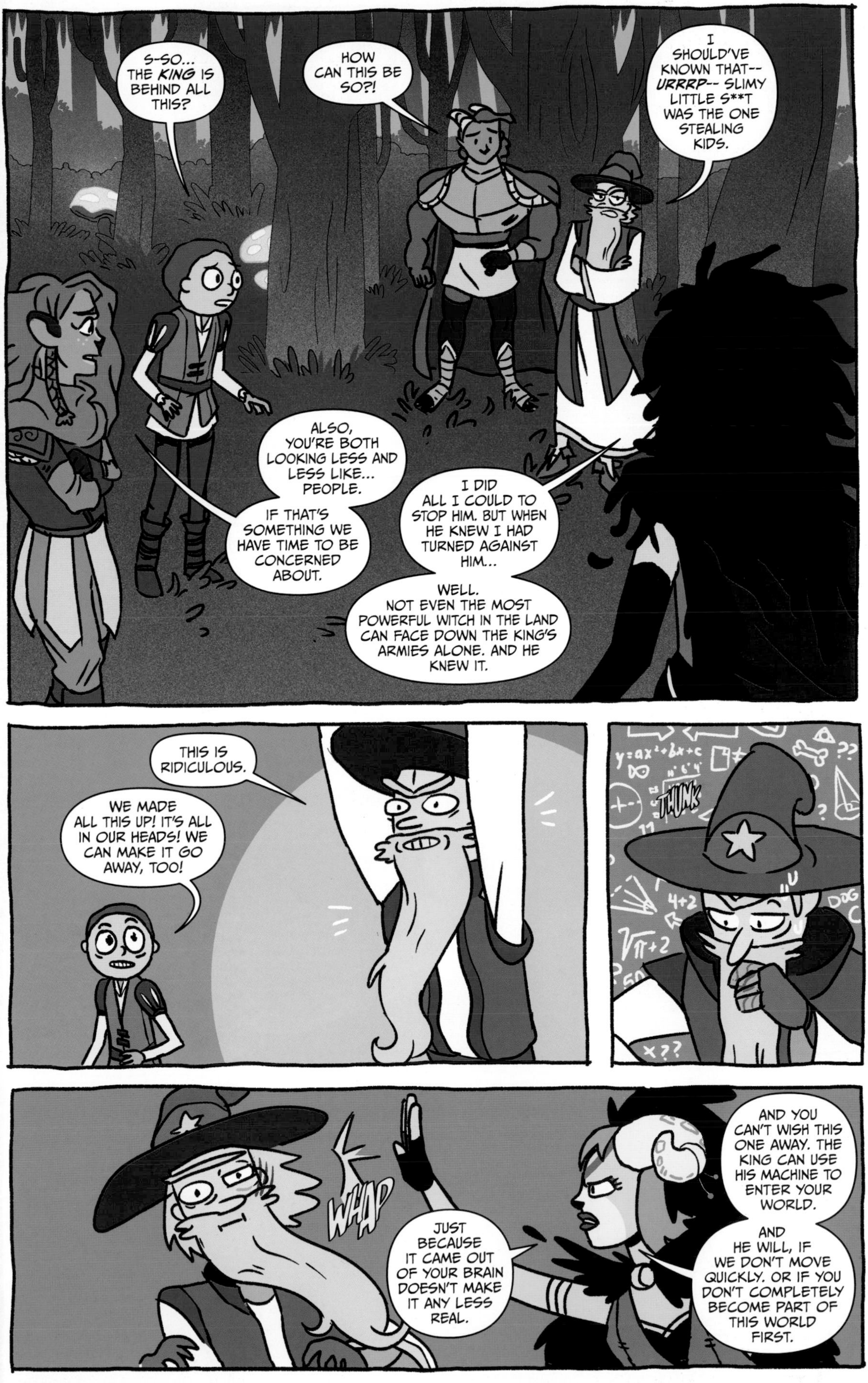
S-SO... THE KING IS BEHIND ALL THIS?
HOW CAN THIS BE SO?!
I SHOULD'VE KNOWN THAT-- URRRP-- SLIMY LITTLE S**T WAS THE ONE STEALING KIDS.
ALSO, YOU'RE BOTH LOOKING LESS AND LESS LIKE... PEOPLE.
IF THAT'S SOMETHING WE HAVE TIME TO BE CONCERNED ABOUT.
I DID ALL I COULD TO STOP HIM. BUT WHEN HE KNEW I HAD TURNED AGAINST HIM...
WELL. NOT EVEN THE MOST POWERFUL WITCH IN THE LAND CAN FACE DOWN THE KING'S ARMIES ALONE. AND HE KNEW IT.
THIS IS RIDICULOUS.
WE MADE ALL THIS UP! IT'S ALL IN OUR HEADS! WE CAN MAKE IT GO AWAY, TOO!
THUNK
WHAP
JUST BECAUSE IT CAME OUT OF YOUR BRAIN DOESN'T MAKE IT ANY LESS REAL.
AND YOU CAN'T WISH THIS ONE AWAY. THE KING CAN USE HIS MACHINE TO ENTER YOUR WORLD.
AND HE WILL, IF WE DON'T MOVE QUICKLY. OR IF YOU DON'T COMPLETELY BECOME PART OF THIS WORLD FIRST.

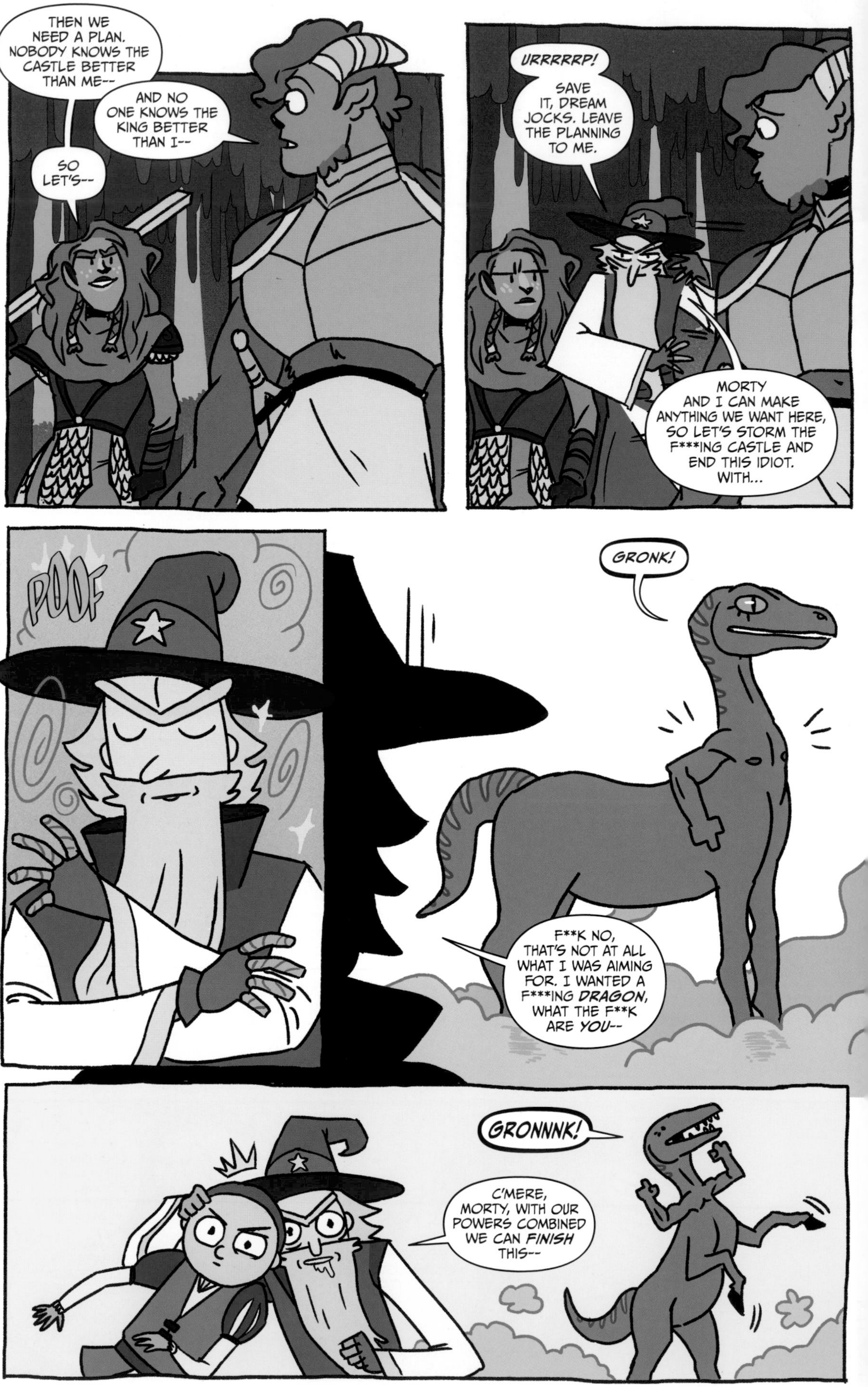
THEN WE NEED A PLAN. NOBODY KNOWS THE CASTLE BETTER THAN ME--
AND NO ONE KNOWS THE KING BETTER THAN I--
SO LET'S--
URRRRRP!
SAVE IT, DREAM JOCKS. LEAVE THE PLANNING TO ME.
MORTY AND I CAN MAKE ANYTHING WE WANT HERE, SO LET'S STORM THE F***ING CASTLE AND END THIS IDIOT. WITH...
POOF
GRONK!
F**K NO, THAT'S NOT AT ALL WHAT I WAS AIMING FOR. I WANTED A F***ING *DRAGON*, WHAT THE F**K ARE *YOU*--
GRONNNK!
C'MERE, MORTY, WITH OUR POWERS COMBINED WE CAN *FINISH* THIS--

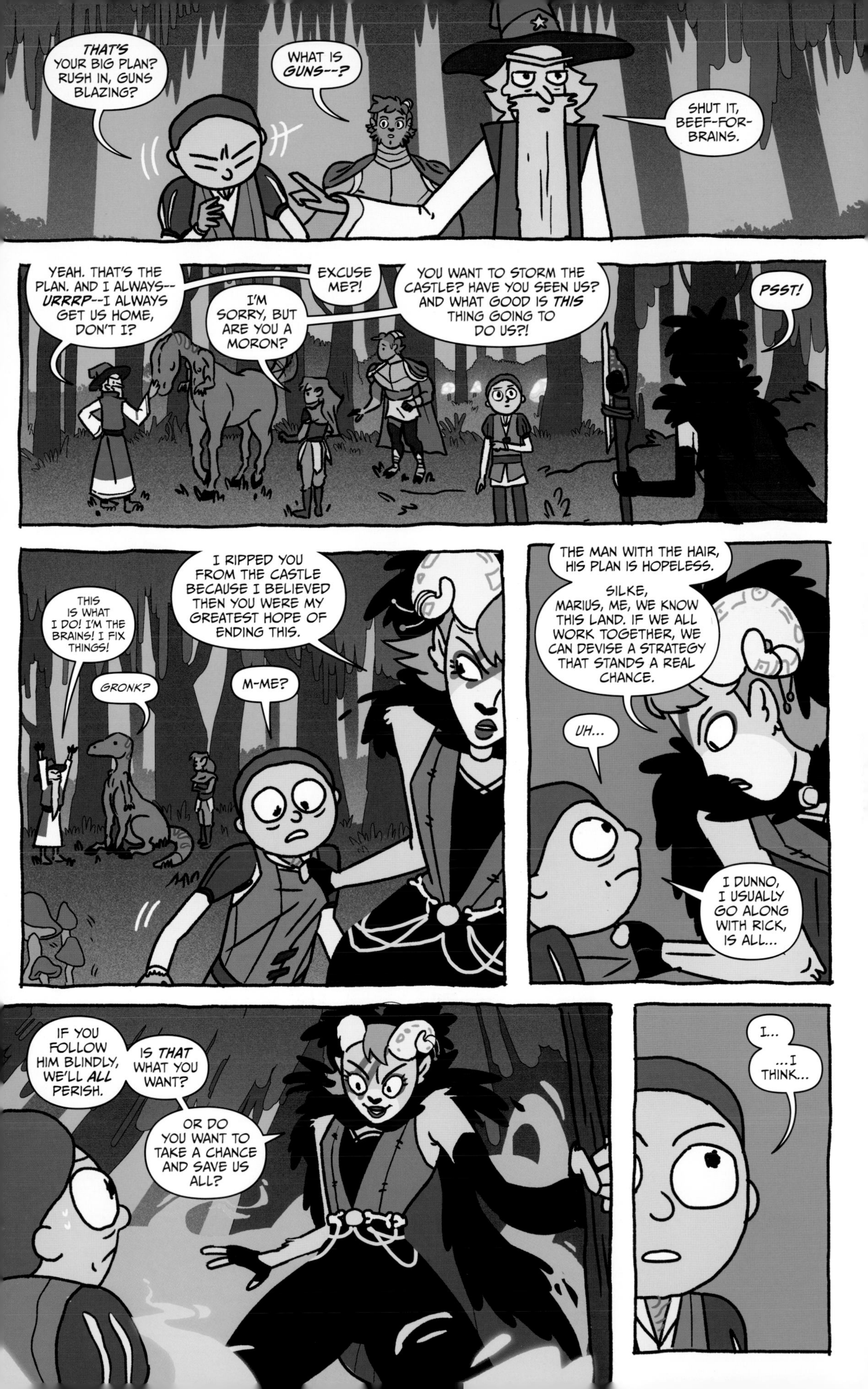
THAT'S YOUR BIG PLAN? RUSH IN, GUNS BLAZING?
WHAT IS GUNS--?
SHUT IT, BEEF-FOR-BRAINS.
YEAH. THAT'S THE PLAN. AND I ALWAYS--URRRP--I ALWAYS GET US HOME, DON'T I?
EXCUSE ME?!
I'M SORRY, BUT ARE YOU A MORON?
YOU WANT TO STORM THE CASTLE? HAVE YOU SEEN US? AND WHAT GOOD IS THIS THING GOING TO DO US?!
PSST!
THIS IS WHAT I DO! I'M THE BRAINS! I FIX THINGS!
GRONK?
I RIPPED YOU FROM THE CASTLE BECAUSE I BELIEVED THEN YOU WERE MY GREATEST HOPE OF ENDING THIS.
M-ME?
THE MAN WITH THE HAIR, HIS PLAN IS HOPELESS.
SILKE, MARIUS, ME, WE KNOW THIS LAND. IF WE ALL WORK TOGETHER, WE CAN DEVISE A STRATEGY THAT STANDS A REAL CHANCE.
UH...
I DUNNO, I USUALLY GO ALONG WITH RICK, IS ALL...
IF YOU FOLLOW HIM BLINDLY, WE'LL ALL PERISH.
IS THAT WHAT YOU WANT?
OR DO YOU WANT TO TAKE A CHANCE AND SAVE US ALL?
I...
...I THINK...

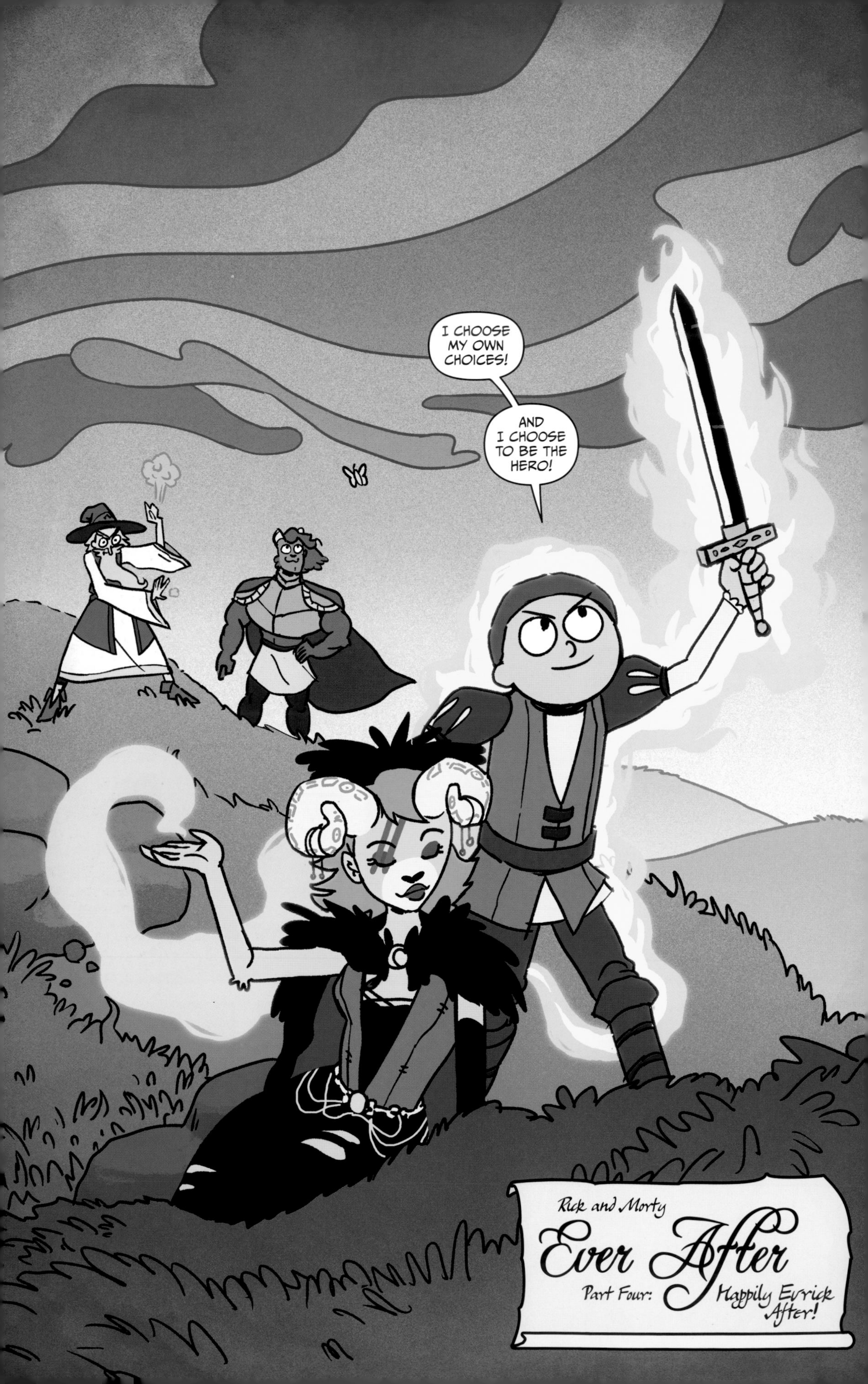
I CHOOSE MY OWN CHOICES!
AND I CHOOSE TO BE THE HERO!
Rick and Morty
Ever After
Part Four: Happily Evrick After!

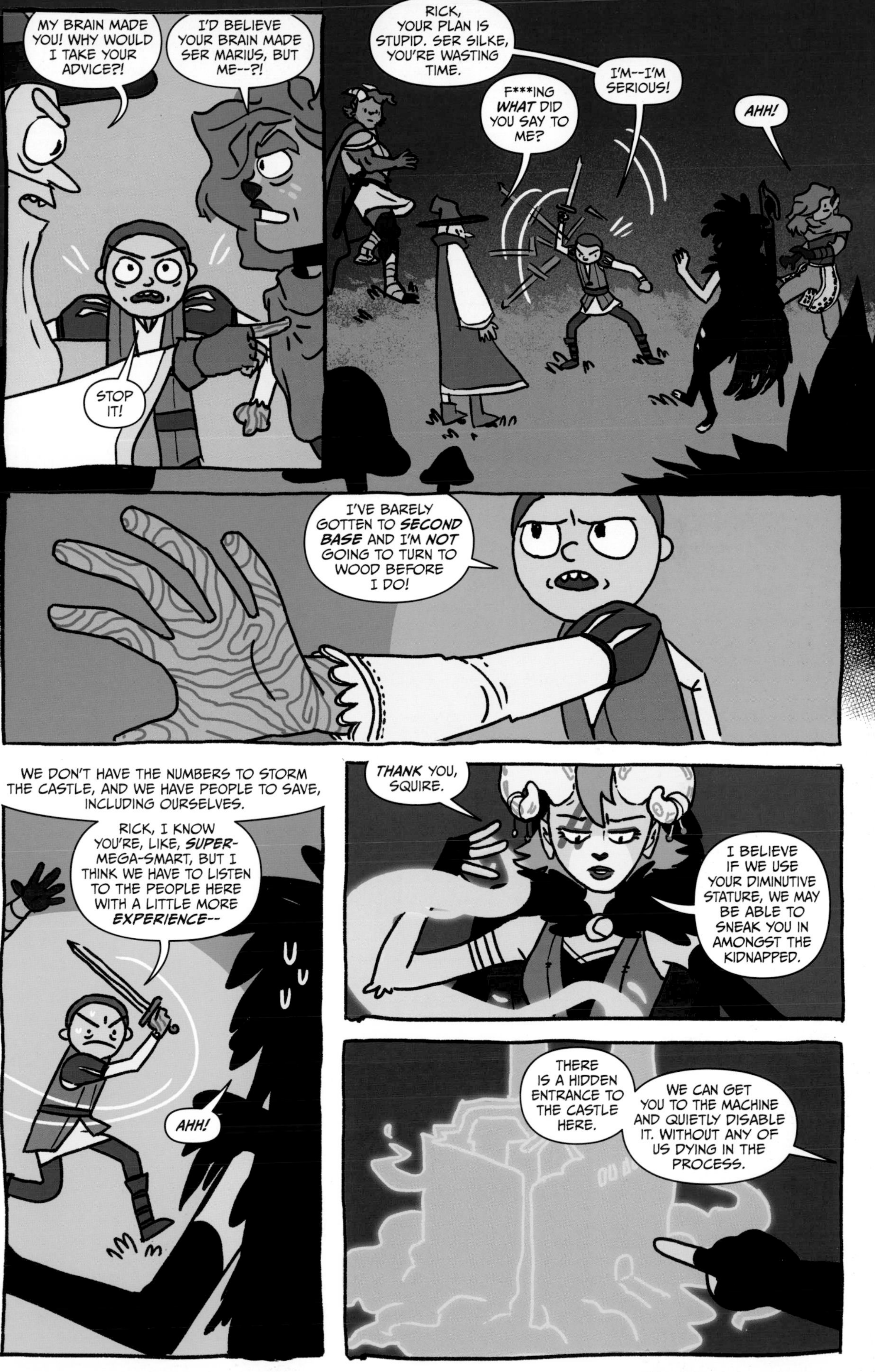
MY BRAIN MADE YOU! WHY WOULD I TAKE YOUR ADVICE?!
I'D BELIEVE YOUR BRAIN MADE SER MARIUS, BUT ME--?!
STOP IT!
RICK, YOUR PLAN IS STUPID. SER SILKE, YOU'RE WASTING TIME.
F***ING WHAT DID YOU SAY TO ME?
I'M--I'M SERIOUS!
AHH!
I'VE BARELY GOTTEN TO SECOND BASE AND I'M NOT GOING TO TURN TO WOOD BEFORE I DO!
WE DON'T HAVE THE NUMBERS TO STORM THE CASTLE, AND WE HAVE PEOPLE TO SAVE, INCLUDING OURSELVES.
RICK, I KNOW YOU'RE, LIKE, SUPER-MEGA-SMART, BUT I THINK WE HAVE TO LISTEN TO THE PEOPLE HERE WITH A LITTLE MORE EXPERIENCE--
AHH!
THANK YOU, SQUIRE.
I BELIEVE IF WE USE YOUR DIMINUTIVE STATURE, WE MAY BE ABLE TO SNEAK YOU IN AMONGST THE KIDNAPPED.
THERE IS A HIDDEN ENTRANCE TO THE CASTLE HERE.
WE CAN GET YOU TO THE MACHINE AND QUIETLY DISABLE IT. WITHOUT ANY OF US DYING IN THE PROCESS.

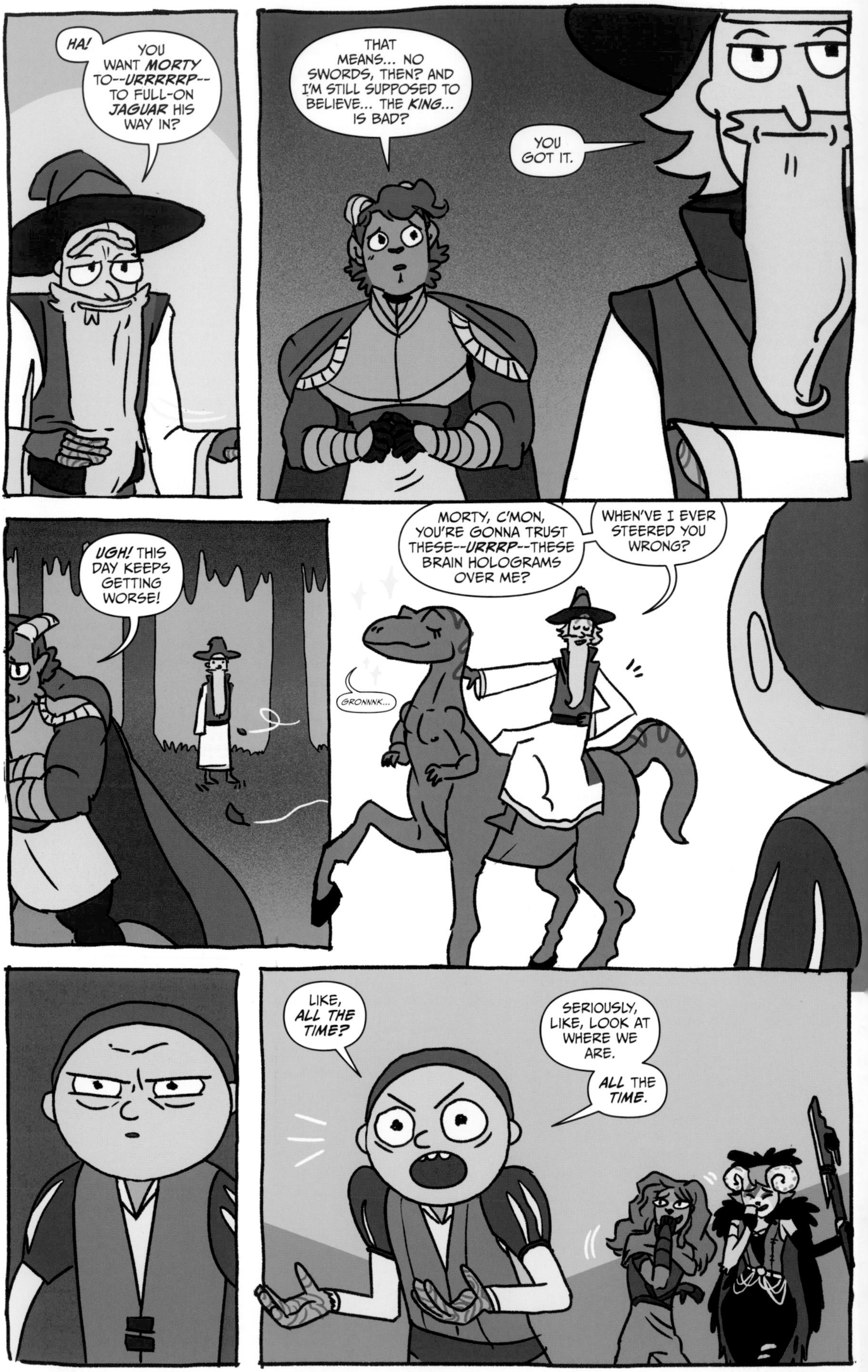
HA!
YOU WANT MORTY TO--URRRRRP--TO FULL-ON JAGUAR HIS WAY IN?
THAT MEANS... NO SWORDS, THEN? AND I'M STILL SUPPOSED TO BELIEVE... THE KING... IS BAD?
YOU GOT IT.
UGH! THIS DAY KEEPS GETTING WORSE!
MORTY, C'MON, YOU'RE GONNA TRUST THESE--URRRP--THESE BRAIN HOLOGRAMS OVER ME?
WHEN'VE I EVER STEERED YOU WRONG?
GRONNNK...
LIKE, ALL THE TIME?
SERIOUSLY, LIKE, LOOK AT WHERE WE ARE.
ALL THE TIME.

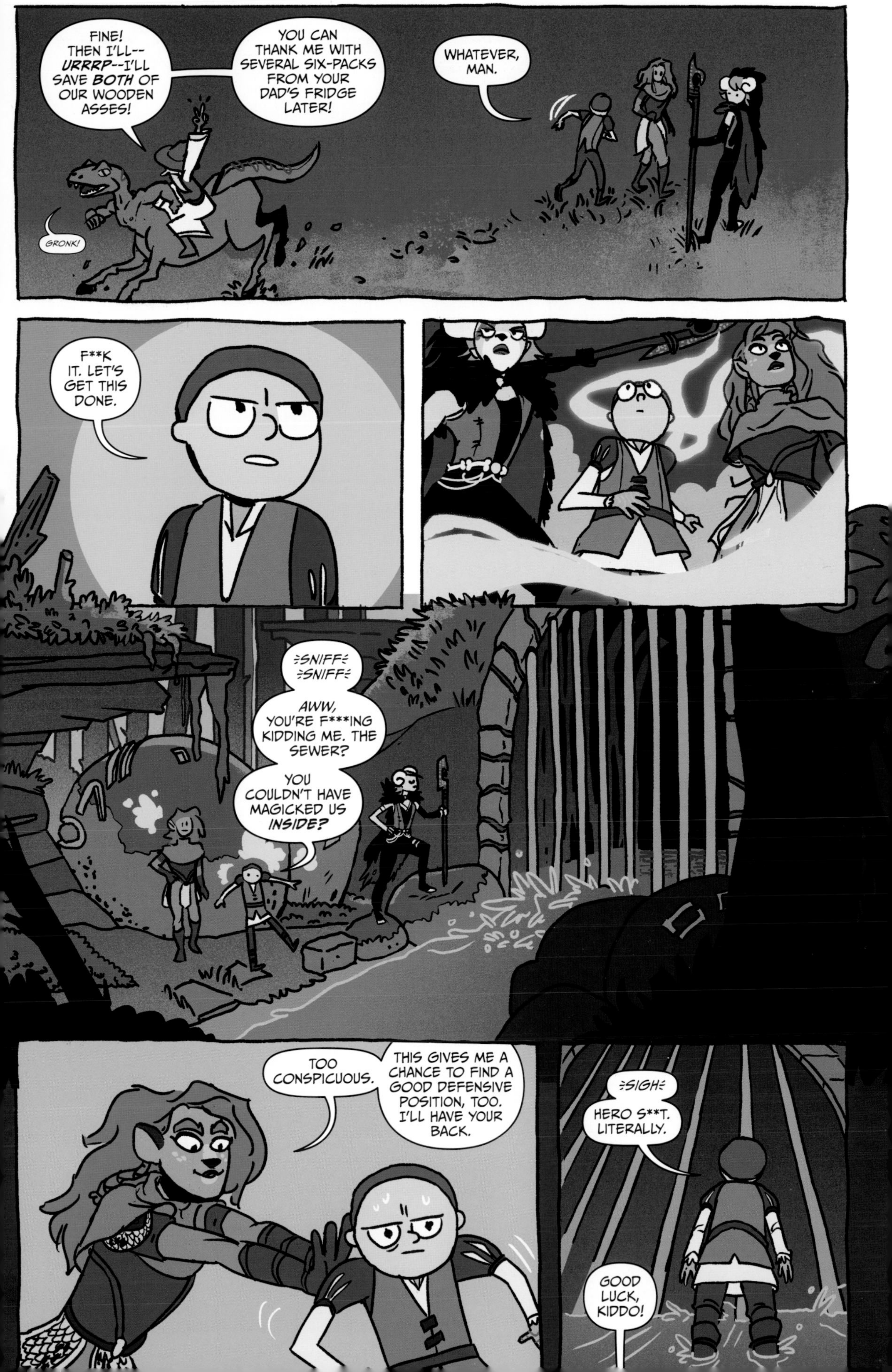

FINE! THEN I'LL-- URRRP--I'LL SAVE BOTH OF OUR WOODEN ASSES!
YOU CAN THANK ME WITH SEVERAL SIX-PACKS FROM YOUR DAD'S FRIDGE LATER!
GRONK!
WHATEVER, MAN.
F**K IT. LET'S GET THIS DONE.
SNIFF SNIFF
AWW, YOU'RE F***ING KIDDING ME. THE SEWER?
YOU COULDN'T HAVE MAGICKED US INSIDE?
TOO CONSPICUOUS.
THIS GIVES ME A CHANCE TO FIND A GOOD DEFENSIVE POSITION, TOO. I'LL HAVE YOUR BACK.
SIGH
HERO S**T. LITERALLY.
GOOD LUCK, KIDDO!

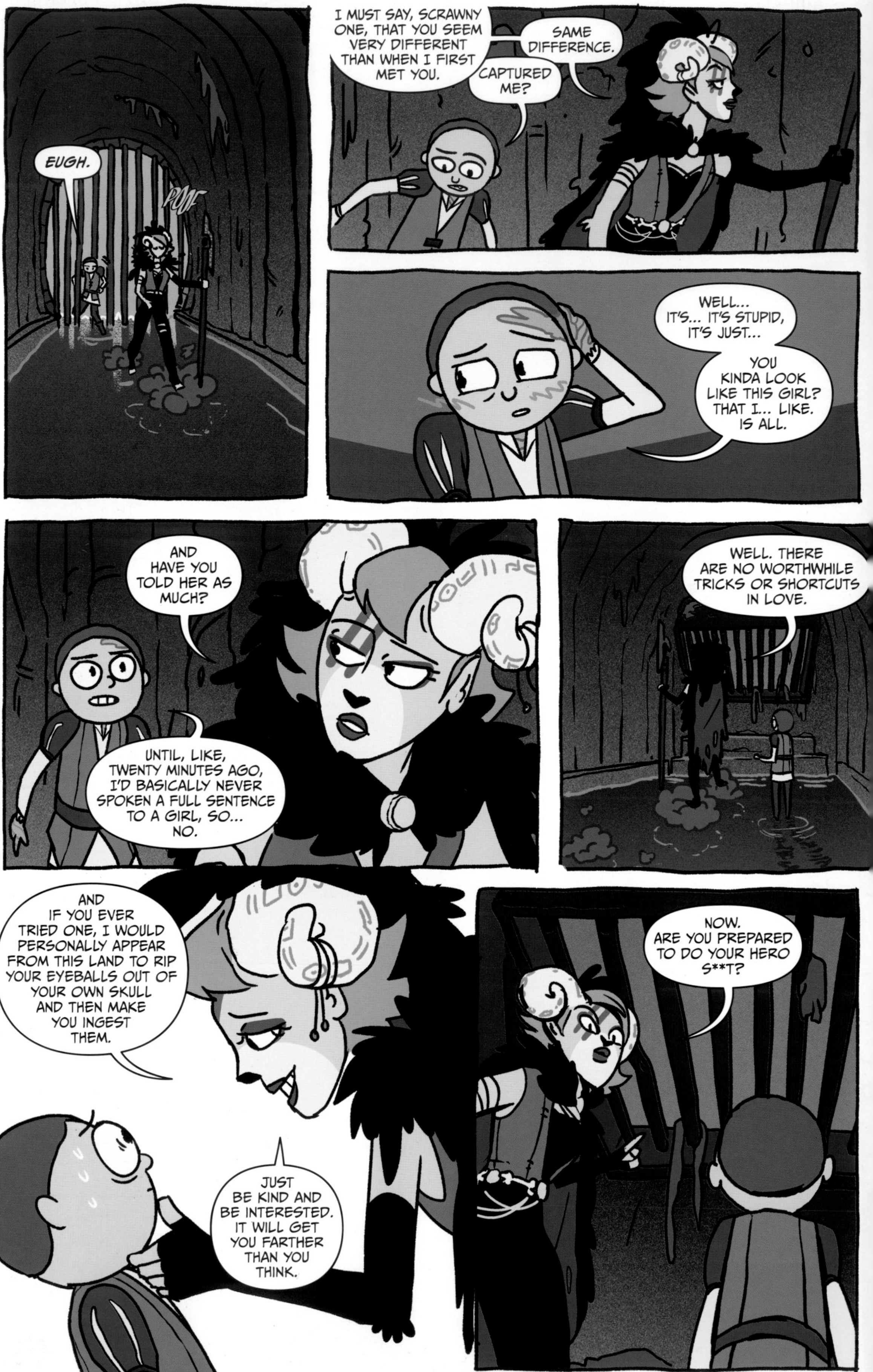
EUGH.
POOF
I MUST SAY, SCRAWNY ONE, THAT YOU SEEM VERY DIFFERENT THAN WHEN I FIRST MET YOU.
CAPTURED ME?
SAME DIFFERENCE.
WELL... IT'S... IT'S STUPID, IT'S JUST...
YOU KINDA LOOK LIKE THIS GIRL? THAT I... LIKE. IS ALL.
AND HAVE YOU TOLD HER AS MUCH?
UNTIL, LIKE, TWENTY MINUTES AGO, I'D BASICALLY NEVER SPOKEN A FULL SENTENCE TO A GIRL, SO... NO.
WELL. THERE ARE NO WORTHWHILE TRICKS OR SHORTCUTS IN LOVE.
AND IF YOU EVER TRIED ONE, I WOULD PERSONALLY APPEAR FROM THIS LAND TO RIP YOUR EYEBALLS OUT OF YOUR OWN SKULL AND THEN MAKE YOU INGEST THEM.
JUST BE KIND AND BE INTERESTED. IT WILL GET YOU FARTHER THAN YOU THINK.
NOW. ARE YOU PREPARED TO DO YOUR HERO S**T?

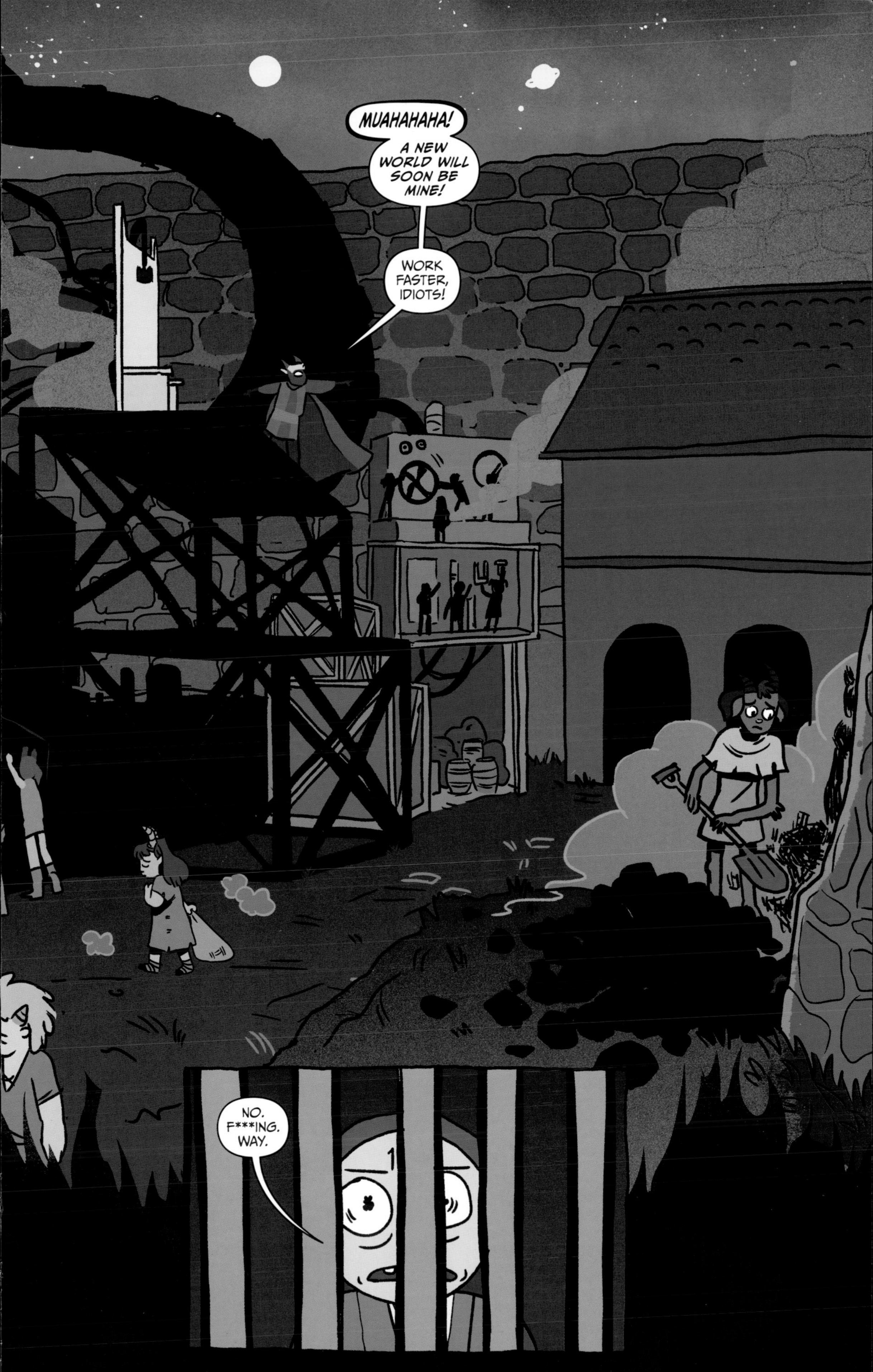
MUAHAHAHA!
A NEW WORLD WILL SOON BE MINE!
WORK FASTER, IDIOTS!
NO. F***ING. WAY.

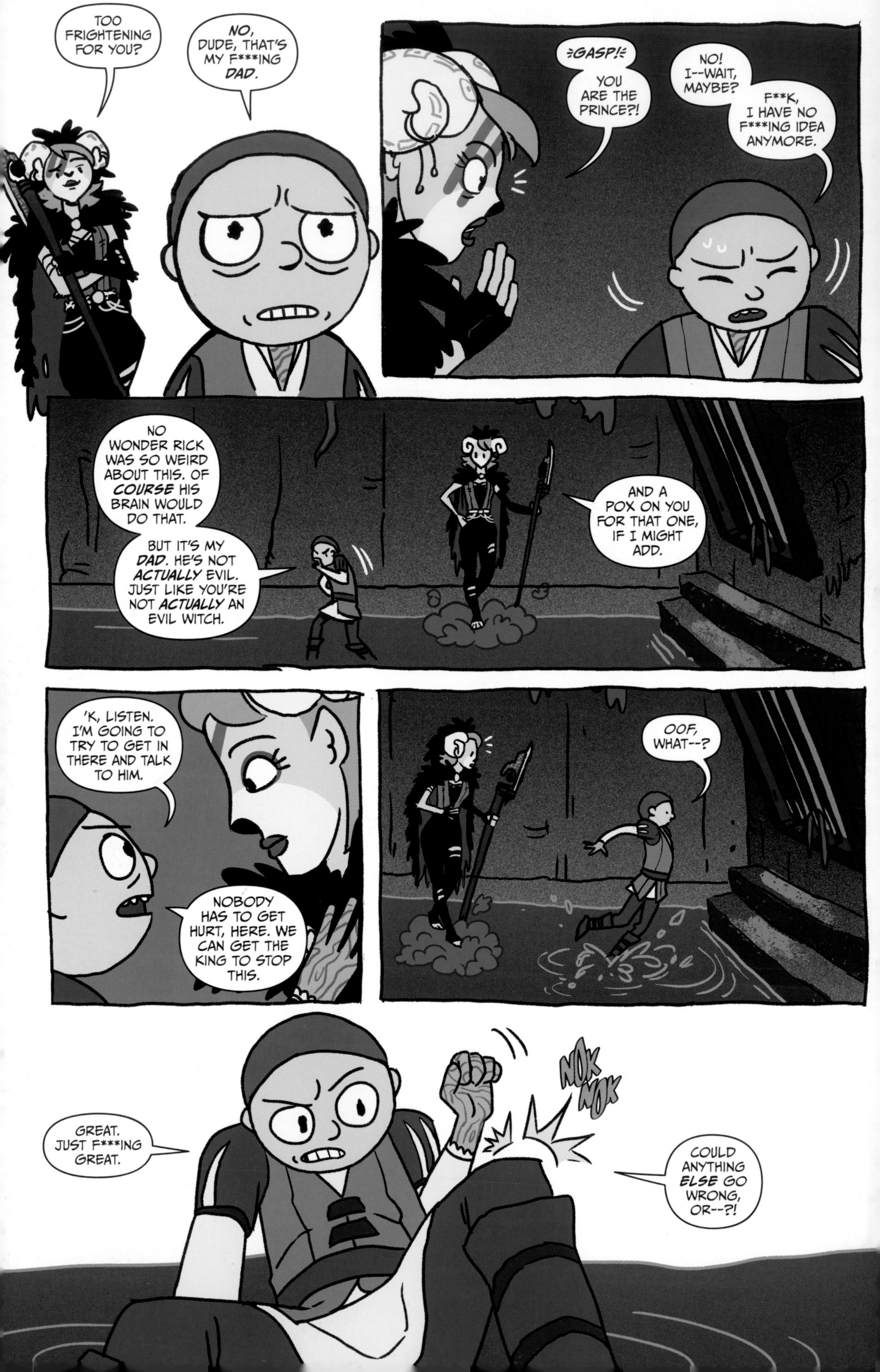
TOO FRIGHTENING FOR YOU?
NO, DUDE, THAT'S MY F***ING DAD.
GASP! YOU ARE THE PRINCE?!
NO! I--WAIT, MAYBE?
F**K, I HAVE NO F***ING IDEA ANYMORE.
NO WONDER RICK WAS SO WEIRD ABOUT THIS. OF COURSE HIS BRAIN WOULD DO THAT.
BUT IT'S MY DAD. HE'S NOT ACTUALLY EVIL. JUST LIKE YOU'RE NOT ACTUALLY AN EVIL WITCH.
AND A POX ON YOU FOR THAT ONE, IF I MIGHT ADD.
'K, LISTEN. I'M GOING TO TRY TO GET IN THERE AND TALK TO HIM.
NOBODY HAS TO GET HURT, HERE. WE CAN GET THE KING TO STOP THIS.
OOF, WHAT--?
GREAT. JUST F***ING GREAT.
NOK NOK
COULD ANYTHING ELSE GO WRONG, OR--?!

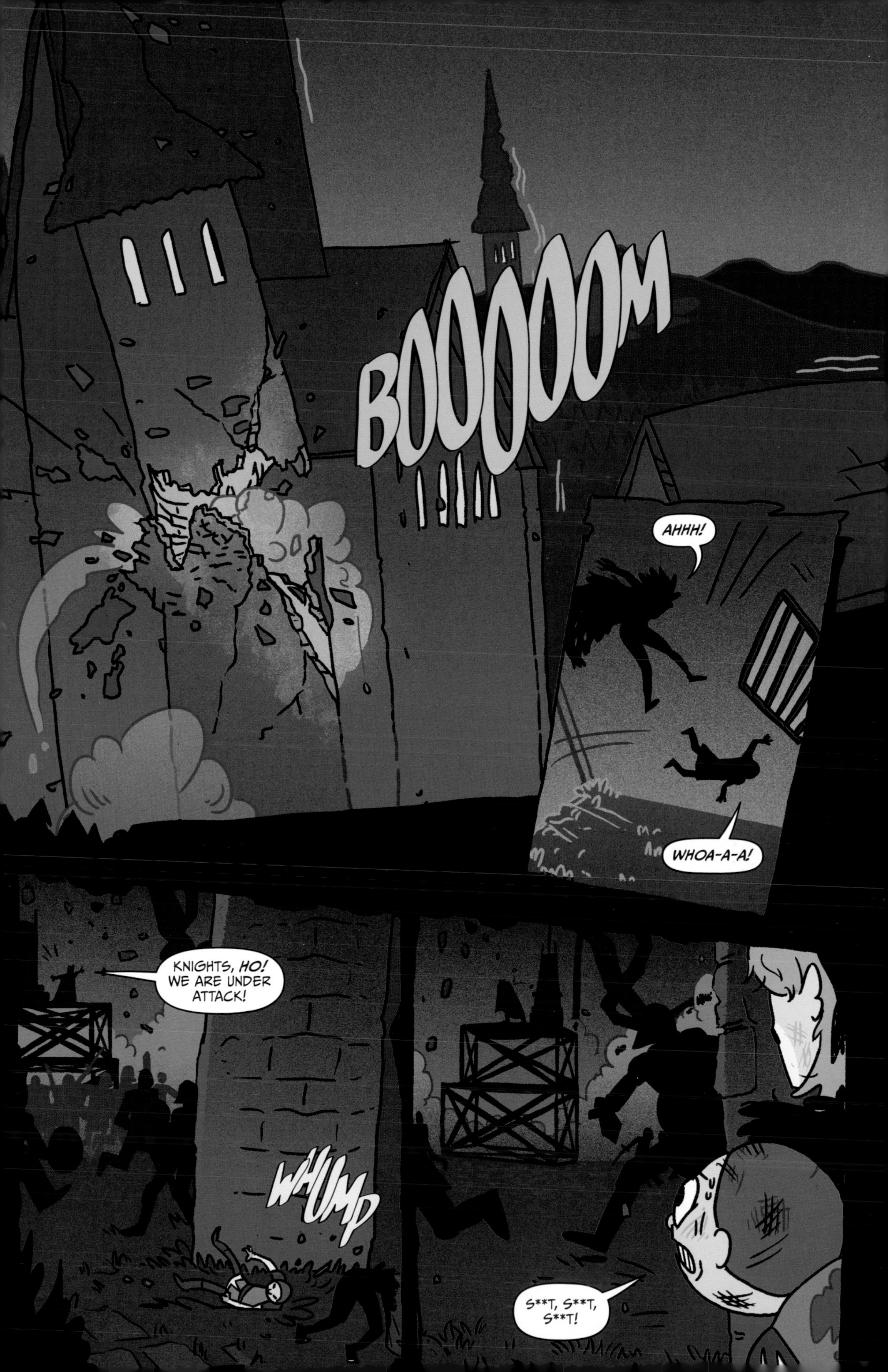
BOOOOOM
AHHH!
WHOA-A-A!
KNIGHTS, HO! WE ARE UNDER ATTACK!
WHUMP
S**T, S**T, S**T!

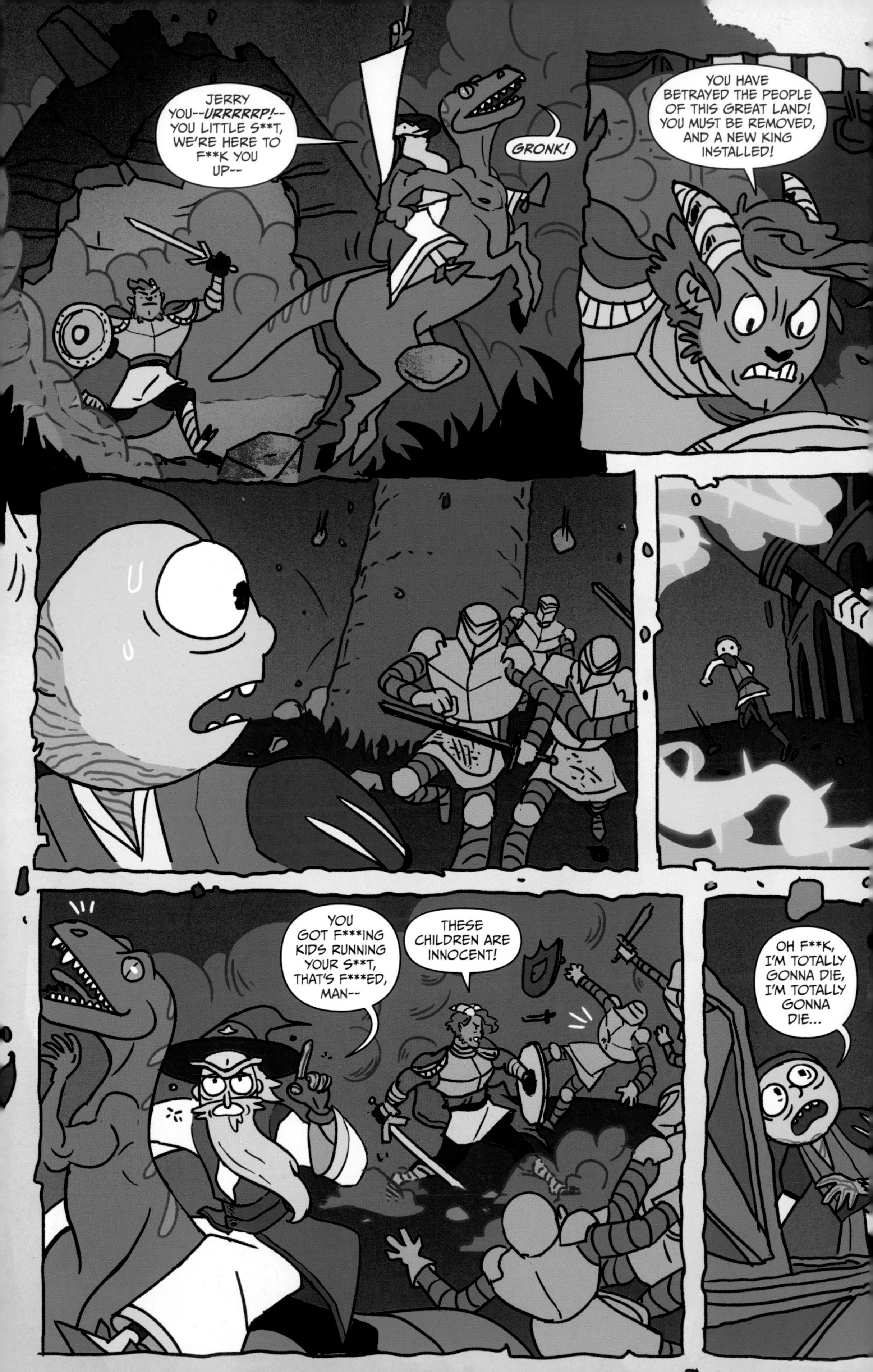

JERRY YOU--URRRRRP!-- YOU LITTLE S**T, WE'RE HERE TO F**K YOU UP--
GRONK!
YOU HAVE BETRAYED THE PEOPLE OF THIS GREAT LAND! YOU MUST BE REMOVED, AND A NEW KING INSTALLED!
YOU GOT F***ING KIDS RUNNING YOUR S**T, THAT'S F***ED, MAN--
THESE CHILDREN ARE INNOCENT!
OH F**K, I'M TOTALLY GONNA DIE, I'M TOTALLY GONNA DIE...

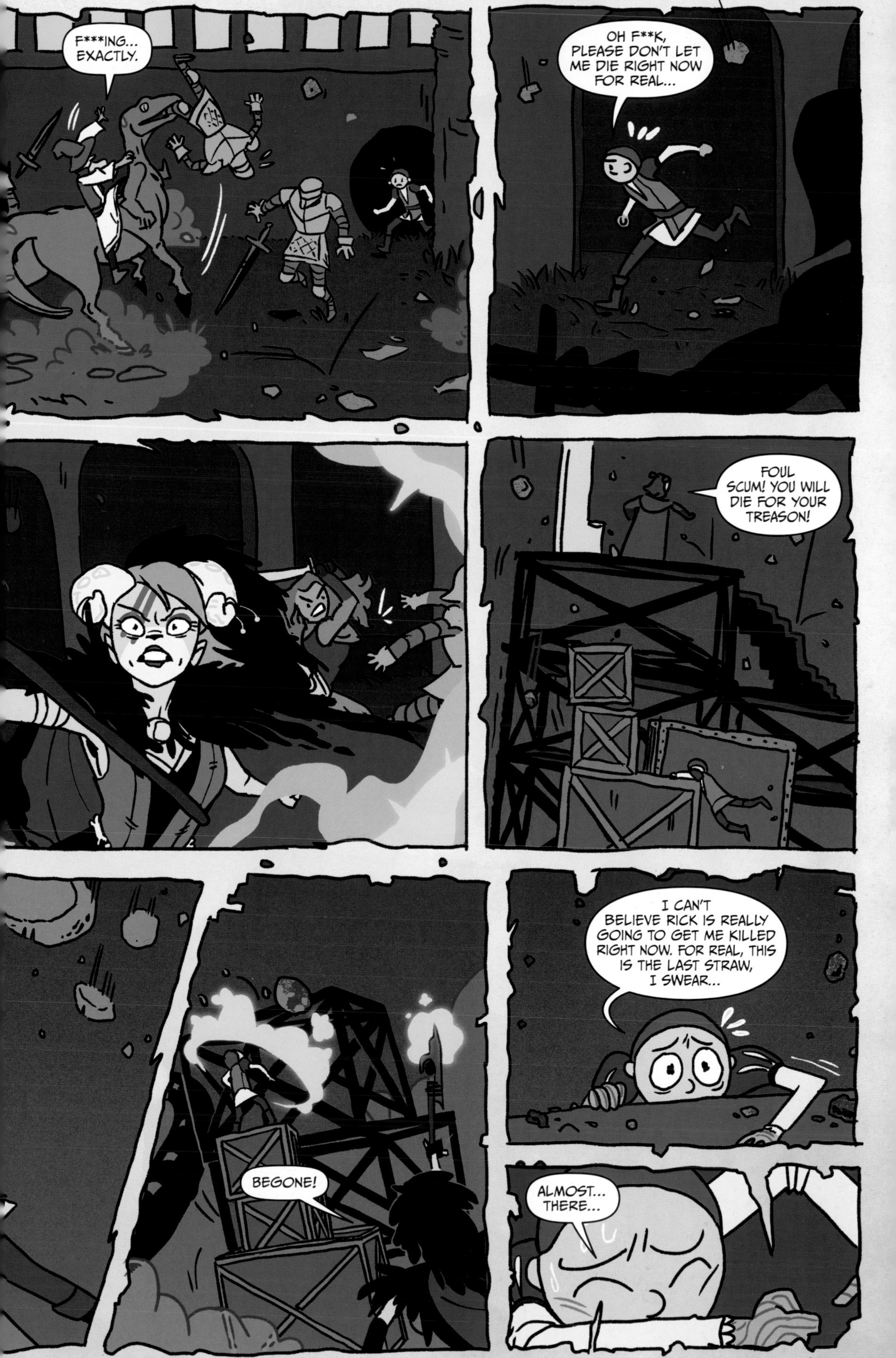
F***ING... EXACTLY.
OH F**K, PLEASE DON'T LET ME DIE RIGHT NOW FOR REAL...
FOUL SCUM! YOU WILL DIE FOR YOUR TREASON!
BEGONE!
I CAN'T BELIEVE RICK IS REALLY GOING TO GET ME KILLED RIGHT NOW. FOR REAL, THIS IS THE LAST STRAW, I SWEAR...
ALMOST... THERE...

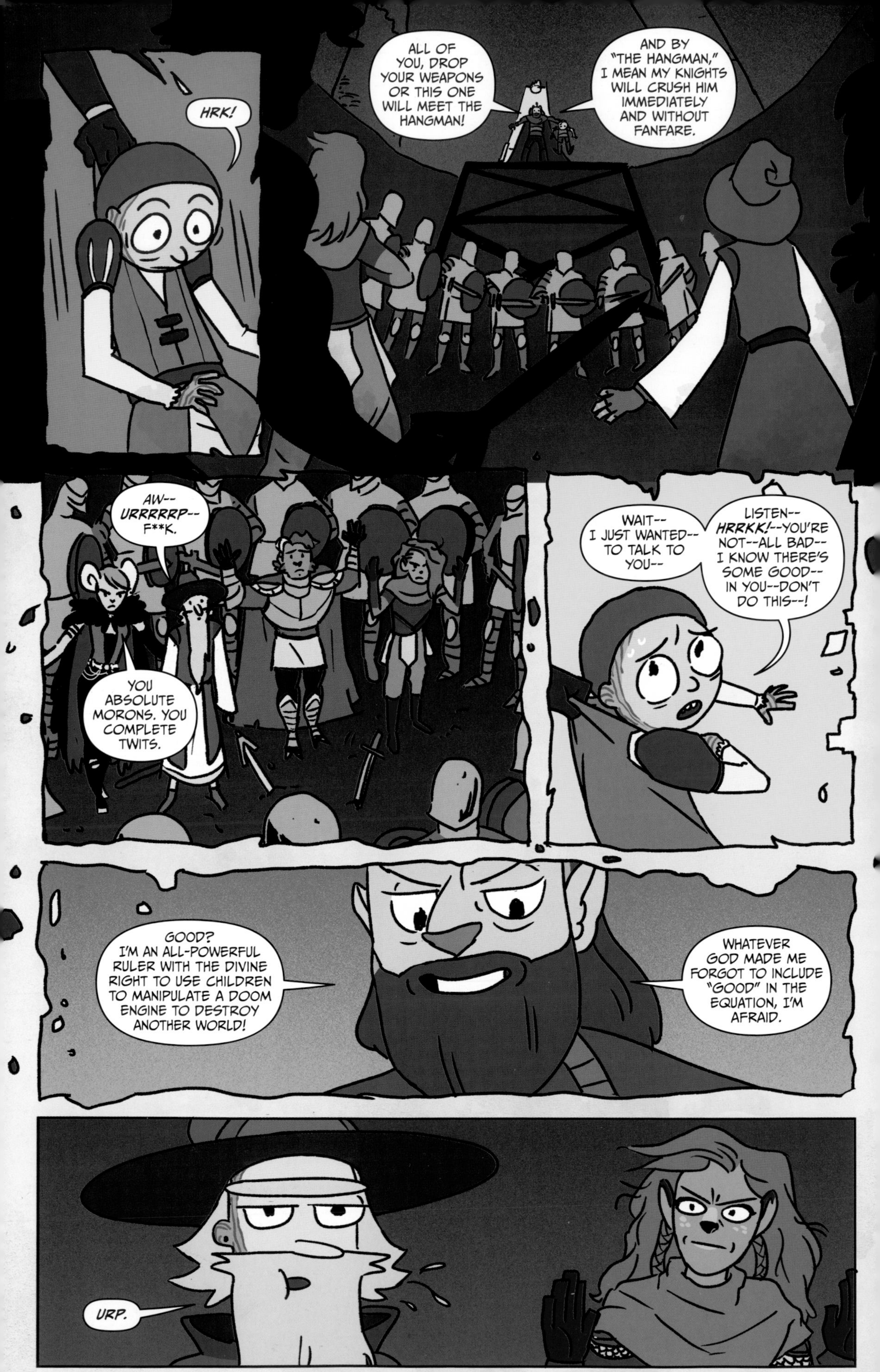

HRK!
ALL OF YOU, DROP YOUR WEAPONS OR THIS ONE WILL MEET THE HANGMAN!
AND BY "THE HANGMAN," I MEAN MY KNIGHTS WILL CRUSH HIM IMMEDIATELY AND WITHOUT FANFARE.
AW-- URRRRRP-- F**K.
YOU ABSOLUTE MORONS. YOU COMPLETE TWITS.
WAIT-- I JUST WANTED-- TO TALK TO YOU--
LISTEN-- HRRKK!--YOU'RE NOT--ALL BAD-- I KNOW THERE'S SOME GOOD-- IN YOU--DON'T DO THIS--!
GOOD? I'M AN ALL-POWERFUL RULER WITH THE DIVINE RIGHT TO USE CHILDREN TO MANIPULATE A DOOM ENGINE TO DESTROY ANOTHER WORLD!
WHATEVER GOD MADE ME FORGOT TO INCLUDE "GOOD" IN THE EQUATION, I'M AFRAID.
URP.

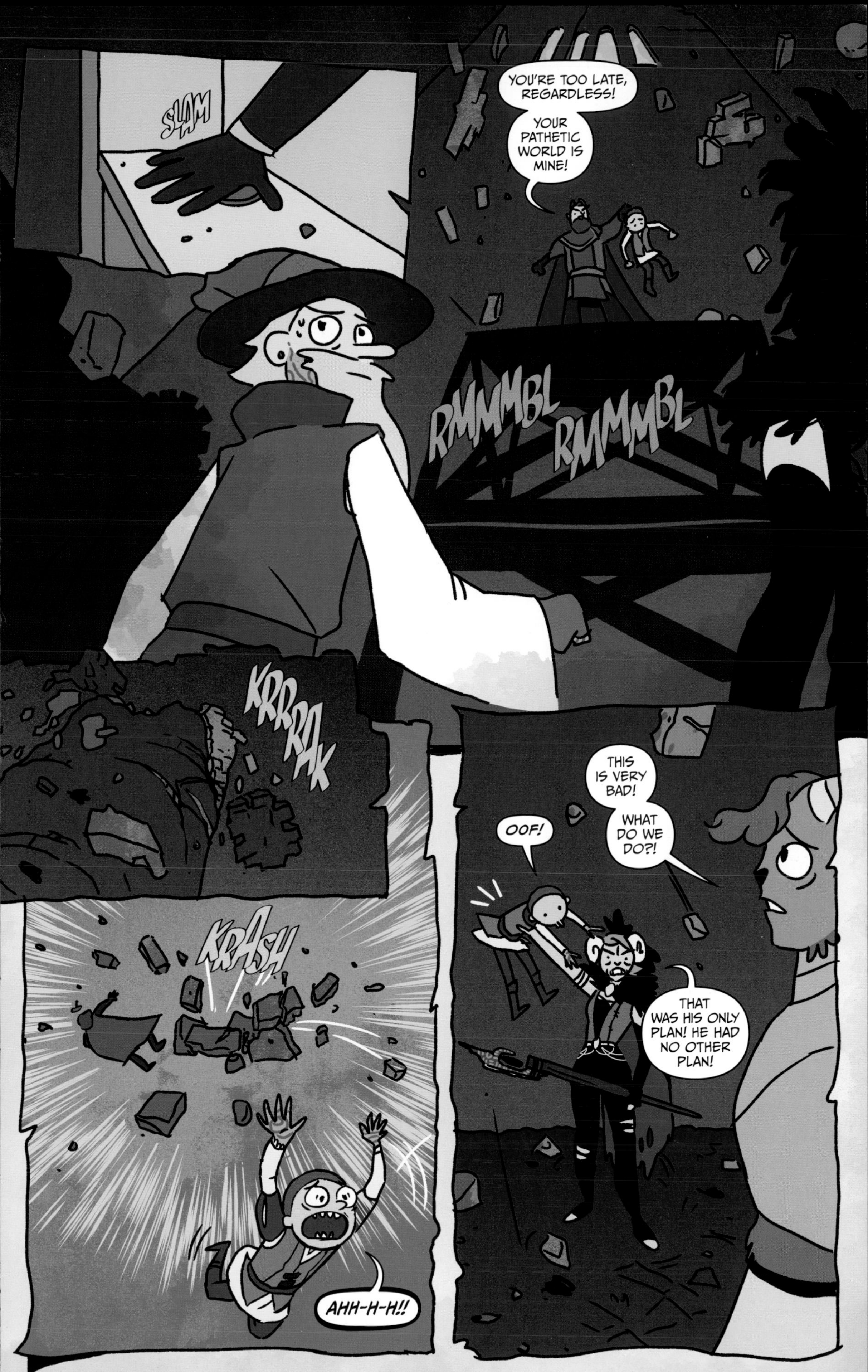
SLAM
YOU'RE TOO LATE, REGARDLESS!
YOUR PATHETIC WORLD IS MINE!
RMMMBL RMMMBL
KRRRAK
KRASH
AHH-H-H!!
THIS IS VERY BAD!
WHAT DO WE DO?!
OOF!
THAT WAS HIS ONLY PLAN! HE HAD NO OTHER PLAN!

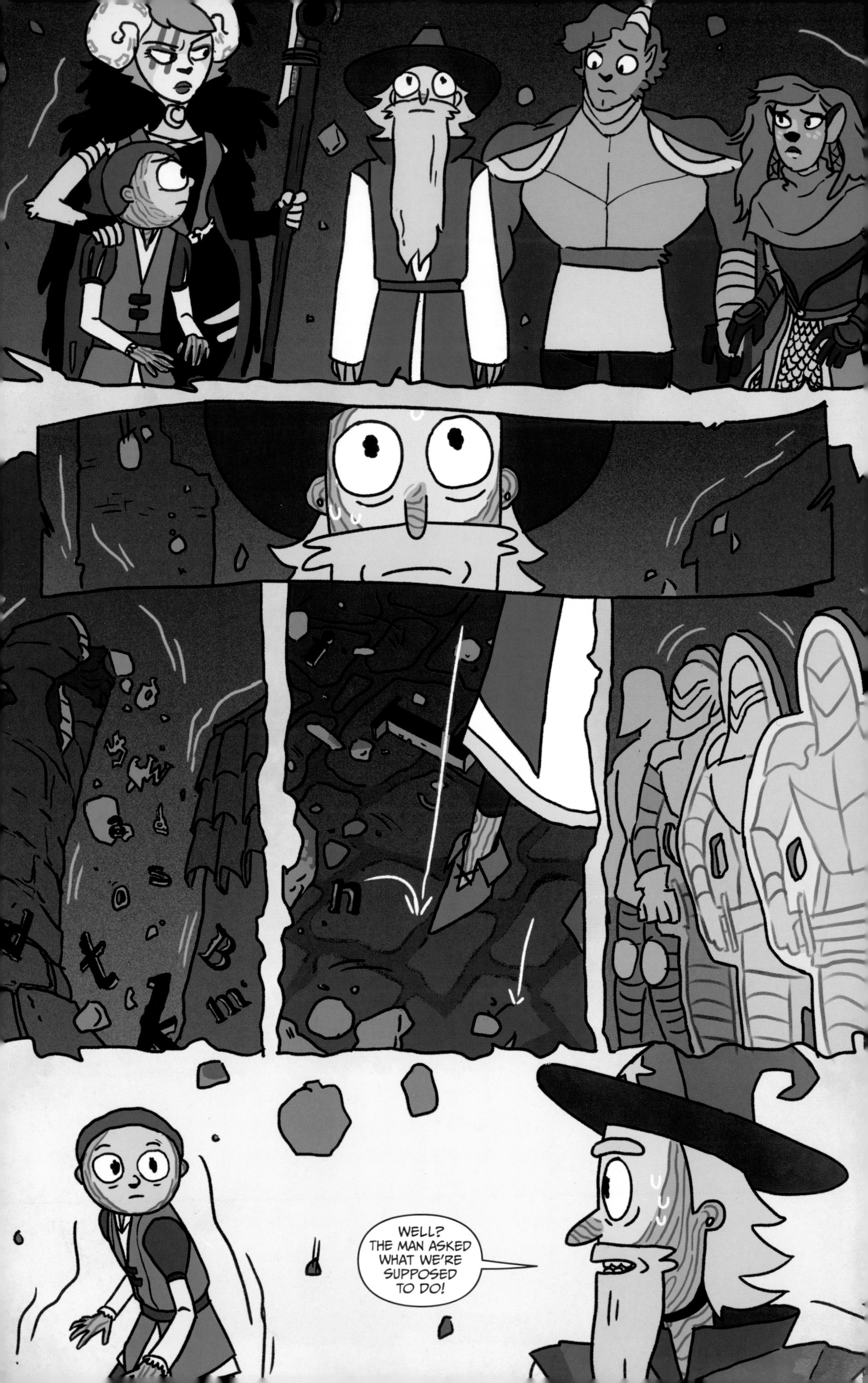
WELL? THE MAN ASKED WHAT WE'RE SUPPOSED TO DO!

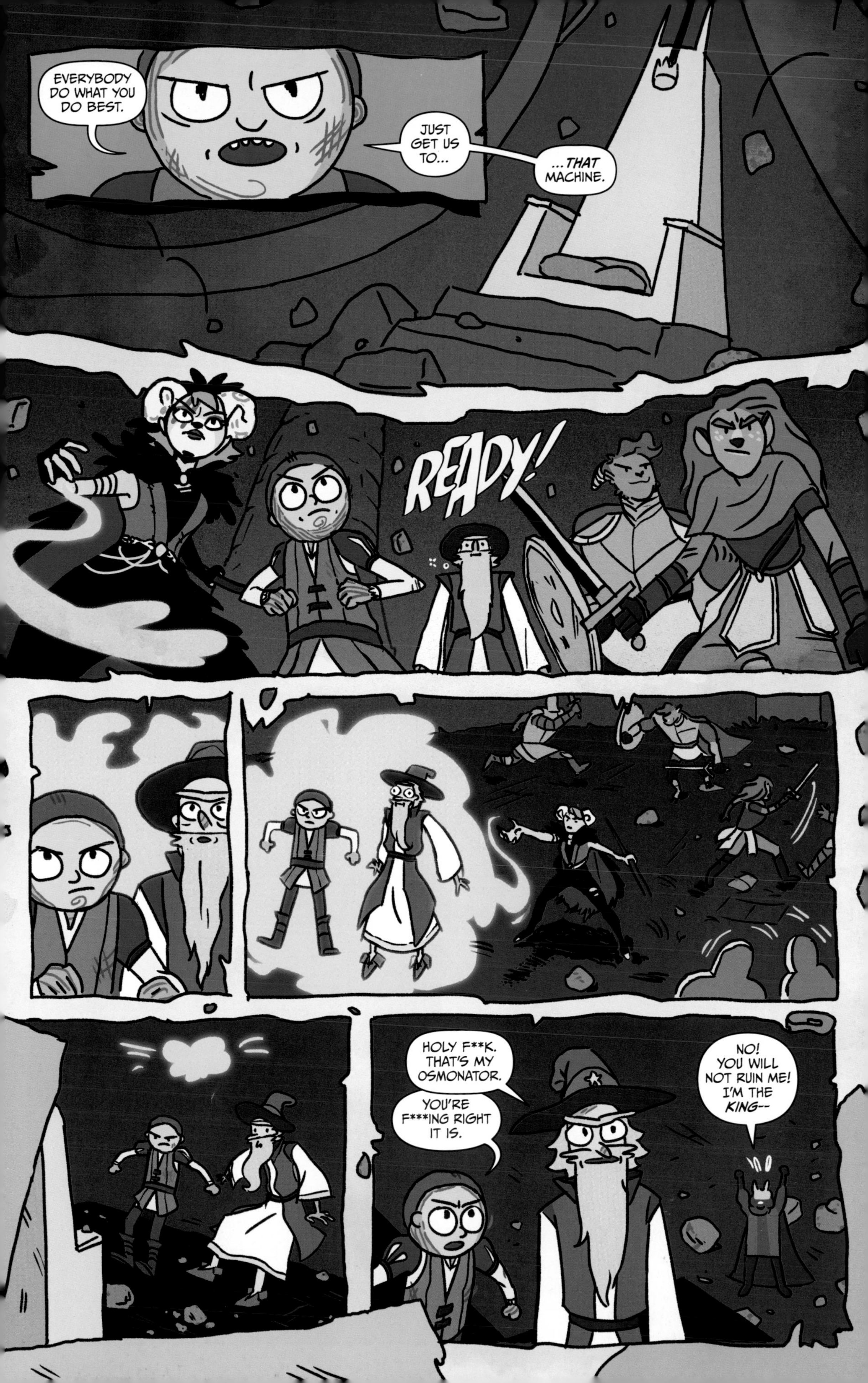
EVERYBODY DO WHAT YOU DO BEST.
JUST GET US TO...
...THAT MACHINE.
READY!
HOLY F**K. THAT'S MY OSMONATOR.
YOU'RE F***ING RIGHT IT IS.
NO! YOU WILL NOT RUIN ME! I'M THE KING--

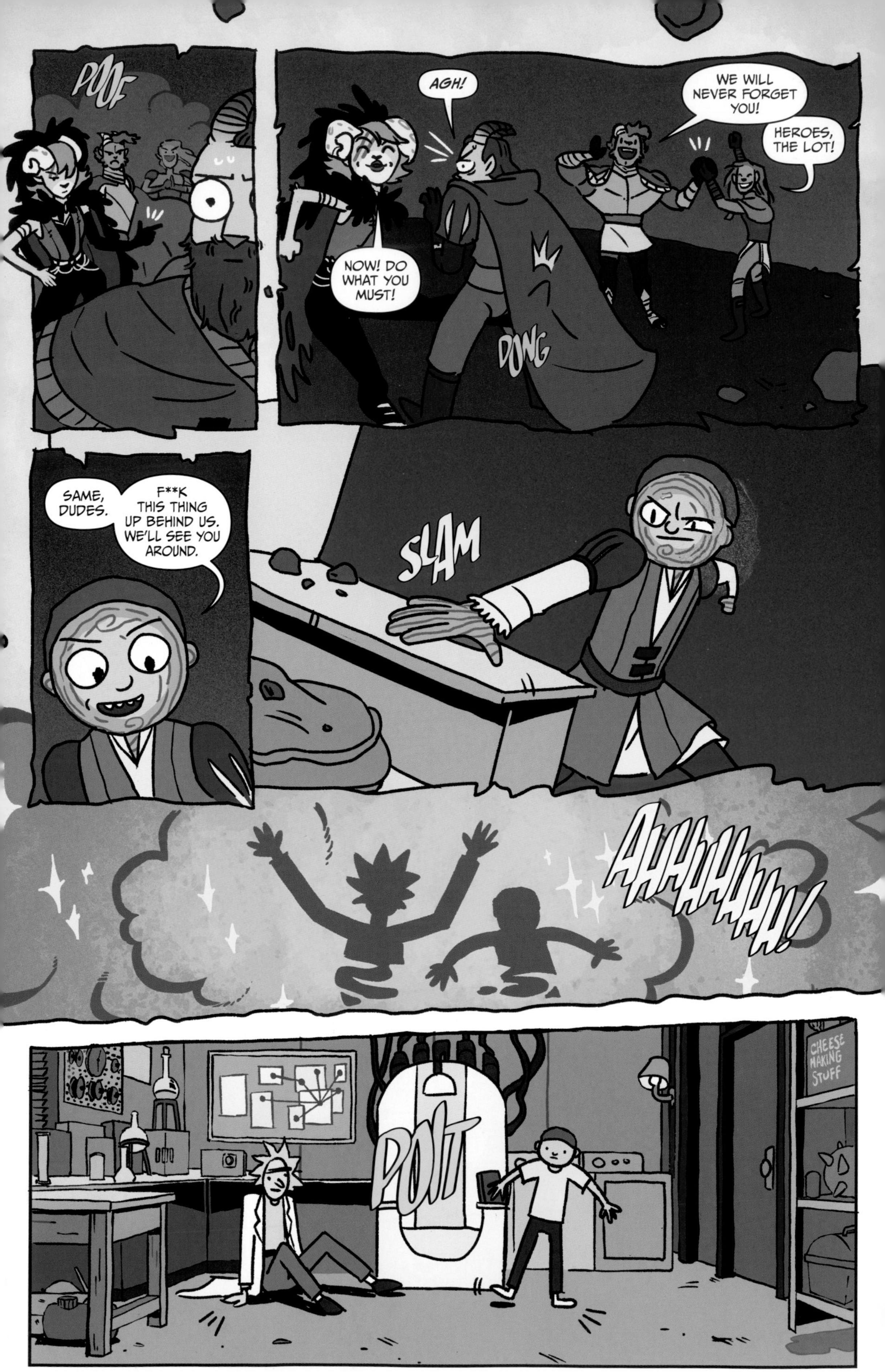
POOF
AGH!
WE WILL NEVER FORGET YOU!
HEROES, THE LOT!
NOW! DO WHAT YOU MUST!
DONG
SAME, DUDES.
F**K THIS THING UP BEHIND US. WE'LL SEE YOU AROUND.
SLAM
AHHHHHHH!
CHEESE MAKING STUFF
POIT

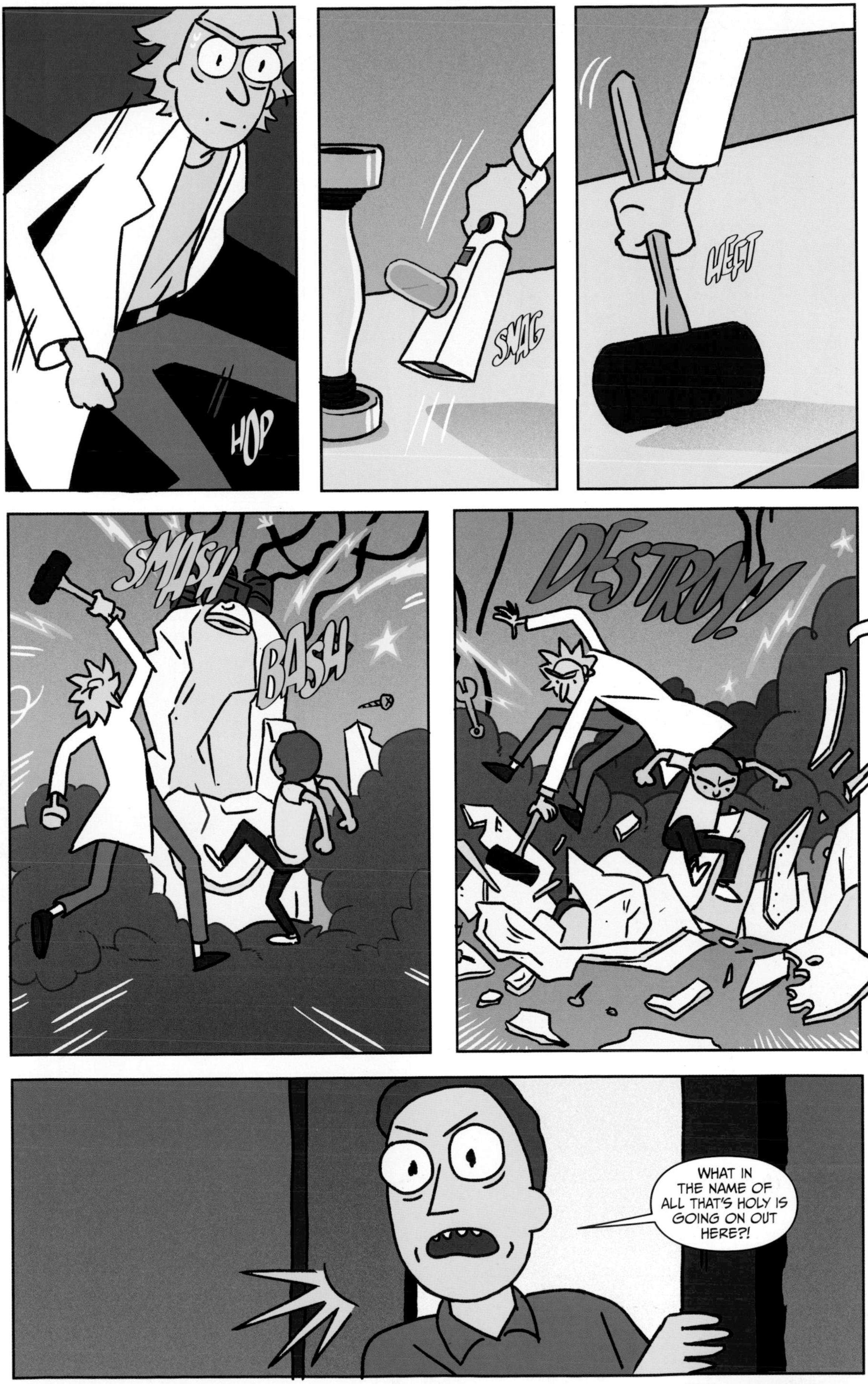
HOP
SNAG
HEFT
SMASH
BASH
DESTROY!
WHAT IN THE NAME OF ALL THAT'S HOLY IS GOING ON OUT HERE?!

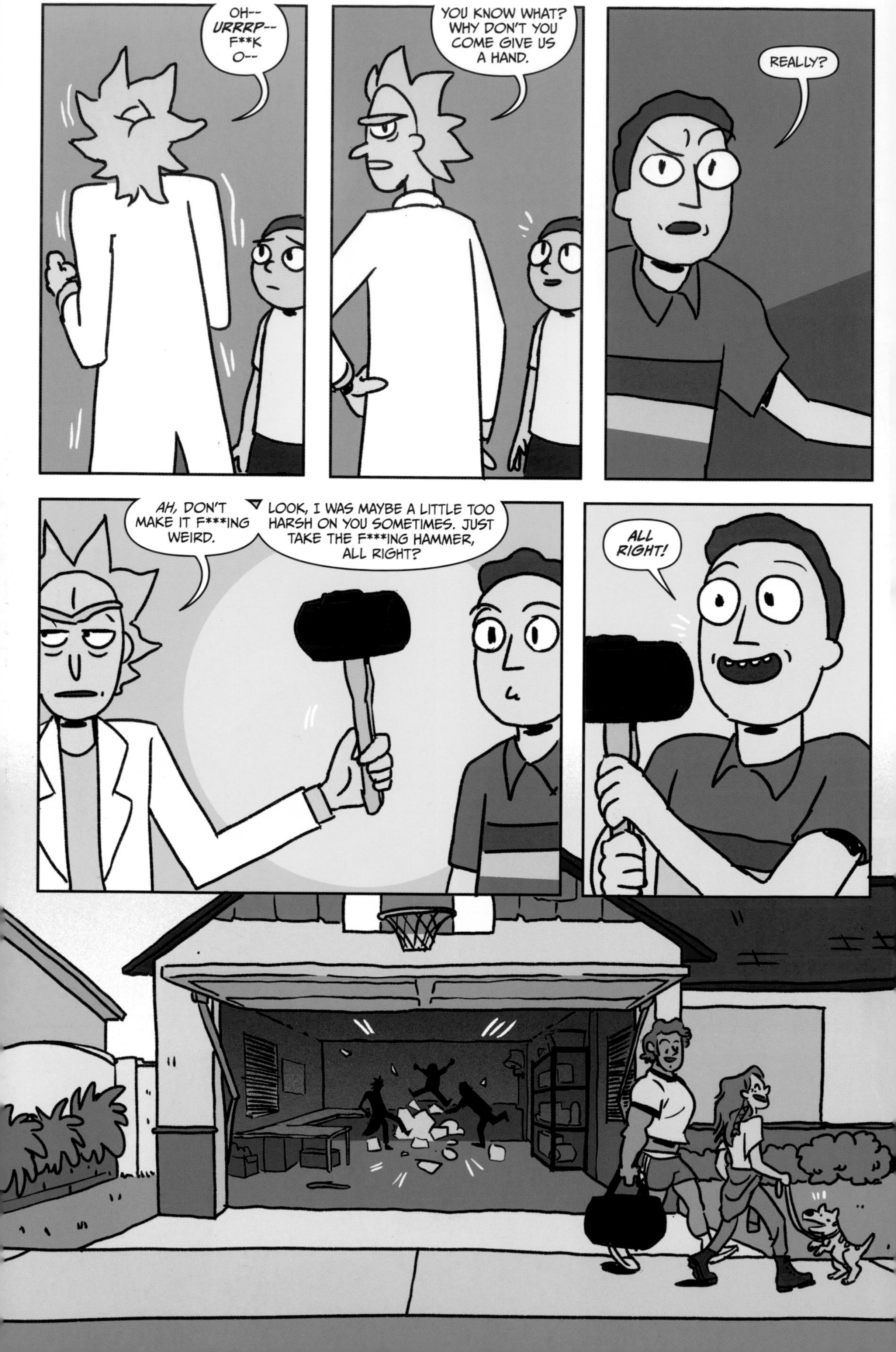
OH-- URRRP-- F**K O--
YOU KNOW WHAT? WHY DON'T YOU COME GIVE US A HAND.
REALLY?
AH, DON'T MAKE IT F***ING WEIRD.
LOOK, I WAS MAYBE A LITTLE TOO HARSH ON YOU SOMETIMES. JUST TAKE THE F***ING HAMMER, ALL RIGHT?
ALL RIGHT!

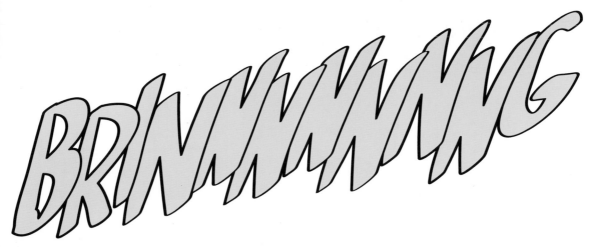

PENCILS DOWN, QUIZ OVER! HAND 'EM IN, FOLKS.

HOW'D IT GO?

DROP

I--UH-- WHA--

ACTUALLY, I THINK I DID OKAY. DID YOU LIKE THE BOOK?

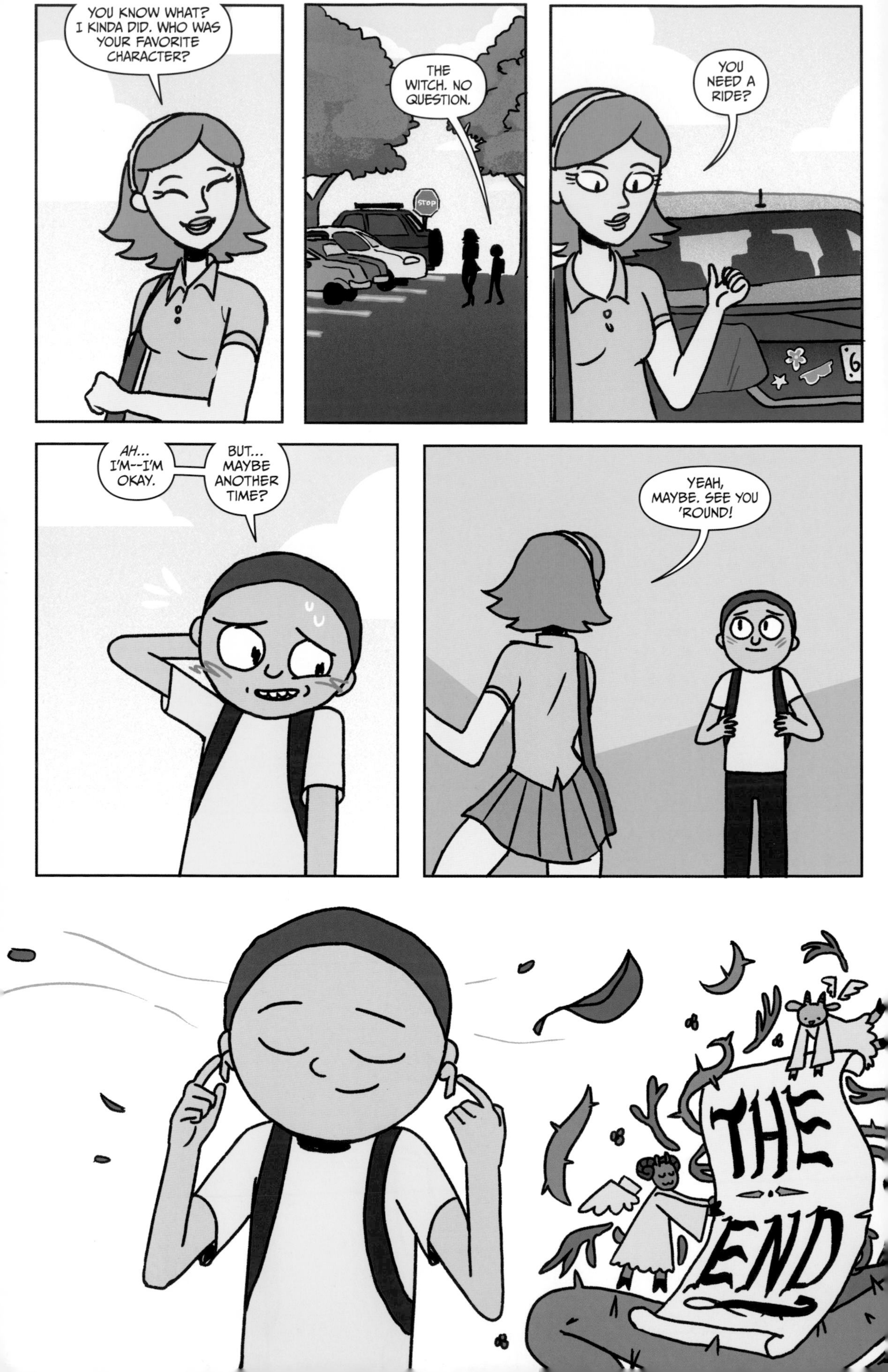
YOU KNOW WHAT? I KINDA DID. WHO WAS YOUR FAVORITE CHARACTER?
THE WITCH. NO QUESTION.
STOP
YOU NEED A RIDE?
AH... I'M--I'M OKAY.
BUT... MAYBE ANOTHER TIME?
YEAH, MAYBE. SEE YOU 'ROUND!
THE END

Bonus Materials

Creating the world of Ever After

ART BY SARAH STERN AND EMMETT HELEN

Silke & Marius

Emmett: Sarah and I split dibs on character design. Y'all don't see the script, but Marius's character was pitched as "Himbo Knight," and I have never called dibs on something so fast. One of my biggest gripes with this archetype in fiction is that the hot meathead knight is usually played as kind of silly for caring about his appearance, and the team was adamant on subverting that. So we went with a guy who looks really hard-core and hot, wearing thigh highs and a crop top chestplate, but is cute and tender, and could be funny without coming across as a caricature. Like a gym bro that volunteers at the animal shelter.

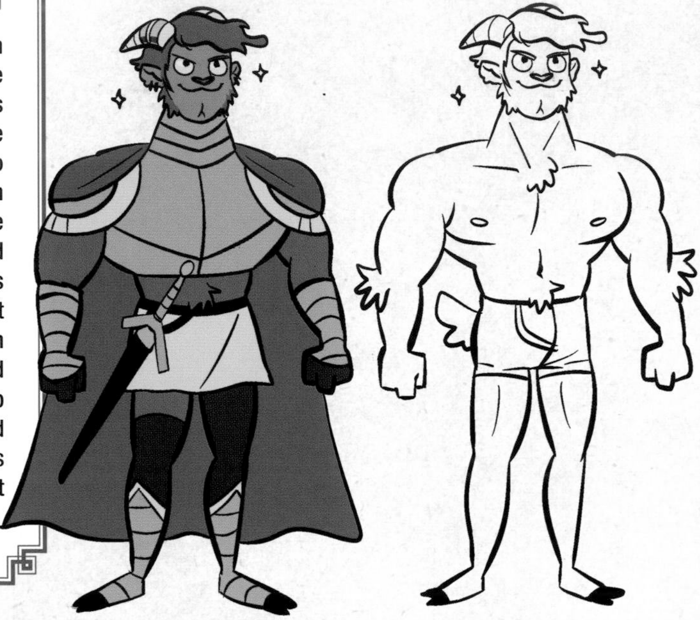

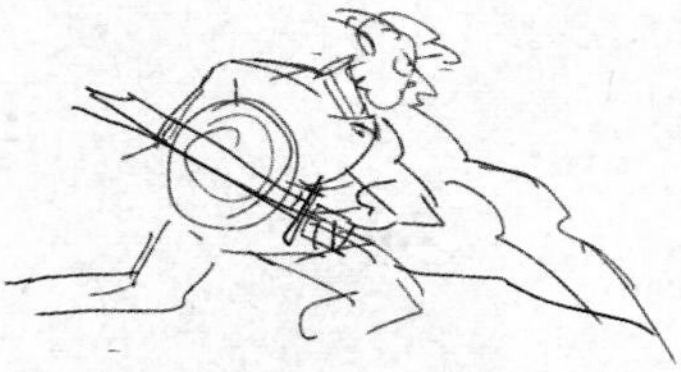

Sam: There's no combo more powerful than a lesbian and her emotional-support himbo, and that's what I really wanted to create for the knights Silke and Marius. Silke is the perfect balance of beefcake, brains, and beauty; Marius is all cake, and crucially falls right in the center of the Big and/or Strong—No Think—Respect Women Venn diagram. Sarah and Emmett absolutely crushed it with both of them. I want them to come to life and cuddle me while also protecting me from home invaders. They're perfect.

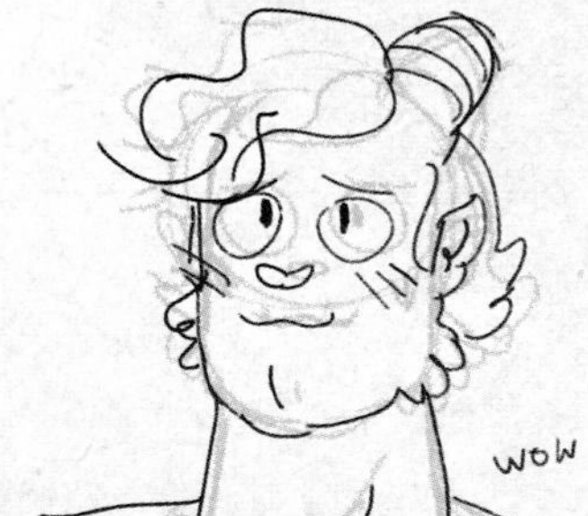
wow

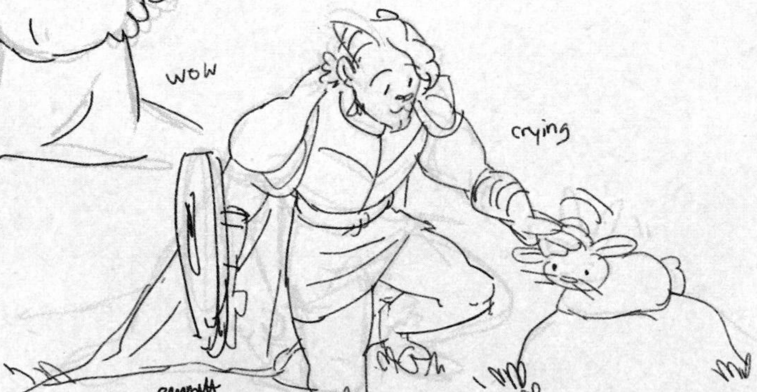
crying
emmett helen

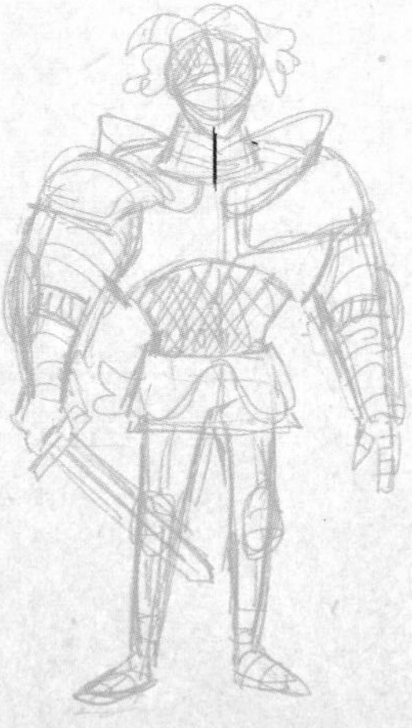

Emmett: Silke was fun to design after Marius, because both are high-ranking knights, but are so totally different. Silke is a clever and tough field agent and needed to look genderless at first, so we packed leather and scalemail armor onto her shoulders for a more masculine silhouette. One of my favorite things about Silke is that she has a playful streak, so the huge hair, freckles, and deer-like features made her a little cute, so like Marius, she could seem really well-rounded and not a stereotype. Sarah helped me dig up reference from a lot of Norse/Viking sources, which you can see especially in the braids.

she is like
a baby deer

kinda
Robin Hood-y
+ viking

Riding
boots

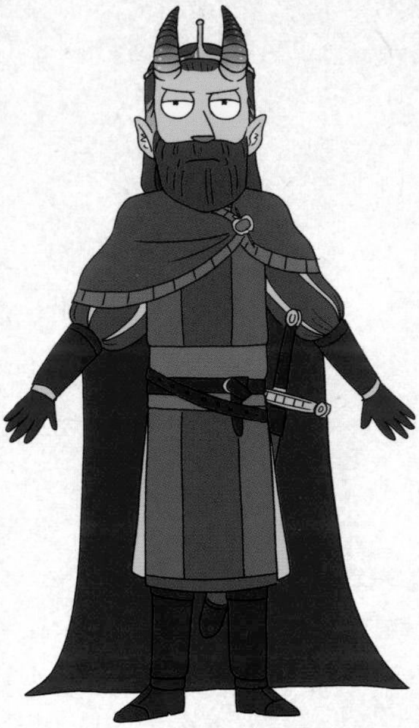

King Jerry

Sarah: King Jerry needed to fit within the fairy-tale world of Avalonia while still being recognizably Jerry, so I did my best to echo his signature station-wagon look enhanced by some regal embellishments. I think the apple cloak pin pulls the whole thing together! Maybe real Jerry should consider growing a beard?

Sam: King Jerry could get it.

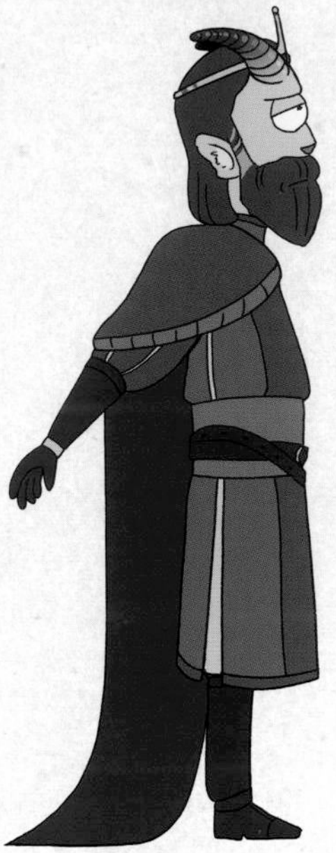

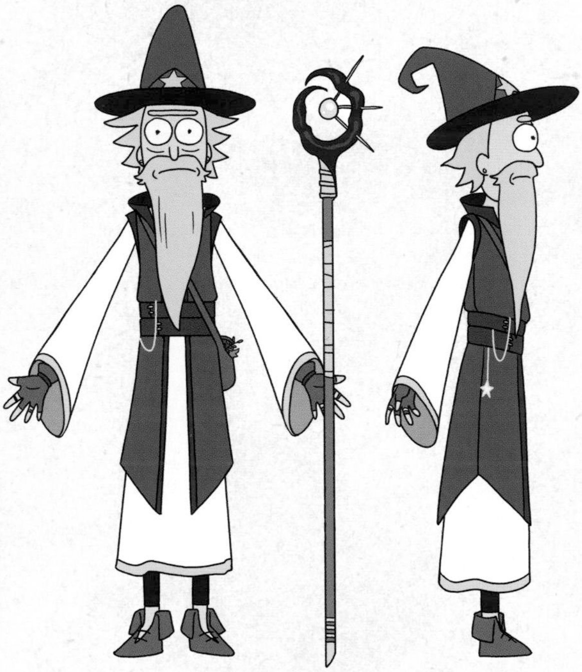

Wizard Rick

Sarah: Wizard Rick needed a look that would read as "wizard" but also be practical enough that he wouldn't immediately throw it off and do the adventure nude. I went with a traditional hat and robe, with a belted overcoat that references the silhouette of his everyday lab coat. As Rick's body is itself a cybernetically altered bag of tricks, I wanted to make sure his fairy-tale look reflected that, as well with some reagent pouches and visible potions.

Sam: Our favorite anti-heroes still needed to be recognizably themselves while also hitting the fish-out-of-fantasy-water mark. Rick's variety of magical vials are absolutely not T-for-Teen-friendly, so we won't get too deep into that, but I love that he looks kind of like a bonkers Gandalf on a bender.

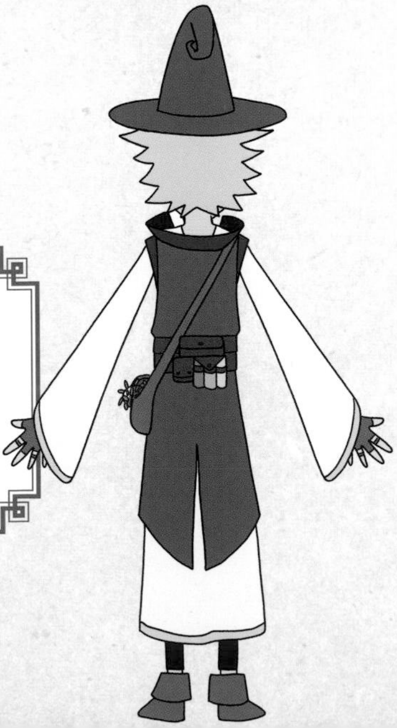

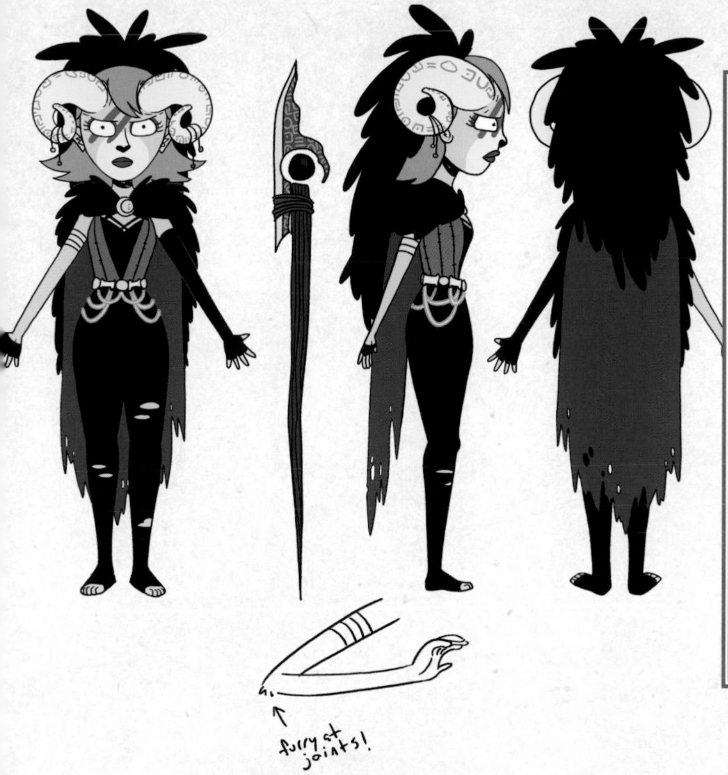

Jessica

Sarah: Witch Jessica is the most enigmatic character in the book, and she needed a look that's both threatening and characteristically stylish. I wanted to give her some fun forest-witch vibes, so I gave her a black bodysuit strung with silver and bone. The big, fluffy feather cloak is very insulating on chilly mornings too, I'm sure!

Sam: I think the best thing about Evil Witch Jessica is how much I would absolutely wear her outfit right now. Hot-Topic-circa-2009 wishes. I wanted threatening but also step-on-me vibes, and that's exactly what Emmett and Sarah gave us. Iconic.

Morty

Sarah: For Tower Morty, we needed to strike a balance between damsel in distress and something practical one could wear while running around terrified in the forest. You can't go wrong with a chunky belt!

Sam: We played around with a bunch of different looks for Morty before settling on the tunic-and-belt combo, but personally, I do think he has a shape-maintaining corset on beneath all that to help with his posture and the courtly "look." How else could one achieve such a flawless standard of medieval beauty?

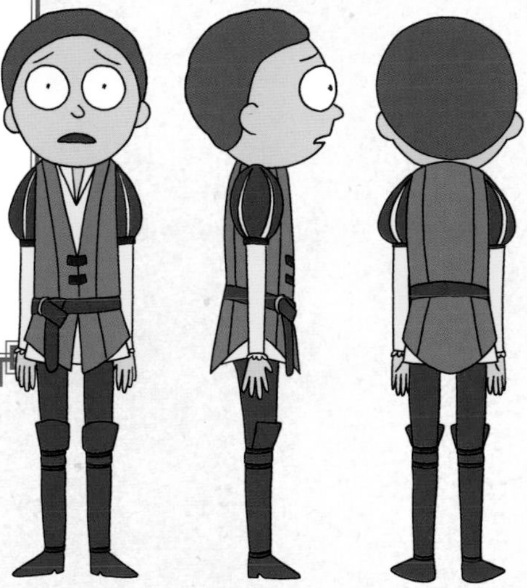

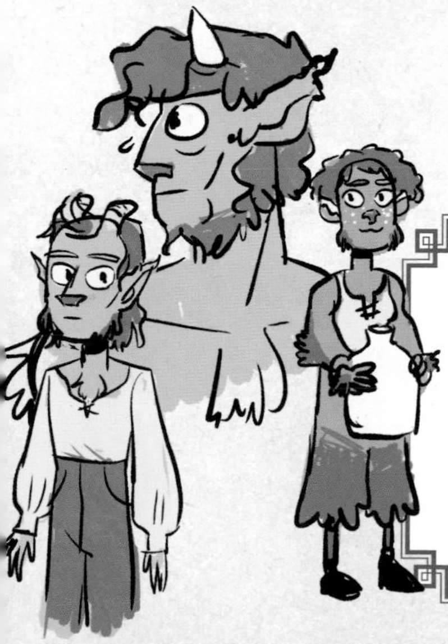

Species

Emmett: One of my favorite things about *Rick and Morty* is how alien species are designed for their environment. Even though this isn't an alien planet, we thought it'd be cool to differentiate the citizens from Rick and Morty. It also allowed us to keep a lot of the recognizable parts of fairy-tale stories without looking generic. Goat, sheep, and deer people just seemed to fit well in this world. Yes, it's weird that they ride horses. Don't think about it.

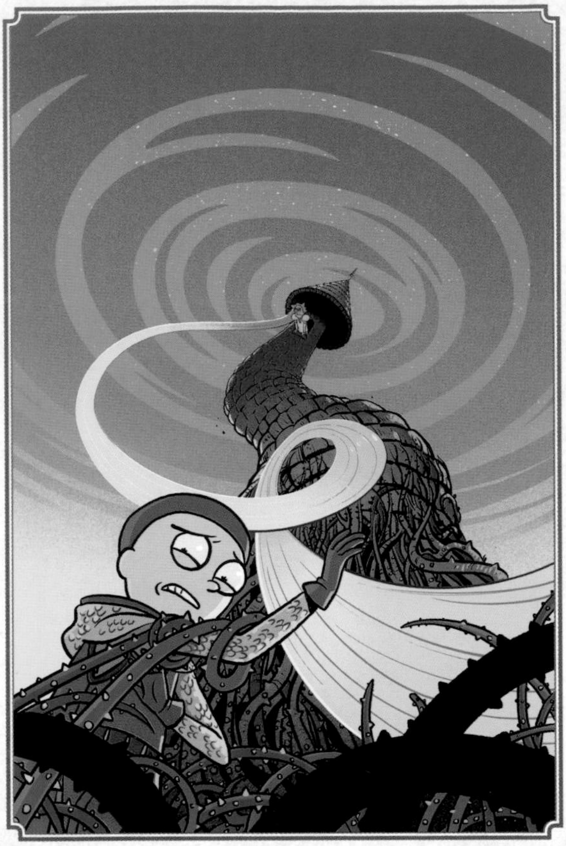
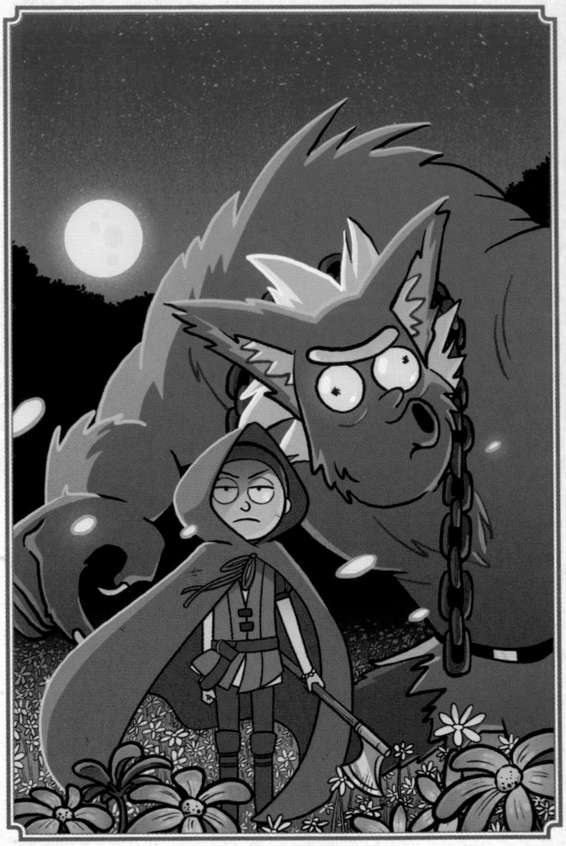
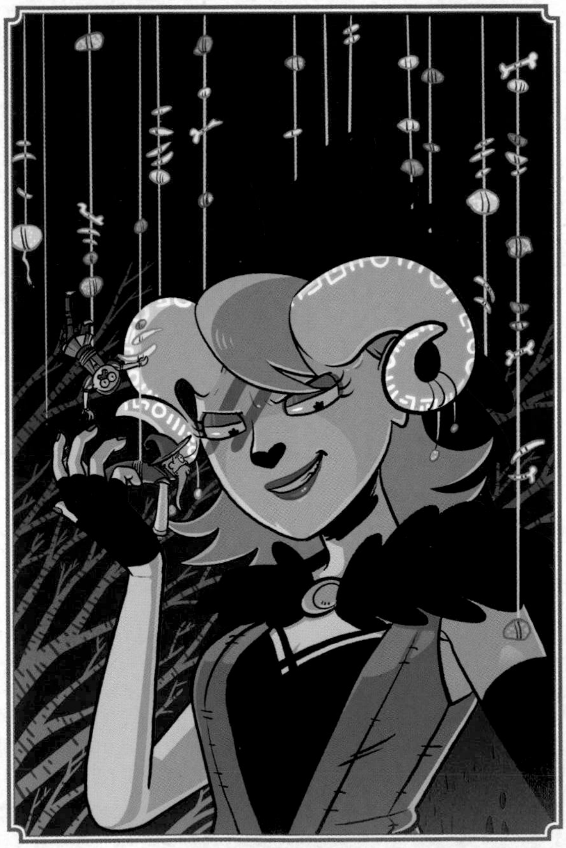
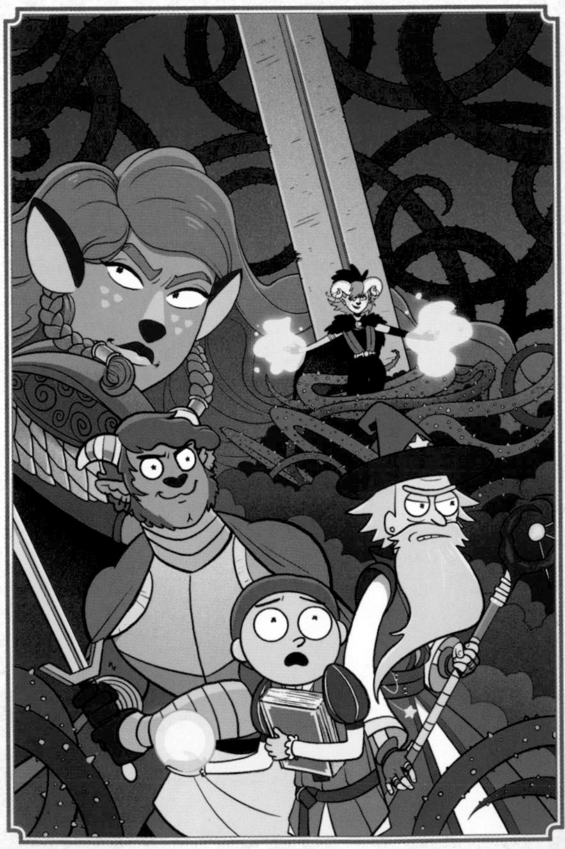

Covers by Sarah Stern

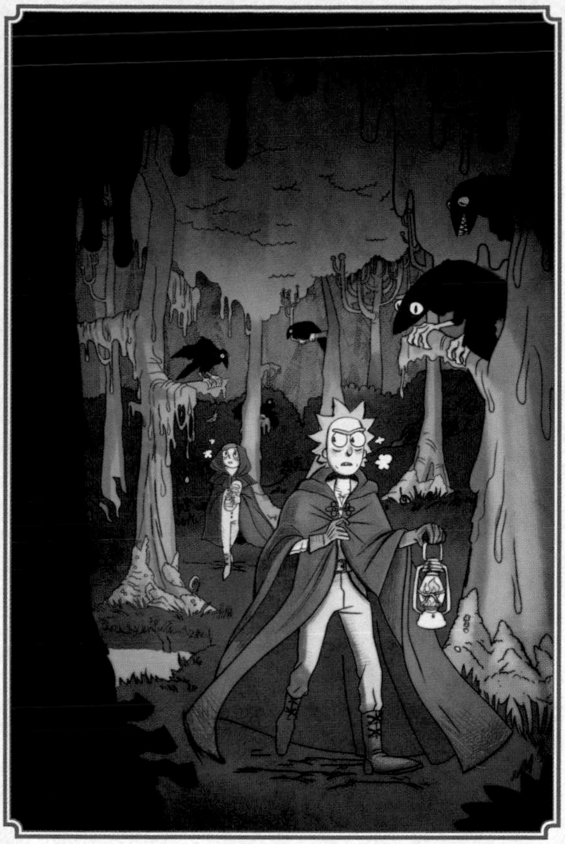

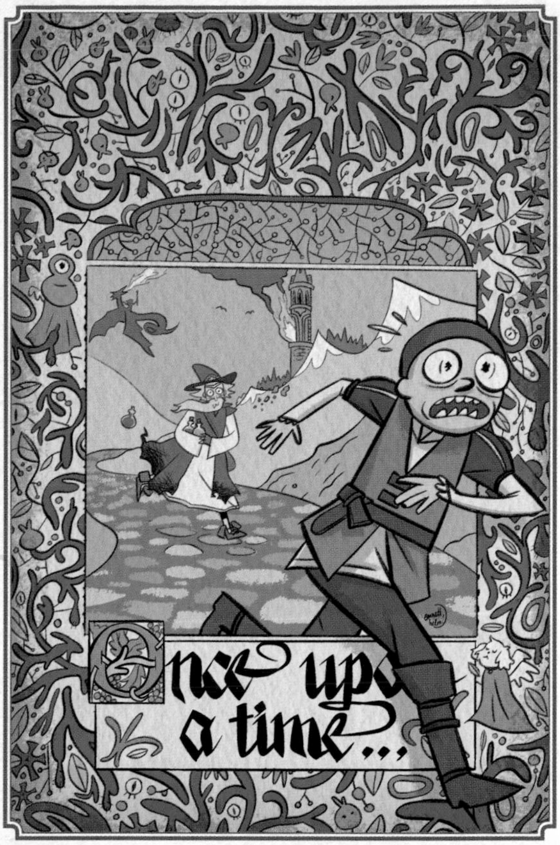
Once upon
a time...

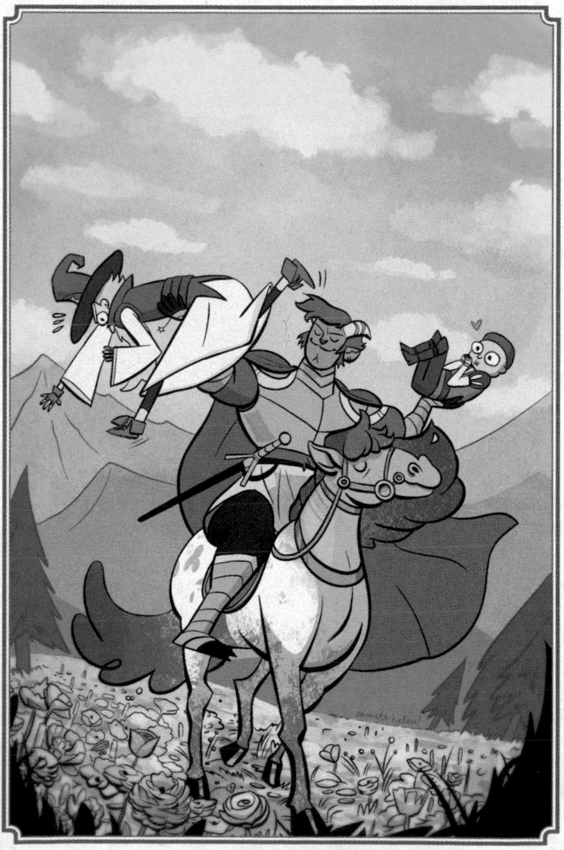

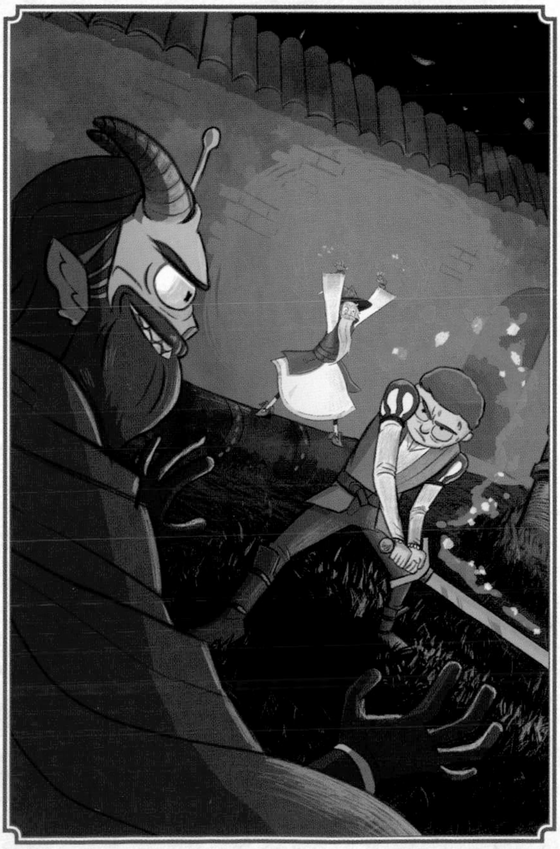

Covers by Emmett Helen

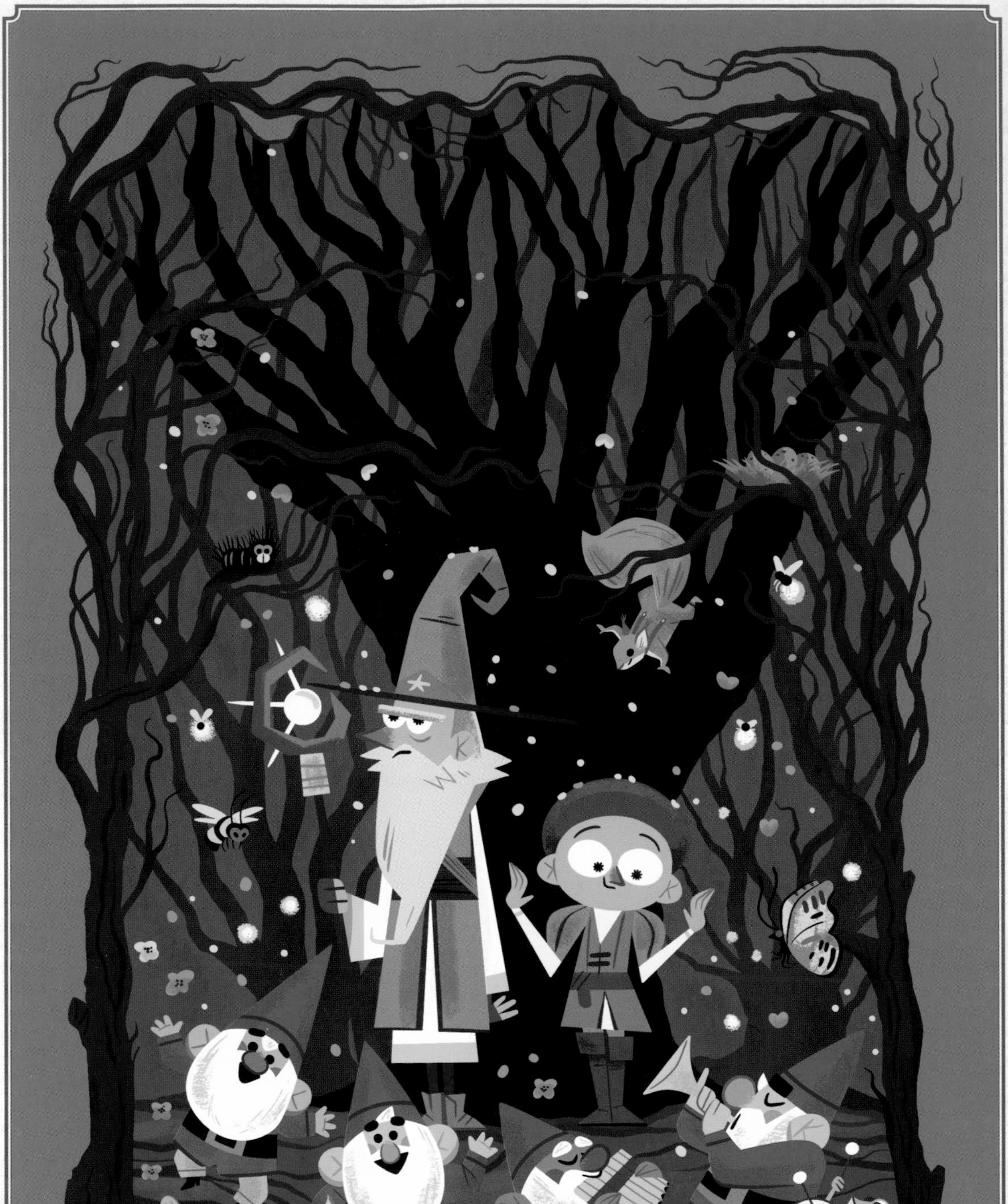

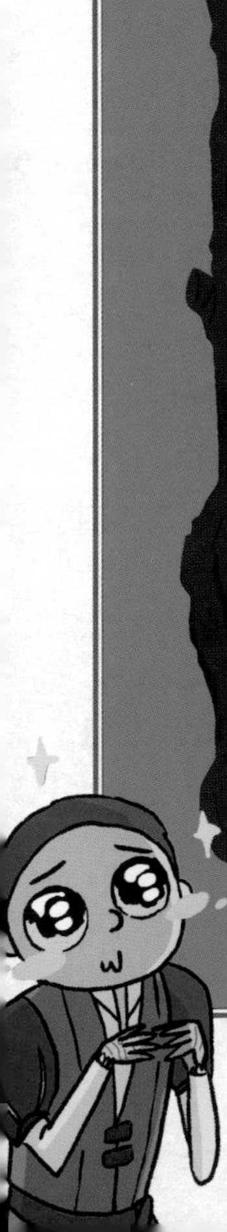

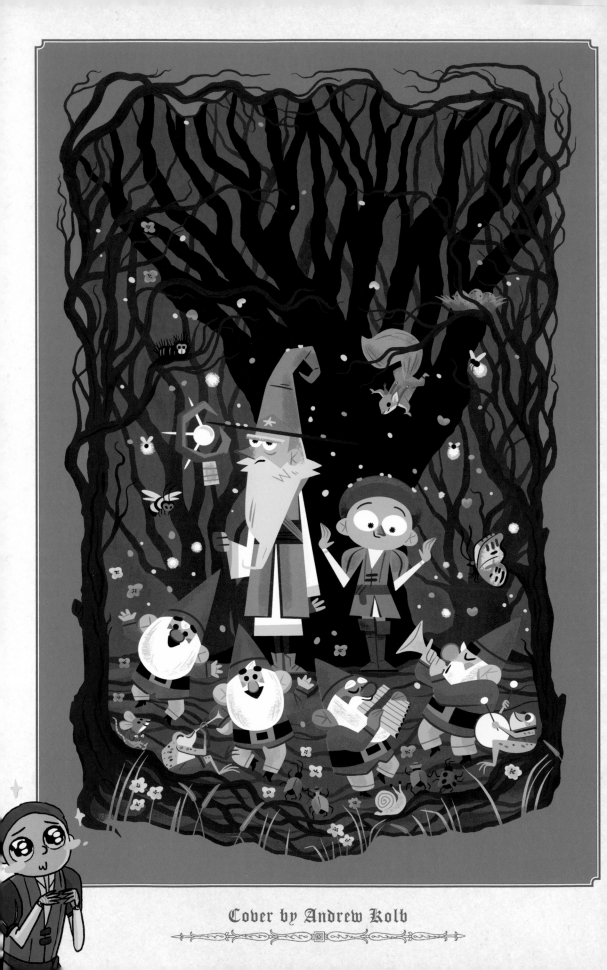

Cover by Andrew Kolb

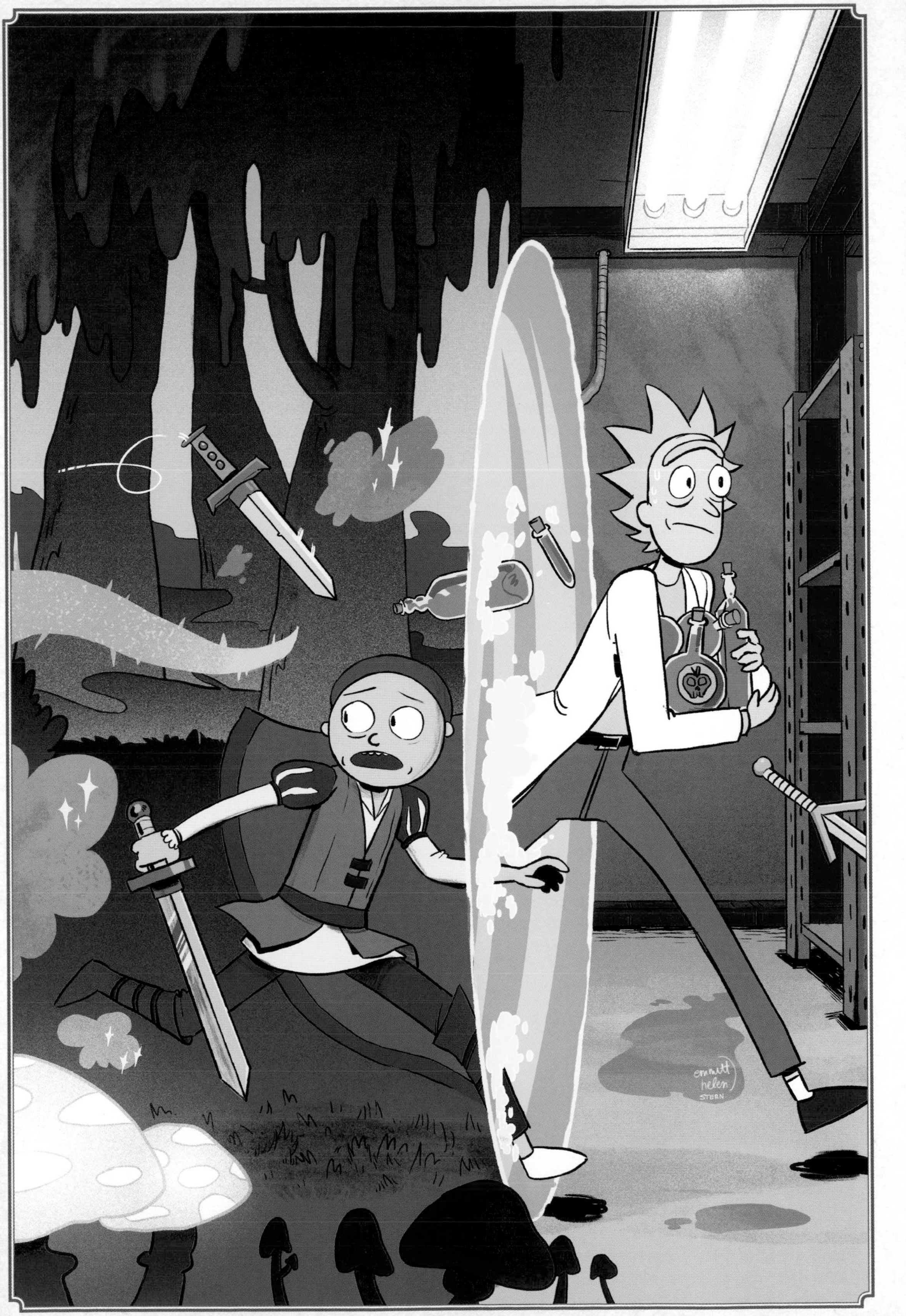
emmett helen
STERN

Cover by Emmett Helen and Sarah Stern

Dan Harmon

Dan Harmon is the Emmy®-winning creator/executive producer of the comedy series *Community*, as well as the co-creator/executive producer of Adult Swim's *Rick and Morty*.

Harmon's pursuit of minimal work for maximum reward took him from stand-up to improv to sketch comedy, then finally to Los Angeles, where he began writing feature screenplays with fellow Milwaukeean Rob Schrab. As part of his deal with Robert Zemeckis at Imagemovers, Harmon co-wrote the feature film *Monster House.* Following this, Harmon co-wrote the Ben Stiller-directed pilot *Heat Vision and Jack,* starring Jack Black and Owen Wilson.

Disillusioned by the legitimate industry, Harmon began attending classes at nearby Glendale Community College. At the same time, Harmon and Schrab founded Channel 101, an untelevised non-profit audience-controlled network for undiscovered filmmakers, many of whom used it to launch mainstream careers, including the boys behind SNL's Digital Shorts. Harmon, along with Schrab, partnered with Sarah Silverman to create her Comedy Central series, *The Sarah Silverman Program,* where he served as head writer for the first season.

Harmon went on to create, write, and perform in the short-lived VH1 sketch series *Acceptable TV* before eventually creating the critically acclaimed and fan-favorite comedy *Community.* The show originally aired on NBC for five seasons before being acquired by Yahoo, which premiered season six of the show in March of 2015. In 2009, he won an Emmy for Outstanding Music and Lyrics for the opening number of the 81st Annual Academy Awards.

Along with Justin Roiland, Harmon created the breakout Adult Swim animated series *Rick and Morty*. The show premiered in December of 2013 and quickly became a ratings hit. In 2014, Harmon was the star of the documentary *Harmontown*, which premiered at the SXSW Film Festival and chronicled his 20-city stand-up/podcast tour of the same name. The documentary was released theatrically in October of 2014.

Justin Roiland

Justin Roiland grew up in Manteca, California, where he did the basic stuff children do. Later in life, he traveled to Los Angeles. Once settled in, he created several popular online shorts for Channel 101. Some notable examples of his work (both animated and live action) include *House of Cosbys* and *Two Girls One Cup: The Show.* Justin is afraid of his mortality and hopes the things he creates will make lots of people happy. Then maybe when modern civilization collapses into chaos, people will remember him and they'll help him survive the bloodshed and violence. Global economic collapse is looming. It's going to be horrible, and honestly, a swift death might be preferable than living in the hell that awaits mankind. Justin also really hates writing about himself in the third person. I hate this. That's right. It's me. I've been writing this whole thing. Hi. The cat's out of the bag. It's just you and me now. There never was a third person. If you want to know anything about me, just ask. Sorry this wasn't more informative.

Sam Maggs

Sam Maggs is a best-selling author of books, comics, and video games. She's the author of many YA and middle-grade books like *The Unstoppable Wasp: Built on Hope, Con Quest!, Tell No Tales,* and *The Fangirl's Guide to the Galaxy*; a senior games writer, including work on Marvel's *Spider-Man*; and a comics writer for titles like *Marvel Action: Captain Marvel, My Little Pony,* and *Transformers.* She is also an on-air host for networks like Nerdist. A Canadian in Los Angeles, she misses Coffee Crisp and bagged milk. Visit her online at sammaggs.com or @SamMaggs!

Sarah Stern

Sarah Stern is a comic artist and colorist from New York. Find her at sarahstern.com or follow her on twitter at @worstwizard.

Emmett Helen

In-between stints as a *Rick and Morty* cover artist, Emmett Helen has created short works for *Sweaty Palms,* the *Life Finds a Way* anthology, *Draw Out the Vote,* and *The Beautiful Book of Exquisite Corpses.* They spend hours in the kitchen and miss the beach just terribly. *My Riot* is their debut graphic novel.

Chris Crank

Hi! I go by crank! You might know my work from several recent Oni books like *The Sixth Gun, Letter 44, Redline,* and *Rick and Morty*. Maybe you've seen my letters in *Revival, HACK/slash, Spread,* or *God Hates Astronauts* (Image). Perhaps you've read *Lady Killer, Ghost Fleet,* or *Sundowners* (Dark Horse). Heck, you might even be reading the award-winning *Battlepug* (battlepug.com) right now! If you're weird you could have heard me online at crankcast.net where I talk with Mike Norton, Tim Seeley, Sean Dove and Jenny Frison weekly about things that are sometimes comics related. If you're super-obscure you've heard me play music with the Vladimirs or Sono Morti (sonomorti.bandcamp.com). Catch me on Twitter: @ccrank.

More Books From Oni Press

**RICK AND MORTY™
VOL. 1**

**RICK AND MORTY™
VOL. 9**

**RICK AND MORTY™
VOL. 10**

**RICK AND MORTY™
VOL. 11**

**RICK AND MORTY™
VOL. 12**

**RICK AND MORTY™
PRESENTS VOL. 1**

**RICK AND MORTY™
PRESENTS VOL. 2**

**RICK AND MORTY™
POCKET LIKE YOU STOLE IT**

**RICK AND MORTY™
VS. D&D VOL. 1**

**RICK AND MORTY™
VS. D&D VOL. 2 PAINSCAPE**

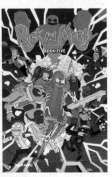

**RICK AND MORTY™
DELUXE EDITION VOL. 1**

**RICK AND MORTY™
DELUXE EDITION VOL. 2**

**RICK AND MORTY™
DELUXE EDITION VOL. 3**

**RICK AND MORTY™
DELUXE EDITION VOL. 4**

**RICK AND MORTY™
DELUXE EDITION VOL. 5**

For more information on these and other fine Oni Press comic books
and graphic novels visit **www.onipress.com.**
To find a comic specialty store in your area visit **www.comicshops.us.**

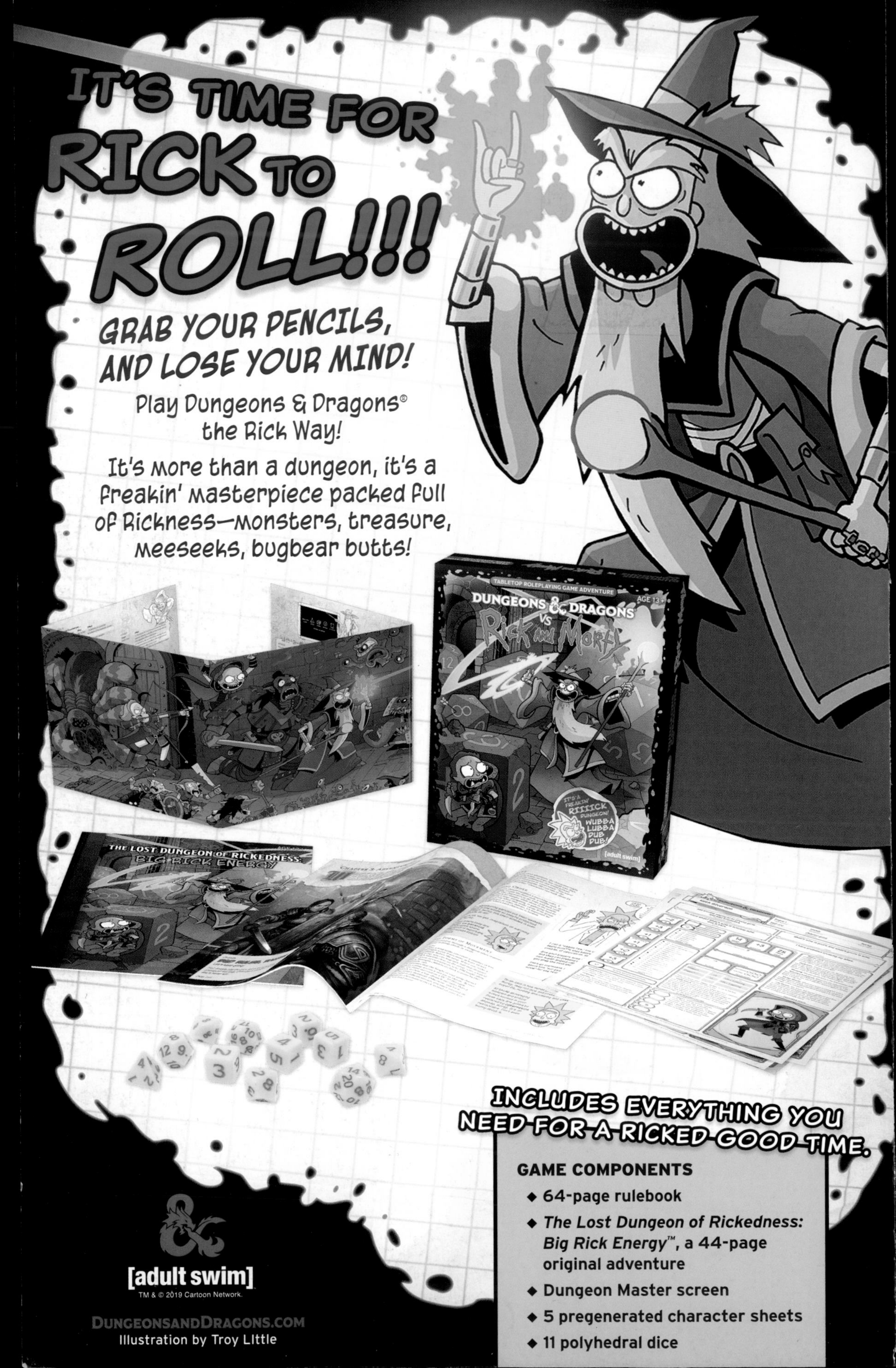

IT'S TIME FOR RICK TO ROLL!!!
GRAB YOUR PENCILS, AND LOSE YOUR MIND!
Play Dungeons & Dragons® the Rick Way!
It's more than a dungeon, it's a freakin' masterpiece packed full of Rickness—monsters, treasure, meeseeks, bugbear butts!
TABLETOP ROLEPLAYING GAME ADVENTURE
DUNGEONS & DRAGONS VS Rick and Morty
AGE 13+
IT'S A FREAKIN' RIIIICK DUNGEON! WUBBA LUBBA DUB DUB!
[adult swim]
THE LOST DUNGEON OF RICKEDNESS: BIG RICK ENERGY
INCLUDES EVERYTHING YOU NEED FOR A RICKED GOOD TIME.
GAME COMPONENTS
◆ 64-page rulebook
◆ *The Lost Dungeon of Rickedness: Big Rick Energy*™, a 44-page original adventure
◆ Dungeon Master screen
◆ 5 pregenerated character sheets
◆ 11 polyhedral dice
[adult swim]
TM & © 2019 Cartoon Network.
DUNGEONSANDDRAGONS.COM
Illustration by Troy Little